"It's safe to say Catholics in North America have had a complicated relationship with the papacy of Pope Francis. In this book, Jeremiah Barker resurrects some of the under-appreciated aspects of Pope Francis' theology and witness. By highlighting the commonalities between Pope Francis and his predecessors, Barker offers a vision of stewardship, justice, and chastity that should challenge and compel Catholics across the ideological aisle."

—PATRICK T. BROWN,
fellow, Ethics and Public Policy Center

"The pope is the vicar of Christ. Faithful Catholics receive the pope's magisterial teaching in a spirit of acceptance and docility. However, too many Catholics regard the pope as just another political figure of the right or the left, whose teaching is judged from one's perspective in the culture wars. Jeremiah Barker presents the teaching of Pope Francis as authentic Catholic doctrine, completely consistent with the teaching of Popes John Paul II and Benedict XVI. A masterful and necessary book!"

—THOMAS BETZ, OFM CAP,
pastor, Saint John the Evangelist Catholic Church, Center City Philadelphia

"Jeremiah Barker persuasively shows the consistency of Pope Francis's theological and anthropological approach—especially to ecology and marriage—with that of his two predecessors. Barker does this with an authoritative but open reading of both familiar and less well-known texts from the three popes. Perhaps even more impressive is Barker's own description of the pontifical understanding of the great modern conflict between what he evocatively calls 'cosmic chastity' and 'technocratic lust.'"

—EDWARD HADAS,
author of *Counsels of Imperfection: Thinking Through Catholic Social Teaching*

"Jeremiah Barker preaches an all-too-rare message: the fullness of the gospel, with all the sharpness of its challenge to our contemporary way of life. For those weary of the constant attempts to assimilate Church teaching to one agenda or another, Barker's book and the deep faith at its roots is just the remedy."

—ZENA HITZ,
author of *Lost in Thought: The Hidden Pleasures of an Intellectual Life*

Cosmic Chastity in an Age of Technocratic Lust

A Song of Three Popes

Cosmic Chastity in an Age of Technocratic Lust

A *Song of Three Popes*

The Legacy of John Paul II and Benedict XVI
in the Francis Papacy: The Theological, Ethical,
and Spiritual Heart of Their Social Message

JEREMIAH BARKER

CASCADE *Books* · Eugene, Oregon

COSMIC CHASTITY IN AN AGE OF TECHNOCRATIC LUST:
A SONG OF THREE POPES
The Legacy of John Paul II and Benedict XVI in the Francis Papacy:
The Theological, Ethical, and Spiritual Heart of Their Social Message

Cascade Books
An Imprint of Wipf and Stock Publishers
199 W. 8th Ave., Suite 3
Eugene, OR 97401

www.wipfandstock.com

PAPERBACK ISBN: 978-1-6667-1700-6
HARDCOVER ISBN: 978-1-6667-1701-3
EBOOK ISBN: 978-1-6667-1702-0

Cataloguing-in-Publication data:

Names: Barker, Jeremiah, author.

Title: Cosmic chastity in an age of technocratic lust: a song of three popes : the legacy of John Paul II and Benedict XVI in the Francis papacy: the theological, ethical, and spiritual heart of their social message / Jeremiah Barker.

Description: Eugene, OR: Cascade Books, 2023 | Includes bibliographical references and index.

Identifiers: ISBN 978-1-6667-1700-6 (paperback) | ISBN 978-1-6667-1701-3 (hardcover) | ISBN 978-1-6667-1702-0 (ebook)

Subjects: LCSH: Benedict XVI, Pope, 1927–2022. | Francis, Pope, 1936–. | John Paul II, Pope, 1920–2005. | Catholic Church—History—20th century. | Catholic Church—History—21st century.

Classification: BX1378.7 B34 2023 (print) | BX1378.7 (ebook)

MARCH 20, 2023 3:26 PM

For my Madonna House family and our guests.

For Ma, Da, Jonny, Carrie, Clara, Felicity, Aminata, Rafe, and River.

For St. Joseph of Nazareth.

For Sts. Joachim and Anne
and the Apocalypse between them.

We ourselves were once foolish, disobedient, slaves to various passions and pleasures, passing our days in malice and envy, hated by men and hating one another; but when the goodness and loving kindness of God our Saviour appeared, he saved us . . .

—TITUS 3:3–5A RSV

Ours is a tragic century where men are faced with tremendous decisions that shake the souls of the strongest. This is also the age of neuroses, of anxiety, of fears, of psychotherapy, tranquilizers, euphoriants—all symbols of man's desire to escape from reality, responsibility and decision-making. This is the age of idol-worship of status, wealth and power. These idols dominate the landscape like idols of old: they are squatty and fat. The First Commandment once again lies broken in the dust. The clouds of war, dark and foreboding—an incredible war of annihilation and utter destruction—come nearer. Dirge-like symphonies surround us and will not let us be.

What is the answer to all these darknesses that press so heavily on us? What are the answers to all these fears that make darkness at noon? What is the answer to the loneliness of men without God? What is the answer to the hatred of man toward God?

—CATHERINE DOHERTY, *POUSTINIA*

Contents

Preface: To My Fellow "JP2 Catholics" ix

Acknowledgments xix

Abbreviations xxi

INTRODUCTION

Introducing Cosmic Chastity 1
Why Interpreting the Popes from within the Culture Wars
Doesn't Work, and an Alternative Hermeneutic That Does

PART I: TRUTH, JUSTICE, AND CHARITY:
THE JP2-B16 LEGACY AND FRANCIS'S SOCIAL TEACHING

1

Resisting Relativism 17
JP2's and B16's Concern for Moral Truth, Justice, and Charity

2

Pope Francis on the Crisis of Communal Commitment 39
Moral Truth and the Truth about Family Life against
the Regime of Relativism

3

A Canticle of Praise against the Logic of Babel 66
The Papal Trio's Liturgical Ontology over
and against the Culture Wars

PART II: ANOTHER SONG, OTHER SINGERS; ANOTHER WAR, OTHER WARRIORS: A FIGHT FOR THE HEART OF CULTURE, THE MEANING OF WORK, AND VOCATIONAL COMMITMENT

4
Benedict and Francis in the Fiery Furnace   91
  A Fight for the Heart of Culture

5
The Truth about Work and the Worker   120
  JP2 and Benedict against Economic Injustice

6
JP2 and Francis on the Call of Christ   139
  A Fight for Love-Fueled Responsibility
  and Vocational Commitment

PART III: THE HARMONY OF MORAL TRUTH AGAINST THE CACOPHONY OF RELATIVISM

7
Francis and the Tradition of Cosmic Chastity
against the Dictatorship of Relativism   167

8
An Ode to Truth   194
  JP2's and Francis's Shared Insistence on Moral
  Truth in the Crucible of Family Life Today

9
A Rehabilitation of Marriage and Family   216
  The Papal Trio on the Summit of Creation

CONCLUSION
Prophetic Outcry and Liturgical Praise
in the Fiery Furnace of Technocratic Lust   243

Bibliography   249

Index   257

Preface

To My Fellow "JP2 Catholics"

"When you want to get to know a sports car, you've got to get inside it, and drive it fast." This is what R. R. Reno, editor of *First Things*, said to a group of Catholic students who were just beginning their studies at Princeton in the fall of 2012. Reno was using the image of "getting to know a sports car" to illustrate what it means to think critically from within a tradition, as opposed to maintaining an allegedly "neutral" and "academic" distance from the truth claims of an inherited tradition. Only by way of tradition are we equipped with a grammar to think critically about our own tradition and other traditions, Reno was proposing. If you want to think critically about your own tradition, Reno was saying, don't stand away from it at a "safe," "objective" distance, as though that'll enable you to think more critically about it. No, get inside of it, and "drive it fast."

After the talk, I made a point of speaking with Reno, whom I had already been following as an eager disciple for several years. I told him about my long-standing existential struggle concerning whether to turn "Romeward." I had just enrolled as an MDiv student at Princeton Theological Seminary, largely on the basis of what Reno had written in the pages of *First Things* about its place in the pantheon of theological "Schools of Thought." Reno had proposed that Princeton Seminary was the best place to study Protestant dogmatics,[1] and so I went in order to deal with the question of whether to embrace Protestantism or become Catholic. After an engaging chat, the conversation came to a natural close, we exchanged farewells, and I turned for the door. "Jeremiah," Reno called to me as I was just about to step out onto the porch, facing Mercer

---

1. Reno, "Schools of Thought," para. 28.

Street. I turned to look back at him. "Don't stay in the antechambers of the Church for too long."

When the First Sunday of Lent came around that spring, I underwent my "first scrutinies" as a part of the Rite of Christian Initiation for Adults (RCIA) program in Princeton University's Catholic chaplaincy. The next morning, as I was eating waffles with my friend Vevian Zaki in the seminary cafeteria, she looked down at her iPhone and said to me with alarm, "The pope is resigning!" I didn't believe her. Vevian knew how much I loved Benedict.

That Lent was the Lent between two popes, the Lent of my scrutinies, the Lent of farewell to a beloved proclaimer of the gospel at the helm of Peter's bark. It was likewise the Lent in which the next pope— Francis—won my heart, and there he struck a symphonic chord. From everything I saw and heard, Francis was rocking it as pope, meeting the needs of a besieged global flock.

By the first autumn of his papacy, Francis was already ruffling some feathers among many of my fellow Catholics involved with Princeton's Catholic chaplaincy, where I had begun serving as coordinator for the "Grad Fellowship" group. While many of my fellow Catholics committed to orthodoxy perceived dissonance in the Francis message, I was hearing something very different, something that came to my ears as music, music in deep harmony with the song I had already learned to love, the song JP2 and Benedict had long been singing.

During Benedict's papacy, his first volume of *Jesus of Nazareth* captured my imagination, and has since maintained its claim upon my heart. The text is dear to me, as it presented anew to my searching soul the figure of the protagonist of the four Gospels. One of the sections of that volume that continually comes to mind is the chapter in which Cardinal Ratzinger—elected as Successor to Peter in the midst of drafting that very volume—enters into conversation with Rabbi Jacob Neusner,[2] author of *A Rabbi Talks with Jesus*. In Neusner's book, the rabbi enters into a dialogue with Jesus of Nazareth as he is presented in Matthew's Gospel.[3] In his own book, Pope Benedict in turn joins Rabbi Neusner and Jesus, among the crowds at a mount in Galilee, where Jesus delivers an extensive sermon, popularly known as the Sermon on the Mount. Following

2. Benedict, *Jesus of Nazareth*, 103–22.
3. See Neusner, *Rabbi Talks with Jesus*, 7–11.

the sermon, as Neusner and Jesus make their way down the dusty roads of Palestine toward Jerusalem, the theologian in the shoes of the fisherman—Benedict XVI—comes alongside Jesus and Neusner, joining in on their conversation. Neusner, for his part, expresses his admiration and astonishment at the words of the new teacher from Nazareth.[4] Yet, he concludes at the end that he cannot follow this compelling rabbi, for his teachings are, he says, a departure from the faith of Abraham and Sarah, Isaac and Rebecca, Jacob, Leah, and Rachel. Ratzinger and Neusner cordially, but decisively, part company: Neusner, on a path more faithful—he firmly believes—to the teachings of Moses, and Ratzinger, for his part, in company with Jesus. Precisely in this following of the rabbi from Galilee, Benedict believes he is following the one whose teaching fulfills the law of Moses and that in this following he is incorporated—as a gentile—into the very family of Abraham.

This conversation between the professor-pope and the professor-rabbi—each in conversation with the carpenter-rabbi—in the pages of *Jesus of Nazareth*, has since served as a model for me. Neusner and Benedict each take seriously the claims of their counterparts, seriously enough to recognize what is distinctive in their respective claims. This is anything but a dialogue built upon the cordiality of relativism. The cordiality is rooted in the mutual desire for truth. My professor Phillip Cary exhorted his students to appropriate postmodern "hospitality" in this very way. That is, we must be hospitable enough to really welcome and orient our conversation partner to our own turf, our own home, with its own distinctive sets of claims, axioms, judgments, and proposals. I hope that in the following pages, I can make a contribution to this style of conversation—a style of engaging in vibrant dialogue with mutual respect rooted in conviction.

In the pages of *Commonweal* magazine, Massimo Faggioli has characterized American Catholicism as the global center of opposition to Pope Francis, and characterized *First Things* as the main intellectual organ of that opposition.[5] This volume is a response to the *First Things* editor-in-chief, Dr. Reno, whom I'm conceiving of as this book's primary conversation partner. It's a student's first response to the professor in a classroom discussion, as it were. And in his response to the teacher's lectures, this

---

4. Benedict, *Jesus of Nazareth*, 114; Neusner, *Rabbi Talks with Jesus*, 155–61.

5. Faggioli, "Whose Rome?," para. 1.

student zeroes in on what he's identifying as the theological, ethical, and spiritual core of the social message of Francis and the two previous popes. The topic of conversation is the legacy of JP2 and Benedict in the Francis papacy. I call that legacy by a single name—*cosmic chastity*, the meaning of which we'll be exploring throughout the rest of this book.

To get a sense of what I'm after, imagine, if you will, that Reno is teaching a class on "The Church and Society Today." Let's say that a number of Reno's lectures for the class include commentary on Pope Francis in relation to current societal trends and in relation to the teaching of the two previous popes. Imagine that I'm one of Professor Reno's students in the back row, a student who to a great extent is a disciple of Reno the theologian. I conceive of this book as a friendly conversation in which I seek to bring to the attention of those listening in on my rebuttal to Dr. Reno a vision of *Catholic social teaching as an integral whole*, rooted as it is in the Church's theological tradition, in direct opposition to what I'm calling *technocracy's regime of lust*. The vision of Catholic social teaching of which I speak is one with a rich theological inheritance. It has been advocated by JP2, Benedict, and Francis together, each of whom draw upon the heritage of that teaching going back to Leo XIII and beyond into the Church's past—a past of long-standing resistance to lust's tyranny.

What initially won this student over to Reno—what compelled him to follow his lead in thinking theologically and in interpreting the signs of the times—was Reno's compelling way of reading the Bible. Reno's eager back-row student has hung on to every word of Reno's series preface to the *Brazos Theological Commentary on the Bible,* as though it were his own personal mandate. Over and against the modern "consensus that classical Christian doctrine distorts interpretive understanding,"[6] Reno proposed that doctrine is, in truth, "a clarifying agent, an enduring tradition of theological judgments that amplifies the living voice of scripture."[7] In opposition to the view that "a noncommitted" reading of Scripture is "the way toward objectivity," Reno boldly observed that "an interpretation unprejudiced" simply invites "the languid intellectual apathy that stands aside to make room for the false truisms and easy answers of the age."[8]

Reno is a representative spokesperson for a vibrant, socially engaged Catholicism that roots itself in orthodoxy. With him I see many

6. Reno, series preface to the *Brazos Theological Commentary*, 11.
7. Reno, series preface to the *Brazos Theological Commentary*, 11.
8. Reno, series preface to the *Brazos Theological Commentary*, 11.

conversation partners whom I seek to engage here through my dialogue with him: Raymond de Souza, Ross Douthat, Douglas Farrow, Matthew Schmitz, George Weigel, and Julia Yost among them, each prominent contributors to the intellectual-social formation of North America's core faithful, and each of whom have found themselves in a position to resist forces of liberalization, secularization, and relativism within and outside the Church in what many call the "culture wars." Each of these theologically informed North American Catholic social commentators are a delight to read and to listen to, each in their own distinctive ways. Among these conversation partners, Reno has been the most formative for me, and is therefore the one I have to reckon with the most in my own heart, in discerning a way of moving as a Catholic in the public square today.

My own steps have taken a distinctive turn away from Reno, particularly with respect to a hermeneutics of the Francis message. Whereas Francis is dismissed by Reno as having entered into a peace pact with the liberal elite, he models for me a way of moving boldly as a Catholic in the public square today. Reno's reading of Francis is a reading I regard as false and misdirected. I've become convinced that Francis's lead takes us in the right direction. But that direction is something that Reno hasn't managed to perceive in his reading of Francis. What Francis actually directs us toward is what I seek to explicate in this book. And I'm convinced that we can clearly perceive what Francis is pointing the way toward if we give him a fair and more thorough hearing on his own hermeneutical playing field; or, to switch metaphors, if we give him a more thorough hearing in what I refer to in this book as the *amphitheater of Catholic social teaching* in which Francis sings his song, according to the acoustical structure of that body of the Church's theological teaching to which Francis submits and to which he consistently appeals.

What I put forward in these pages is an introductory presentation of the theology and accompanying ethos and spirituality of cosmic chastity that grounds the body of the Church's social doctrine as it is presented by Francis and the two previous popes. With respect to interpreting the Francis message, this book offers an alternative hermeneutic to the one exemplified by much of Reno's commentary on Francis in the pages of *First Things*. By way of presenting *cosmic chastity* as the singular social message of the JP2, Benedict, and Francis papacies, I place Francis's thinking in close association with that of the two previous popes. This book, then, doesn't primarily argue for a hermeneutic of continuity; it executes and exemplifies a hermeneutic of continuity.

With respect to how to read the signs of the times, this student in the back row of Reno's classroom is fundamentally a disciple of JP2 and Benedict, two of *the* great heralds of the Catholic faith in his lifetime and in the lifetime of his fellow classmates of committed millennial Catholics. The student writing this volume looks to JP2 and B16 as heralds of Catholic orthodoxy, heralds of the glad tidings of Jesus Christ in the contemporary world, as the Moses and Elijah of Catholic social teaching as it pertains to the present moment. These two figures—this student believes—show the way of moving as a Catholic in the public square. The pressing concern of Vatican II—that of the Church's mission in the modern world—was the concern that animated the missionally driven hearts of these two ecclesial giants when they served as young theological advisors at the council, and throughout their subsequent scholarly and pastoral careers. In a decades-long fraternal collaboration, these two dogmatically rooted Vatican II rock stars forged the way for a New Evangelization and lit the fire of a culture of life in the dark night of a culture of death. As collaborative shepherd-intellectuals and formators of a new generation of the core faithful, they were keenly on guard against the ideological wolves that threatened their ecclesial flock, ever prone as this flock was to wander straight into an ideological den of beasts.

My fellow committed Catholic "classmates" and I are largely formed by JP2's robust Marian spirituality, his zeal for evangelization, and his vision of sexual chastity in an age of endemic and systematically fed sexual lust. We are likewise very much children of Benedict's christocentricity, his love for the liturgy, and his commitment to the Word of God. We are especially formed by JP2's and B16's outspoken commitment to orthodoxy and moral truth in a relativistic age. And Francis, according to my portrayal of him in this book, follows very closely in their footsteps. What impresses this back-row student about JP2 and B16 is very much what impresses him about Francis.

By way of this text, I seek to explain what I'm hearing in the message of Francis and the two previous popes. As many faithful North American Catholics look to JP2 and Benedict as allies in their struggles for social and political influence, and as this book presents JP2 and Benedict as allies of Francis's social concerns, the theological rationale of JP2's and Benedict's social teaching will serve—in this text—a mediating function between *Francis* on the one hand and faithful *conservative North American Catholics* on the other. Both Francis and the core faithful of his flock in North America claim an alliance with JP2 and Benedict, but the relationship between Francis and a significant portion of the core faithful is characterized by tension. Many faithful Catholics perceive Francis as possessing what seem to be undeniable and obvious weaknesses—not just his alleged propensity for doctrinal sloppiness (remarks on airplanes, the "infamous" *AL* footnote, his nonresponse to the *dubia*) but also some of his purportedly preposterous appointments and fellow travelers (e.g., Cardinal Paglia and the JP2 Institute). Though this book is not itself polemical in character, as it does not set out to directly dismantle every suspicion of Francis one by one and explain his every move, it does offer a reckoning with these apparent weaknesses on Francis's part, and it does so by presenting the theological, ethical, and spiritual heart of the Francis message, in the light of which his words and actions can be thoroughly comprehended and in a way that I think can awaken an enthusiasm and support for Francis on the part of those zealously concerned for the preservation and promulgation of the orthodox faith today. Once we can see Francis in the same theological, ethical, and spiritual space as JP2 and Benedict, it will be easier, I suggest, to see him in relation to the concerns that animate the faithful Catholics who are concerned that Francis is a threat to orthodoxy. My hope is that any JP2 Catholics reading this book can walk away from the text with a sense that the heart of the Francis message is something that they can get behind, something that calls for a serious and much-needed societal conversion. Indeed, it's my hope that readers will find in Francis, by way of this text, an enlightening guide through the confusing and tumultuous landscape of our day, as I have found him to be in my own life as a millennial Catholic who considers himself a child of JP2 and Benedict.

I would like to identify at the outset an aspect of the papal trio's social teaching that runs as a red thread throughout this volume's theological, ethical, and spiritual meditation on the singular message of the three popes, particularly as it manifests itself in the message of Francis. This book harps strongly upon cosmic chastity's demand upon the human heart to make a definitive gift-of-self according to a theology of creation-as-gift, in direct opposition to the lustful urgings of our consumeristic, relativistic, and technocratic society. That is to say, this book harps upon cosmic chastity's vision of sexuality, marriage, family, and vocational commitment as part of a larger logic of integral ecology according to a theology of creation-as-gift in thorough opposition to relativism, technocracy, and consumerism. An integral vision of sexuality, marriage, family, and vocation as part of a larger logic of integral ecology is a vision that interprets human sexuality as fundamentally about *making a definitive gift-of-self*. Human sexuality is conceived of in this book as itself a revelation of creation's built-in demand upon the human heart that we do everything in our power to find a way of making a gift of ourselves. Hence, *the demand* (that we strive to make a gift of ourselves) and *the icon of that demand* (human sexuality, expressed primarily in marriage and family as well as in vocational commitment in consecrated life and holy orders) stand in opposition to the same evil triplets which in turn conspire *against* chastity and *for* lust, namely, relativism, technocracy, and consumerism.

According to this book's hermeneutic, Francis's *LS* is read as a companion encyclical to Benedict's *CV*. Both sound an insistent indictment upon business as usual in a culture that finds itself in the clutches of the market's rationale of use and abuse of the world's people and things. The singular *CV-LS* social platform of Benedict and Francis in the JP2 tradition of social thought calls for serious social change—change that many people today, conservatives and progressives alike, intuitively know we need. There is an intuitive sense among many millennials and Gen Zers that there is a serious problem with business as usual in the global market. That is to say, there is a widespread conviction in society today that there is a serious problem with how we manage (or mismanage) our household as a society, in how we manage (or mismanage) our common home.

For the papal trio and the radical left, our household mismanagement is largely a matter of ecology and economics. And for the papal trio, our economic and ecological crisis of household mismanagement is deeply related to our society-wide misunderstanding of the micro-household, and particularly, our misunderstanding of the bedroom, of the marriage bed, of family, of sexuality, of our bodies in relation to other bodies, as well as our misunderstanding of the integral relation between the sacred matter of the body and the marriage bed on the one hand and, on the other hand, household management as a whole—on micro and macro levels. The very concern which unites the papal trio's concern with the fundamental concern of the radical left—the shared papal and leftist objection to the neoliberal logic of the market and the shared papal and leftist concern for the environmental crisis—is for the papal trio deeply connected with a false understanding of sexuality, which has duped much of the political left, and which, I dare say, has duped much of the political right, as well. The ecological crisis, the economic crisis, and the crisis in sexuality is, for the papal trio, a singular crisis in failing to perceive the implications of the Christian doctrine of creation-as-gift.

The problem with business as usual in the liberal market, which is a problem with our societal practices of household mismanagement, is fundamentally about our need for the virtue of chastity over and against the vice of lust. And in using the terms "chastity" and "lust," I mean to apply them in the broadest sense, with meaning inclusive of but not restricted to their explicitly sexual aspects. The problem with business as usual, I suggest, is that it lacks the criteria of love rooted in truth, a love which is inherently chaste—which is what Benedict called for in *CV*, and what Francis has consistently called for after him. The problem with business as usual in society today is that it is governed by the technocratic paradigm, which in turn is harnessed to feed the lusts of our hearts. The technocratic paradigm feeds into our disordered desires, and further deforms our hearts, furthering the disorder of our already-disordered impulses. And the prophetic outcry of the Francis papacy, in deep continuity with the message of the two popes before him, is fundamentally an outcry against this paradigm with the lusts that it feeds upon and which it feeds.

In much of popular discourse today, the distinction that is thought to be of import is the distinction between liberal and conservative. And by way of popular (mis)perceptions, we drag our discussions about what the popes have to say into the superficial spats of the culture wars that divide social perspectives into these two categories. I propose *another divide, one that I think is more fundamental, more important, and more relevant to a Catholic worldview*, namely, the divide between the rationale of technocratic lust on the one hand, and the rationale of cosmic chastity on the other. With respect to this divide, Francis stands securely alongside the two previous popes, singing a prophetic song of truth, justice, love, and peace, a song that shall ultimately prevail—eschatologically speaking—over the dissonant clamor of technocracy and lust.

Jeremiah Barker
Combermere, Ontario
Solemnity of St. Joseph, Husband of Mary, 2023
Tenth Anniversary of the Beginning of the Francis Pontificate

Acknowledgments

THOSE WHO HAVE SHARED a home with me, in work and recreation, have given me a glimpse of what it is to love chastely. This began with the faith and the love for the Church I received from my parents. It likewise began with my older brother Jonathan, apart from whom everything about me and this book is inexplicable. This book is a fruit of an extensive, vibrant conversation we've been having our whole lives, and which became a conversation with our brothers in spirit Adam Beach and Joshua Lore. Austen Detweiler likewise became a key part of this conversation in the early years of Francis's papacy. This conversation's development owes a great deal to the integrated sexual ethic that Phillip Cary, Christopher C. Roberts, and R. J. Snell were passing on to their eager searching students at Eastern University and Villanova.

Without Teresa Gehred's initial affirmation of my vision for this book, I would not have perceived its composition as falling within the purview of my Madonna House vocation. Without Phillip Cary's significant help in kick-starting this book's early development, and without his practical advice throughout the drafting process, this project would not have come to fruition. Christina Milan provided the occasion for me to crack open JP2's *Theology of the Body* just as the book was beginning to develop in outline form. Scott Sanderson's encouragement as the book began to take shape in my heart was key to getting me kick-started in the task. Alejandro Lozano was instrumental in helping me think out the shape of the book at its genesis. Veronica Ferri and Ana Sofia Corona Gaxiola helped me perceive the pathway that lay ahead in the manuscript's development, and Sara Matthews came in with some helpful feedback at the end. Joey Alfano, Amy Barnes, Meaghan Boyd, Jeff George, L. Gordon Graham, Solomon Ip, Brian Nafarrette, Nicholas Parrott, Scott Pichard, Fr. Robert Wild, and Daniel Wildish at various

xix

stages of the drafting process engaged portions of the text and provided helpful feedback. One conversation with Daniel Perren helped me identify what's at stake in some of the controversies surrounding *AL* chapter 8. Chris Hanlon and the brothers at Noreen's provided the much-needed ambiance and fraternity in our own "Hell's Kitchen." And many thanks to Rodney Clapp, editor at Cascade, for taking on my first book and seeing it through to publication.

Working with Doug Guss and Michael Amaral in the H.E.L.P. (Heating, Electrical, Landscaping, Plumbing) Department afforded me the opportunity to be accompanied by two grounded laborers in the vineyard of the Lord, who put flesh on the bones of integral human development as grateful stewards of the gifts of God. Doug with chain saw, backhoe, tractor, and dump truck displays a rough-and-ready *poustinik's* cosmic tenderness that I can't cherish enough, combined with his unmatchable attention to the ways of the cosmos as they manifest themselves in a cat on the prowl, a doe and fawns crossing the road, a frenzied squirrel, a chickadee begging for peanuts in a nearby shrub, a juicy grub ripe to be hooked as bait for a trout. Doug, along with Fr. Louis Labrecque and Darrin Prowse, consistently demonstrates for me the ethos of chaste love at work in that "bright sadness" of the sugar bush, that outpost of the redemption that is nigh and that embassy of the resurrection on Carmel Hill.

Those with whom I have collaborated in the Madonna House "veggie basement" have been irreplaceable for me in ongoingly forming and reforming my heart—my steadfast sisters and brothers who have labored closely with me in that context have taught me so much about what love is like through thick and thin.

Elizabeth Bassarear, Theresa Davis, Steve Heroux, Fr. Kieran Kilcommons, Larry Klein, and Fr. David Linder have provided ever-treasured life direction during the time of this book's development, direction that's been indispensable for writing in the midst of the concrete circumstances of our shared life "hidden with Christ in God."[9]

The Barker family and my MH family with our guests have provided the immediate social circumstances for me to begin to catch a glimpse of the meaning of the Church's social teaching. This book's dedication honors them as a part of that tradition of the Christian social vision inaugurated in the homes of Joachim and Anne, of Joseph and Mary, in that small village on the fringes of the Roman Empire.

9. Col 3:3.

Abbreviations

AL   *Amoris laetitia*. Pope Francis. Apostolic exhortation. The Vatican, March 19, 2016. https://www.vatican.va/content/francesco/en/apost_exhortations/documents/papa-francesco_esortazione-ap_20160319_amoris-laetitia.html.

CA   *Centesimus annus*. Pope John Paul II. Encyclical letter. The Vatican, May 1, 1991. https://www.vatican.va/content/john-paul-ii/en/encyclicals/documents/hf_jp-ii_enc_01051991_centesimus-annus.html.

"CM"   "Colombo to Manila." Pope Francis, interviewed by Jerry O'Connell. "Press Conference of His Holiness Pope Francis Onboard the Flight from Colombo to Manila." The Vatican, January 15, 2015. https://www.vatican.va/content/francesco/en/speeches/2015/january/documents/papa-francesco_20150115_srilanka-filippine-incontro-giornalisti.html.

"CR"   "Czech Republic." Pope Francis. "Address of Pope Francis to the Bishops of the Episcopal Conference of the Czech Republic on their '*Ad Limina*' Visit." The Vatican, February 14, 2014. https://www.vatican.va/content/francesco/en/speeches/2014/february/documents/papa-francesco_20140214_ad-limina-rep-ceca.html.

CV   *Caritas in veritate*. Pope Benedict XVI. Encyclical letter. The Vatican, June 29, 2009. https://www.vatican.va/content/benedict-xvi/en/encyclicals/documents/hf_ben-xvi_enc_20090629_caritas-in-veritate.html.

EG   *Evangelii gaudium*. Pope Francis. Apostolic exhortation. The Vatican, November 24, 2013. https://www.vatican.

va/content/francesco/en/apost_exhortations/documents/
papa-francesco_esortazione-ap_20131124_evangelii-gaud-
ium.html.

EV   *Evangelium vitae*. Pope John Paul II. Encyclical letter.
           The Vatican, March 25, 1995. https://www.vatican.va/
           content/john-paul-ii/en/encyclicals/documents/hf_jp-
           ii_enc_25031995_evangelium-vitae.html.

FC   *Familiaris consortio*. Pope John Paul II. Apostolic exhor-
           tation. The Vatican, November 22, 1981. https://www.
           vatican.va/content/john-paul-ii/en/apost_exhortations/
           documents/hf_jp-ii_exh_19811122_familiaris-consortio.
           html.

"FMW"   "A Future More Worthy of the Human Person." General
           audience. January 24, 2001. https://www.vatican.va/con-
           tent/john-paul-ii/en/audiences/2001/documents/hf_jp-
           ii_aud_20010124.html.

FT   *Fratelli tutti*. Pope Francis. Encyclical letter. The Vatican,
           October 3, 2020. https://www.vatican.va/content/francesco/
           en/encyclicals/documents/papa-francesco_20201003_en-
           ciclica-fratelli-tutti.html.

HV   *Humanae vitae*. Pope Paul VI. Encyclical letter. The Vatican,
           July 25, 1968. https://www.vatican.va/content/paul-vi/en/
           encyclicals/documents/hf_p-vi_enc_25071968_humanae-
           vitae.html.

LE   *Laborem exercens*. Pope John Paul II. Encyclical letter.
           The Vatican, September 14, 1981. https://www.vatican.
           va/content/john-paul-ii/en/encyclicals/documents/hf_jp-
           ii_enc_14091981_laborem-exercens.html.

"L&E"   "Latvia and Estonia." Pope Francis. "Address of His Holi-
           ness Pope Francis to the Bishops of the Episcopal Confer-
           ence of Latvia and Estonia on their '*Ad Limina*' Visit." The
           Vatican, June 11, 2015. https://www.vatican.va/content/
           francesco/en/speeches/2015/june/documents/papa-fran-
           cesco_20150611_adlimina-lettonia-estonia.html.

LR1   *Love and Responsibility*. Karol Wojtyla. Translated by Grzer-
           gorz Ignatik. Boston: Pauline, 2013.

LR2   *Love and Responsibility*. Karol Wojtyla. Translated by H. T. Willetts. San Francisco: Ignatius, 1993.

LS   *Laudato si'*. Pope Francis. Encyclical letter. The Vatican, May 24, 2015. https://www.vatican.va/content/francesco/en/encyclicals/documents/papa-francesco_20150524_enciclica-laudato-si.html.

LUD   *Let Us Dream: The Path to a Better Future*. Pope Francis. In conversation with Austen Ivereigh. New York: Simon and Schuster, 2020.

"M&F1"   "Male and Female, Catechesis I." Pope Francis. "The Family: Male and Female (I)." General audience. The Vatican, April 15, 2015. https://www.vatican.va/content/francesco/en/audiences/2015/documents/papa-francesco_20150415_udienza-generale.html.

"M&F2"   "Male and Female, Catechesis II." Pope Francis. "The Family: Male and Female (II)." General audience. The Vatican, April 22, 2015. https://www.vatican.va/content/francesco/en/audiences/2015/documents/papa-francesco_20150422_udienza-generale.html.

MW   *Man and Woman*. Pope John Paul II. *Man and Woman He Created Them: A Theology of the Body*. Translated by Michael Waldstein. Boston: Pauline, 2006.

OA   *Octogessima adveniens*. Pope Paul VI. Apostolic letter. The Vatican, May 14, 1971. https://www.vatican.va/content/paul-vi/en/apost_letters/documents/hf_p-vi_apl_19710514_octogesima-adveniens.html.

PC   *Patris corde*. Pope Francis. Apostolic letter. The Vatican, December 8, 2020. https://www.vatican.va/content/francesco/en/apost_letters/documents/papa-francesco-lettera-ap_20201208_patris-corde.html.

PP   *Populorum progressio*. Pope Paul VI. Encyclical letter. The Vatican, March 26, 1967. https://www.vatican.va/content/paul-vi/en/encyclicals/documents/hf_p-vi_enc_26031967_populorum.html.

RH   *Redemptoris hominis.* Pope John Paul II. Encyclical letter. The Vatican. March 4, 1979. https://www.vatican.va/content/john-paul-ii/en/encyclicals/documents/hf_jp-ii_enc_04031979_redemptor-hominis.html.

RN   *Rereum novarum.* Pope Leo XIII. Encyclical letter. The Vatican, May 15, 1891. https://www.vatican.va/content/leo-xiii/en/encyclicals/documents/hf_l-xiii_enc_15051891_rerum-novarum.html.

RSV   Revised Standard Version, Catholic Edition, copyrighted 1965 and 1966 by the Division of Christian Education of the National Council of the Churches of Christ in the U.S.A. *The Navarre Bible: New Testament, Compact Edition*, Scepter: Princeton, 2001.

SC   *Sign of Contradiction.* Pope John Paul. New York: Seabury, 1979.

SRS   *Solicitudo rei socialis.* Pope John Paul II. Encyclical letter. The Vatican, December 30, 1987. https://www.vatican.va/content/john-paul-ii/en/encyclicals/documents/hf_jp-ii_enc_30121987_sollicitudo-rei-socialis.html.

SS   *Spe salvi.* Pope Benedict XVI. Encyclical letter. The Vatican, November 30, 2007. https://www.vatican.va/content/benedict-xvi/en/encyclicals/documents/hf_ben-xvi_enc_20071130_spe-salvi.html.

TOB   *Theology of the Body.* Pope John Paul II. *The Theology of the Body: Human Love in the Divine Plan.* Reprinted translations of *L'Osservatore Romano.* Boston: Pauline, 1997.

VS   *Veritatis splendor.* Pope John Paul II. Encyclical letter. The Vatican, August 6, 1993. https://www.vatican.va/content/john-paul-ii/en/encyclicals/documents/hf_jp-ii_enc_06081993_veritatis-splendor.html.

"WMF" "World Meeting of Families." Pope Francis. "Meeting with Bishops Taking Part in the World Meeting of Families, Philadelphia." The Vatican, September 27, 2015. https://www.vatican.va/content/francesco/en/speeches/2015/september/documents/papa-francesco_20150927_usa-vescovi-festa-famiglie.html.

INTRODUCTION

· · · · ·

Introducing Cosmic Chastity

Why Interpreting the Popes from within the Culture Wars Doesn't Work, and an Alternative Hermeneutic That Does

THE PROBLEM WITH PAPAL HERMENEUTICS in North America today is that we easily fall into the trap of reading the popes as if they're players in a game they're not actually playing. Or, to return to the metaphor of music: Reno, as a papal music critic representative of many a faithful Catholic, thinks that Francis is singing from a dated 1970s hymnbook.[1] I am proposing an alternative reading of the Francis soundtrack. Francis is singing, I am convinced, from the perennial prophetic hymnbook of Catholic social teaching. The song of Francis's papal message, which has a particular resonance in this progressive millennial moment, is structured by the philosophical and dogmatic pattern of the social teaching of JP2 and Benedict, and has no resemblance to the shallow moral relativism

---

1. In 2013, Reno was still presenting Francis as merely *perceived* by *National Catholic Reporter* and *Huffington Post* as singing from their hymnal. See Reno, "How to Limit Government," sec. "Popes and Interviews," paras. 9–13. By the time of "Crisis of Solidarity" (November 2015), "Francis's Improv Theology" (June 2016), para. 10, "A Militant Church" (July 2017), "Building Bridges," (November 2017), "Failing Papacy" (February 2019), and "Francis Stands Firm" (February 2020), Reno has become more direct in characterizing Francis as a cliché-laden ally of the liberal elite. Reno's reflection on Francis's alleged defense of "Bourgeois Religion" in December 2017 is particularly biting. If there's one article in response to which I seek to offer an alternative hermeneutic of the Francis message, it's this one (Reno, "Liberal Tradition, Yes; Ideology, No," sec. "Bourgeois Religion," paras. 6–8).

1

of old liberal Catholics who get a kick out of distributing condoms and celebrating mass around a coffee table with pita bread and wine in a mug.

Whereas the words of JP2 and Benedict were regularly mined for ammunition on the part of the right against the left, Francis leaves very little ammo for the right, providing arms, it seems, for the right's most rabid opponents. Indeed, from the perspective of those most worried about Francis, it seems that he is driven by the very impulses that drive those popularly derided as "social justice warriors" in their "neo-Marxist" fight for truth and justice. For many Francis critics, it is taken for granted that those are accurate descriptions for the important social dynamics at play in our world, and therefore, it is taken for granted that the bishop of Rome is "categorizable" in relation to those very dynamics—either for or against millennial "social justice warriors" (SJWs) and the boomer Woodstock idealists.[2] Francis is indeed dismissed as an ally of today's "SJWs" by many of North American Catholicism's ardent defenders of orthodoxy, who likewise take it for granted that this is a legitimate label for progressives and not just a polemical slur at the ready in the auto-suggest ammo magazine of online conservative social commentators. Francis sounds like one of these radical leftist democratic socialists and Black Lives Matter activists, or like one of their boomer predecessors at Woodstock, according to the categories appealed to on a popular level on the "conservative" side of the culture wars. For much of his papacy, Francis has been portrayed by both sides of the culture wars as something of a Bernie Sanders of Rome. And depending on whether Bernie is a symbol of progress or regress, Francis, too, is a symbol of the same. During his first presidential campaign (for the 2016 election), Bernie even found it expedient to make regular appeal to the figure of Francis, and made a point of shaking his hand in the Vatican during the height of the campaign season. And that's what worries the "conservative" culture warriors. Francis seems a little too cozy with the left.

What is needed is a more serious and attentive theological engagement of Francis's teaching in direct interaction with that of JP2 and B16, in view of the thoughtful concerns of Francis's sharpest critics. It is the aim of this book to begin taking some steps toward meeting that need. This student in the back row of Reno's class raises his hand to speak, concerned that many of his classmates are ill-equipped to receive—in the message of Francis—the best transmission on offer of the JP2-B16

---

2. See Reno, "Failing Papacy," para. 12.

message into this present cultural moment. This student's classmates are ill-equipped to receive a message that he thinks is very important for us to be hearing at this moment in history, a message that stands up boldly against the forces of technocracy, relativism, and the commercial logic.[3]

I'm making a distinction here between my *conversation partners* (represented primarily by Professor Reno) on the one hand and my *audience* on the other, my fellow "classmates" in the lecture hall of North American Catholicism, listening in, as it were, as I respond to the professor's commentary on the current pontificate. It is for this audience of faithful Catholics who are ambivalent about Francis that I want to articulate the theological social vision at the core of the papacies of JP2, Benedict, and Francis, and which, when identified, brings to light the profundity of the message of the Francis pontificate.

My audience for this book, whom, as I have said, I envision as "classmates" listening in on my response to Professor Reno, are devoted Catholics who have a beautiful culturally formed "instinct" for sexual chastity, formed as they have been by JP2's theology of the body. Their hearts have been formed to cherish various key aspects of the message of JP2. These young Catholics have an innate fidelity to B16, given his obvious connection and continuity with JP2. They are now left with very little to say about Francis, with an ambivalence toward him, with a big question mark regarding this papacy, and lacking an appetite for the culture wars and for the spats in the press and on online platforms. They are unequipped to navigate the varying claims about the meaning and message of this pontificate. They feel the bite of an aggressive anti-Christian culture, and they want a pontiff who stands up for the truth of the faith in the face of aggressive secularization.

A primary question for this student in Reno's "course" on Catholicism and society today is whether the content of Francis's message is to be dismissed as strung-together dated clichés from the seventies,[4] contribut-

---

3. As Benedict states, "Economic activity cannot solve all social problems through the simple application of *commercial logic*." Economic activity, Benedict insists, "needs to be *directed towards the pursuit of the common good*, for which the political community in particular must also take responsibility . . . [G]rave imbalances are produced when economic action conceived merely as an engine for wealth creation, is detached from political action" (*CV*, sec. 36). Emphasis in quotes are original, unless indicated otherwise.

4. See Reno, "Francis Stands Firm," para. 4, where Reno identifies in JP2 and Benedict the same weakness for dialogue that characterizes Francis. For Reno's take on why Francis's appeals to dialogue and bridge-building are untimely, see also Reno,

ing to a process of liberalization and secularization in the Church by way of a confusing refusal of precision (like the project of the loosey-goosey rule-breaking Jesuits at Creighton University with whom Reno has come to associate Francis),[5] or if Francis's message is to be embraced as belonging to the same genre of robustly orthodox prophetic social criticism proper to JP2 and B16.[6] To which intellectual family tree does Francis's message belong? Reno associates Francis's message with the former, while his student in the back row associates it with the latter. Part of what I'm hoping readers of this book will come to see is that connecting Francis with the two previous popes gets him right in a way that connecting him with loosey-goosey liberalizers gets him wrong.

If we take it for granted that JP2 and B16 more or less had an alliance with the cause of the religious right in North America, and if the religious right is under fire in the Francis pontificate, then we take it for granted that Francis is an enemy of the very causes for which JP2 and B16 fought. This is a taken-for-granted story line with which many of my Catholic classmates are familiar. It's precisely this story line that I seek to deconstruct in this book, and in opposition to which I seek to tell the narrative in an alternative manner, in a manner truer to the categories that matter to the Church's social doctrine. In the assessment of some of my classmates, however, the story of the popes since the opening of Vatican II can be told in the following way: we had a Democrat in the Chair of Peter in the person of John XXIII, followed by the Republican Paul VI (whose Republican platform was particularly clear in his preemptive strike against the HHS mandate in the encyclical *HV*), followed by a movie star Republican JP2 (who with Ronald Reagan smashed the left, the communist regime, and the pro-choice caucus in one fell swoop), followed by the alt-right Republican B16, who in turn was followed by the return of the Democratic Party—with a socialistic vengeance!—to the Throne of Saint Peter in the person of Jorge Bergoglio.

Associating John XXIII and Francis with the Left in today's culture wars and Paul VI, JP2, and B16 with the Right is a caricature of what I take to be a popular narrative to which many of my *classmates* are susceptible, not the professor. But Reno is not clarifying for my classmates the distinction between the wars fought between Left and Right on the

---

"Building Bridges," para. 4, and Reno, "Crisis of Solidarity," para. 2.

5. See Reno, "Failing Papacy," para. 10, for the ambiguous "pastoral approach" of the Jesuits whom Reno knew at Creighton.

6. See Reno, "Francis's Improv Theology," para. 10.

one hand and, on the other hand, the war that John XXIII, Paul VI, JP2, B16, and Francis have each been fighting together as a singular force, joined as they are against a common opposition. And for what are these warriors fighting, from the perspective of Reno's back-row student? And against what do they stand in opposition? They're fighting on behalf of *cosmic chastity* over and against the *technocratic lust* that reigns supreme in society today.

This book arises from the conviction that the ways in which JP2 and B16 were confused as allies with American conservatism is as misleading, unclear, and confusing as any misapprehension of Francis's orthodoxy. As I don't have a stake in reacting against a liberal Catholicism that is dying out anyway, the bigger threat, in my view, sociologically, for the North American Church, is that we fall into a right-wing tribalism—and I love that Francis resists precisely that, all the while offering a viable and robustly Catholic alternative to the liberal and conservative sides of the culture wars.

Reno, highly critical of Francis, has called for a redemption of hints and suggestions of a cogent argument in the Francis message.[7] I reappropriate Reno's call as a call for me to draw out or highlight what I take to be the underlying rationale of the Francis message. That underlying rationale is strikingly similar to that of the two previous popes, and I'm surprised that Reno is missing it. This one student of Reno is in fact inspired by Francis's call and teaching, and it is the aim of this book to draw out what inspires me, and to identify what I hope Reno and my classmates don't miss in the Francis message. But as things stand, I think Reno is missing it, and is telling the Francis story in a false and misleading manner.

The Francis story as I perceive it and as I tell it in these pages is a story of proclaiming the message of cosmic chastity. "Cosmic chastity" is a name I assign to a theological perspective to which Francis subscribes and which precedes him. In accordance with this all-encompassing theology of creation-as-gift, if creaturely existence means existence-as-gift (mirroring the trinitarian interpersonal Existence-as-Gift), then my relationship to the gift and the dignity inherent to the gift has to be safeguarded by chastity, so as to honor the meaning of creaturely existence in relation to the Creator, and so as not to dishonor the meaning

---

7. Reno identifies a need for theologians to "apply themselves to redeem the hints and suggestions of a cogent argument" in *LS* specifically (Reno, "Weakness of *Laudato Si*," para. 30).

of creaturely existence, and thereby dishonor the Creator. Technocratic unchastity, or lust, refers to a posture that does not safeguard the dignity of creation-as-gift. Such unchastity, or lust, expresses itself across every sector of social life. It is precisely an all-encompassing technocratic *lust* that JP2, Benedict, and Francis have together opposed in the late twenti- eth and early twenty-first centuries.

Cosmic chastity calls us to overcome what is derived from what JP2 refers to as *lust in its three forms.*[8] That is, cosmic chastity stands over and against the lust of the eyes, the lust of the flesh, and the pride of life. A chastity that is cosmic, I propose, can be spoken of in terms of *chastity in its three forms*—chastity of the eyes, chastity of the flesh, and the humility of life, by which I mean a posture of love informed by an understanding of the truth of the meaning of our own creaturely status in relation to the Creator and in relation to the rest of creation. Cosmic chastity, i.e., chas- tity in its three forms, stands in corollary distinction from lust in its three forms. The posture of chaste love is the posture proper to the true, just, and loving humility of grateful creatures who know themselves to be the recipients of the gifts of the Creator who bestows gifts upon us in utter gratuity. The call to cosmic chastity in society is a call to overcome, in particular, aspects of human behavior arising from lust in its three forms as lust in its three forms manifests itself by way of what Pope Francis calls *the technocratic paradigm.* The technocratic paradigm fuels lust, and lust fuels the technocratic paradigm. Cosmic chastity, on the other hand, gets at the splendor of truth as perceived in every aspect of life in the light of the gospel.[9]

---

8. *TOB*, 10.29.1980. This *L'Osservatore Romano* English translation of the Italian word *concupiscenza* as "lust" is translated by Waldstein as "concupiscence." Whereas Waldstein, for good reason, establishes a technical distinction between concupiscence and lust, for the purposes of this book I use the word "lust" more broadly in reference to both the notion of *concupiscenza* as well as the notion of *lussuria* and *lussurioso* (Waldstein consistently translates the latter two words as "lust"). For an explanation of Waldstein's nuanced translation of these words in comparison with the *L'Osservatore* translation, see Waldstein, introduction to *Man and Woman*, 13. "Lust in its three forms" is translated by Waldstein as "*the threefold concupiscence*" (*MW*, 46:1).

9. My use of the word "chastity" here is akin to that of Walker and Caldecott. Walker explains Caldecott's contextual understanding of chastity thus: "By setting chastity within the solemn play of conjugal communion, Caldecott recovers the true splendor of sexual purity" (Walker, foreword to *Not as the World Gives*, xvi). For Caldecott, Walker explains, "chastity . . . both shapes and reflects the luminous pattern of all truly human polity" (Walker, foreword to *Not as the World Gives*, xvi). For Caldecott, "personal purity, social justice, and worship coinhere" (Walker, foreword to *Not as the World Gives*, xvi).

Presenting a snapshot of Catholic social teaching as articulated by the papal trio is the fundamental goal of this book. It is my hope that the theologically rooted social vision promoted by the papal trio will find a more prominent place in the hearts of some of my fellow "JP2 Catholics" who read this book, as it has begun to find a more prominent place within my own heart, thanks to the papal trio's teaching. This book, then, can be conceived of as an introduction to Catholic social teaching at large, as it draws upon JP2, Benedict, and Francis as primary sources for presenting that teaching, by way of engaging some of their encyclicals, exhortations, books, homilies, audiences, addresses, and interviews.

This book arises from a conviction that the JP2-B16 social message is inherently and fundamentally an *ecological* message. The ecological context of every facet of JP2's and B16's message is something we're not paying enough attention to in North America, I think. And this is a big part of why we're not perceiving what Francis is fundamentally up to in his pontificate. The real social project of the Francis pontificate, I contend, is to present the Christian moral vision with the cosmic backdrop of a theology of creation, as JP2 and Benedict had done. This theology of creation, we shall see, is integral to an eschatology, cosmology, and anthropology to which the Church testifies "in order to help people to live their lives in the dimension of authentic meaning," as we shall explore in the coming pages (to reappropriate Renato Martino's description of the aim of articulating the Church's social teaching).[10] This holistic theology of creation demands of us a posture of *cosmic chastity*, a posture whose meaning will become clearer as we engage the social vision of the papal trio. It's a vision that includes within its purview the demands of truth, justice, and love. Central to this posture of cosmic chastity is a posture that honors the dignity of the human person, the dignity of humanity as a whole, and the dignity of creation at large, by way of adhering to the demands of truth, which include the demands of justice and love.

The vision of cosmic chastity espoused by Francis and the two previous popes is an extension of JP2's theology of the body to the whole material creation. JP2 provides a grammar for this extension in his all-encompassing theology of creation-as-gift, which serves as the cosmic backdrop for his anthropology and theology of the human body. A theology of creation is the presupposed context for a theological anthropology of the human body and sexuality.

10. Martino and Crepaldi, "Presentation," para. 3.

It is in the context of reverence proper to an authentic integral ecology that JP2 spoke of environmental stewardship. He consistently spoke of environmental stewardship in terms of the truth of the meaning of creation, and in terms of the imperative of just and charitable relations among human beings and on the part of humanity in relation to the cosmos at large. In his "Meditation on Givenness," JP2 observes that

> nowadays, we often speak of "ecology," i.e., concern for the natural environment. The foundational basis for such ecology, however, is the mystery of creation, which is a great and incessant stream of giving all the goods of the cosmos to man—both those goods he encounters directly as well as those he only discovers through research and experiments utilizing the various methods of science. Man knows more and more about the riches of the cosmos, but at the same time he sometimes fails to recognize that these come from the hand of the Creator. However, there are times when all men, even nonbelievers, glimpse the truth of the givenness of creation and begin to pray, to acknowledge that all is a gift from God.[11]

The *truth of the givenness of creation* is the fundamental truth of cosmic chastity, at the center of the ethos, spirituality, and theology of cosmic chastity. The recognition of this truth is a recognition required for the development of an ethos of cosmic chastity in human hearts and in the heart of society. The truth of the givenness of creation is the foundational truth underlying an ethos of chastity, and is very much the underlying truth for an anthropology and ethos of sexual chastity in particular, which is at the heart of a theological ecology. This truth of the givenness of creation is what demands of us an ethos of chaste love. In what I'm calling JP2's critique of technocratic lust, he lamented the tendency of members of society today "to see no other meaning in their natural environment than what serves for immediate use and consumption"[12]—and this applies to human bodies, to the fruits of the land, to the work of our hands, and to every facet of the earth's ecosystems and the universe at large. JP2's "call for a global ecological conversion"[13] is based upon his theology of creation, and upon his understanding of humanity within creation. For JP2, our relationship with the rest of the cosmos must be determined by an anthropology and cosmology rooted in truth.

11. JP2, "Meditation on Givenness," 872–73.

12. *RH*, sec. 15; quoted in *LS*, sec. 5.

13. LS, sec. 5, citing JP2, "God Made Man," sec. 4.

"Cosmic chastity" is a name I've assigned to a notion according to which the cosmos, by its very nature, makes demands upon us. It demands that we bow our heads to its true meaning as cosmos. The truth of the cosmos demands that we render to every bit of God's creation what is its due, and thus render to the Creator what is his due, in a posture of what Wojtyla calls "justice toward the creator,"[14] according to the integral meaning of the cosmos as a whole and of each of its parts. The very nature of creation is such that creatures contain within themselves the demands of justice. From this perspective, the cause of justice pertains as much to ecology as it pertains to anthropology, within a vision according to which an authentic ecology depends upon an authentic anthropology and vice versa. JP2's anthropology (and notably, his theology of the human body) belongs within a larger theology of creation, his *theology of the cosmic body*.[15]

Immediately following his last visit with JP2—on the eve of JP2's death—Joseph Ratzinger gave a speech at the Benedictine convent of Subiaco.[16] There, Ratzinger sounded a call for men and women of our day to follow the example of St. Benedict of Norcia, who showed "the way that leads on high, beyond the crisis and the ruins" in "a time of dissipation and decadence."[17] Consistent with the overall message of Catholic social teaching, Ratzinger discussed in this context both the "great dangers" and "the great opportunities for man and the world" in these times.[18] In this address that Ratzinger gave at the threshold of his papacy, without using the term, he clearly presents the technocratic paradigm as *the* major threat to the common good in contemporary society.[19] For Ratzinger, the figure of St. Benedict served as an icon and model for the very theological, ethical, and spiritual vision that I'm calling the vision of "cosmic chastity," the vision which he advocated throughout his papacy under the patronage of St. Benedict.

14. *LR2*, 209–61. This is the title of *Love and Responsibility's* fourth chapter in the Willetts translation. Ignatik translates it "Justice with Respect to the Creator" (*LR1*, 193).

15. For the relationship between ecology and Catholic social teaching at large, see Schindler, "Habits of Presence," 575.

16. Peter Seewald recounts this address in relation to JP2's death and Ratzinger's subsequent election and papal ministry in Seewald, *Benedict XVI*, 2:249–52, and Seewald, *Light of the World*, 5.

17. Ratzinger, "Europe's Crisis of Culture," 326.

18. Ratzinger, "Europe's Crisis of Culture," 335.

19. Ratzinger, "Europe's Crisis of Culture," 325–36.

The notion of cosmic chastity found within the thinking of Pope Benedict rests upon his insistence—which he shares with JP2—that we must ensure that the natural environment receives the respect that is its due, according to the truth of its being.[20] For Benedict, it is precisely "the notion that there are no indisputable truths to guide our lives"[21] that has resulted in the degradation of both the natural environment and the social environment. Benedict insists that "the misuse of creation begins when we no longer recognize any higher instance than ourselves, when we see nothing else but ourselves."[22] The environmental crisis, for Benedict, is a consequence of a relativistic outlook, and as such is a part of the crisis in truth.

Another central icon of cosmic chastity alongside St. Benedict is the image of St. Francis of Assisi, which Pope Francis places before our eyes in the pages of LS.[23] According to Pope Francis, St. Francis's "response to the world around him was so much more than intellectual appreciation or economic calculus, for to him each and every creature was a sister united to him by bonds of affection. That is why he felt called to care for all that exists."[24] St. Francis's love was a chaste love which extended to the entirety of the cosmos, on all levels, both macro and micro. The Benedict-Francis call for a deepened respect for the environment, i.e., their call for cosmic chastity, is based upon a steadfast insistence on justice, a single-minded refusal of injustice, and a resolute allegiance to the truth of the meaning inherent to creation according to its very being.

20. D. C. Schindler, citing Ratzinger, explains that for the ancient Greeks, God was "the ultimate principle of order, and they saw nature—that is, the given intelligibility, beauty, and goodness of things—as the place wherein divine order culminates . . . When the Greeks called the world 'kosmos,' meaning 'jewel' or 'ornament,' they were setting into relief both this essential order and its divine provenance. Divine order, the presence of the gods, shines forth in the resplendent goodness that inheres in things" (Schindler, "Work," 4–5). My use of the word "cosmos" presupposes this notion.

21. LS, sec. 7. This is Francis's own paraphrase of an insight he attributes to Benedict. Francis cites Benedict, "Bundestag Address."

22. LS, sec. 6, citing Benedict, "Bolzano." As Benedict put it on that occasion, "The brutal consumption of Creation begins where God is not, where matter is henceforth only material for us, where we ourselves are the ultimate demand, where the whole is merely our property and we consume it for ourselves alone. And the wasting of creation begins when we no longer recognize any need superior to our own, but see only ourselves" (see Benedict, "Bolzano," paras. 23–25).

23. LS, secs. 1–2, 10–12, 66, 87, 91, 125, 218, 221.

24. LS, sec. 11.

As Pope Francis warns, we mustn't allow ourselves to stand by as "silent witnesses to terrible injustices" in the face of "environmental deterioration . . . caused by . . . selfish lack of concern."[25] In the opening of his encyclical *FT* as well as in the opening of his encyclical *LS*, Pope Francis points to St. Francis as a figure who reminds us of the truth of who we are within the context of creation.[26] Much of what ails the world today, we see in the teaching of Pope Francis, has to do with the fact that we have forgotten this truth. St. Francis is an icon of one who stands in relation to the cosmos as "a sister with whom we share our life and a beautiful mother who opens her arms to embrace us."[27] St. Francis models for us, then, the chaste alternative to the posture of possessive lust that dominates our use of created materiality today.

In the teaching of Francis and the two previous popes, creaturely existence means existence-as-gift. This means that my relationship to the gift and the dignity inherent to the gift has to be safeguarded by chastity, so as to honor the meaning of creaturely existence. Technocratic unchastity, or lust, refers to a posture that does not safeguard the dignity of creation-as-gift, specifically by way of a technocratic approach to creation. This technocratic approach is inherently unchaste in that it "exalts the concept of a subject who, using logical and rational procedures, progressively approaches and gains control over an external object," to use Pope Francis's description of the technocratic paradigm in *LS*.[28] This "control" is a mechanistic control that refuses to bow before and collaborate with an external object according to its nature and meaning as gift, and rather manipulates it according to the lusts of the human heart disfigured by sin, reduced as we so often are to the falsifying category of mere *consumer*. In systemic technocracy, we turn our brothers and sisters—and we ourselves are turned into—mere *commodities* and mere *consumers* to consume and be consumed in the mechanisms of a "free" market.

Reverence for the cosmos, in the shared vision of JP2, Benedict, and Francis, is inseparable from reverence for truth. A commitment to truth includes a commitment to the correct teaching concerning the meaning of the cosmos. That is, a commitment to truth entails a commitment to a true ecology. That's why this book dwells so extensively upon the papal

25. *LS*, sec. 36.

26. *FT*, secs. 1–4, 48.

27. *LS*, sec. 1.

28. *LS*, sec. 106.

trio's commitment to *truth* as a key aspect of their teaching on cosmic chastity. Bowing our heads in submission to the truth of the meaning of the cosmos in the nitty-gritty details of social life is an integral aspect of a practically applied allegiance to the truth at large, which transcends my own subjectivity as an individual, and includes truth as it pertains directly and specifically to me in particular as a subject.

If we look at the societal landscape through the lens of the social teaching of Francis and the two previous popes, the significant social divide, as I have already suggested in the preface, is not between liberal and conservative, but between technocratic lust and cosmic chastity. Each chapter of this book presents a particular angle on the contest in society today between the vice of lust on the one hand and the virtue of chastity on the other, each vying to gain the upper hand of allegiance in our hearts. Each chapter draws attention to this contest by zeroing in on particular aspects of cosmic chastity as alternatives to particular aspects of technocratic lust. Each chapter allows JP2, Benedict, or Francis (and some chapters combine two or all three of them) to take the lead by way of their ethical social teaching and integral theological vision and spirituality.

Part 1 of this book, consisting of chapters 1–3, presents the framework of the theologically rooted social teaching of the papal trio, zeroing in on the role of truth, justice, and charity[29] in relation to marriage, family, and Christian vocation at large as the primary context in which chaste love is to be lived out in society. Chaste love is primarily expressed by way of self-gift in the context of family life. Self-gift in family life is an integral aspect of humanity's overall vocation within the cosmos as *liturgists* leading all creatures in a song of universal praise to the Creator. In chapter 1, I present the papal trio's song of cosmic chastity in opposition to the din of technocratic lust by way of presenting JP2's and Benedict's vision of justice and charity rooted in truth over and against technocratic lust's inherent falsehood, injustice, and failure in charity. Chapter 2 presents Francis's call to vocational commitment, particularly his call for young adults today to take the risk of marrying and having children. I present Francis's vision of family as the locus point in society for the exercise of the very notions of justice and charity rooted in truth, in opposition to the fear of commitment so prevalent in the hearts of young men and women raised in the shadow of relativism's regime. It is

29. In this book, the terms "love" and "charity" are used interchangeably.

this regime of relativism that makes up the conditions for the festering of the technocratic rationale in the hearts of young adults who, though called to give themselves away in the form of a definitive vocational commitment, have become de-capacitated in their ability to do so. Chapter 3 goes on to present the papal trio's liturgical ontology as an alternative to the outlook of the culture wars and as an alternative to the endemic economic injustices proper to the neoliberal commercial logic.

Chapters 4–6 make up part II of this book, and keep firmly in view the book's main presupposition that the real divide in society today is between the harmony of cosmic chastity on the one hand and the cacophony of technocratic lust on the other, not between liberalism and conservatism. The discord of technocratic lust is part of the discord of the culture wars, as both sides of the culture wars have been dragged into the rationale of technocracy, and tend to carry out these wars according to its dissonant reasoning. In chapter 4, I locate Benedict and Francis in the tradition of Henri de Lubac and Romano Guardini, who engage in a genre of cultural warfare altogether different from what is found in popular culture today. Chapter 5 presents the papal trio's socially radical and distinctively Catholic song of justice and charity in economics and particularly, in a vision of work, while chapter 6 returns to the theme of vocation, i.e., Christ's call to make a gift of ourselves—as one of the main acoustical features of the amphitheater of Catholic social teaching in which the papal trio sings, focusing on JP2's and Francis's reflections on Christ's call to young adults in the US. In this context, we hear the harmony between JP2's and Francis's *call to chaste love by way of vocational commitment* in following Christ—precisely as social beings called to an utterly dispossessive love.

Part 3 of this book zeroes in on how the papal trio's song is a song of truth in direct opposition to relativism, beginning with chapter 7's examination of Francis's strategically fought war on relativism's dictatorship. There, we'll hear how Francis contributes his own tenor line to the harmony of truth sung with JP2 and Benedict, each against relativism's disharmony and discord. We continue, in chapter 8, with an examination of JP2's and Francis's ardent commitment to and harmony with the melody of moral truth, and at last end with chapter 9's survey of Francis's integral ecology and theology of marriage and family.

The notion of "cosmic chastity" as a singular term identifying the singular theology, ethos, and spirituality of the social-ecological "song" that Francis and the two previous popes "sing" initially began to take

shape within my heart when I encountered the notion of "cosmic tenderness" and "cosmic gentleness" introduced by Catherine Doherty in her
spiritual classic, *Poustinia*.[30] While Doherty never used the term "cosmic
chastity," she articulated the notion I'm getting at in her presentation of
the Russian *poustinik*—a desert dweller devoted to a life of prayer and
service[31]—who is animated by *a love for all that is* according to an ethos
of that fruit of the Spirit, gentleness, which along with the other fruits of
the Spirit stands in distinction from what St. Paul calls the "works of the
flesh"—immorality, impurity, licentiousness, idolatry, sorcery, enmity,
strife, jealousy, anger, selfishness, dissension, party spirit, envy, drunken-
ness, and carousing.[32] The *poustinik* was for me, then, the initial icon of
cosmic chastity as the notion began to take shape in my heart. The figures
of St. Benedict and St. Francis, as presented by their papal namesakes, as
icons of cosmic chastity—began to transpose themselves upon my heart
along with the figure of the Russian *poustinik*, who beholds before his
chaste gaze all that proceeds from the hand of God as gift.

The popes going back to Leo XIII, like Doherty, proposed the very
notion of cosmic gentleness and tenderness in their social teaching as
they navigate the multitude of challenges and opportunities characteristic of what Doherty referred to as "our growing, changing, technological,
urban civilization."[33] Doherty's presentation of the *poustinik*, then, played
a key role in providing the acoustical hermeneutical context in which I
began to hear the harmony of the song of the three popes.

---

30. Doherty, *Poustinia*, 76–77. Catherine likewise connects the notion of "cosmic
charity" with the spirituality of the *poustinik* (143).

31. See Barker, "Poustinik Option."

32. Gal 5:19–23 RSV.

33. Doherty, *Poustinia*, 3.

PART I

· · · · ·

Truth, Justice, and Charity
The "JP2-B16" Legacy and Francis's Social Teaching

1

. . . . .

Resisting Relativism

*JP2's and B16's Concern for Moral Truth,
Justice, and Charity*

POPE FRANCIS'S SONG OF cosmic chastity is not a song he wrote, nor is it a song he sings alone. Rather, it's the social-theological song the two previous popes had long been singing before Francis took to the global-ecclesial stage in 2013. In part 1 of this book, I invite my readers to remove the hermeneutical earbuds—with which we hear only the shouts of culture warriors in the media—and to walk with me toward the hermeneutical amphitheater of Catholic social teaching, where we can hear the harmony of the song that Francis sings with the two previous popes. Each of these first three chapters, constituting part 1 of this book, will identify some of the key structural features of the song. Here in chapter 1, as we take a seat in the amphitheater, we'll start by listening for the musical structure of the song as JP2 and Benedict have been singing it. To begin, we'll listen for the roles played by the notions of truth, justice, and charity in that musical structure. The singular commitment of the JP2-B16 duet to an integral vision of justice, charity, and truth—key structural features of the song of cosmic chastity—stands in direct opposition to the cacophony of technocratic lust's injustice, lovelessness, and falsehood.

JP2's Concern for Moral Truth vs. Relativism

When Cardinal Karol Wojtyla preached the annual Lenten retreat to the papal household and the Curia at the request of Paul VI in 1976, he gave to the Pope and to the rest of his audience a snapshot of his pastoral context as a shepherd in Soviet-occupied Poland.[1] At that very time, the faithful Catholic youth of the Archdiocese of Krakow—so Wojtyla recounted—found themselves in the midst of a "great darkness," namely, "the darkness devised by the whole of the secularizing, anti-religious system of state education."[2] Directing the attention of the Pope, his household, and the Curia, then, to Psalm 139—where the psalmist declares to God that "even the darkness is light for you / and night is as brilliant as day"[3]—Wojtyla related that during the weeks of Lent, as well as during the summer months, the youth of Wojtyla's archdiocese eagerly seek out the opportunity to attend the youth retreats offered by the Polish Church. The youth do this, Wojtyla said, in order to rediscover "God and themselves."[4] The Polish youth perceive these retreats as an opportunity "that brings with it fresh discovery of the meaning of life."[5] Wojtyla reflected that by way of these spiritually fortifying times of retreat, the faithful youth of Krakow, under an aggressively atheistic communist regime, knew in their bones the truth of the psalmist's prayer to God: "I shall take the wings of daybreak, and dwell at the uttermost bounds of the sea. Even there your hand still leads me / Your right hand holds me fast."[6]

At the papal Lenten retreat in Rome, Wojtyla recounted for Paul VI and the other retreatants with him that "though surrounded by that darkness" of secularism "these young people" of Krakow "journey on, trusting in God's presence, trusting the meaning of this world, trusting in the beauty of creation which they seek to know and understand as they wend their way through the forests and across mountain ranges."[7] Wojtyla truly had the heart of a shepherd in relation to the youth of Poland. He was a guardian, warding off the powers of atheism and secularism—which, like a pack of wolves, threatened his flock. As a preacher of the gospel,

1. *SC*, 5–6.
2. *SC*, 6.
3. Ps 139:12, as quoted in *SC*, 6.
4. *SC*, 6.
5. *SC*, 6.
6. Ps 139:9–10, as quoted in *SC*, 6.
7. *SC*, 6.

Wojtyla kept alive the fire of faith in the hearts of these youth, surrounded as they were by the darkness of anti-Christian ideologies. He did this primarily by guiding them in an encounter with God's presence. Wojtyla directed his young flock toward the true "meaning of this world," toward "the beauty of creation," so that they might "know and understand" that meaning and that beauty as they made "their way through the forests and across mountain ranges."[8] As Pope, Wojtyla continued the same task, but on a global scale. JP2 guided the members of his flock to see through the darkness that surrounded them in the midst of secularization. At a time when much of the world was turning its back on God, JP2 invited his global flock to look to God, to the true meaning of the world, to the beauty of creation, and he elucidated that meaning so that his flock could more deeply "know and understand" that meaning and beauty, as he hiked along with them, as it were, leading them through the forests and mountain ranges of God's creation, equipping them to perceive—precisely by way of creation's beauty—the splendor of the Creator.

A few decades into his papacy, on the Feast of the Transfiguration, a day on which the Church especially commemorates the splendor of Christ revealed to three of his disciples on the peak of Mount Tabor, JP2 gave to the world his encyclical *VS*. In this encyclical, we can see that the encounter with God—which JP2 facilitated for his flock as a shepherd of the youth of Krakow and later as shepherd of the universal flock—is an encounter with Christ the Truth, who dispels all darkness and falsehood.[9] As JP2 said in *VS*, "the splendour of truth shines forth in all the works of the Creator and, in a special way, in man, created in the image and likeness of God."[10] The cosmos itself is a bearer of divine truth, a bearer of truth's beauty, a testimony to divine truth. And within that cosmos, humanity has a particular place as both perceiver and revealer of God and his truth. In the order of creation, humanity is peculiarly disposed to be receptive to and cognizant of truth, and uniquely capable of responding to this truth with love for the author of truth. "Truth enlightens man's intelligence and shapes his freedom, leading him to know and love the Lord,"[11] leading him to love the Creator, JP2 suggested, and to thereby discover true freedom.

8. *SC*, 6.

9. For indeed, as the *Compendium* identifies, "the first of the challenges facing humanity today is that of *the truth itself of the being who is man*" (*Compendium*, sec. 16).

10. *VS*, prefatory blessing.

11. *VS*, prefatory blessing.

In the opening of *VS*, the global "retreat master" offered the universal Church an opportunity to pause and contemplate the splendor of truth, leading his fellow "hikers" to pray with the psalmist: "Let the light of your face shine on us, O Lord."[12] Of the many aspects of darkness that JP2 identified in the midst of secularization, well after the fall of the Soviet bloc, was the darkness of *relativism*. This darkness of relativism is prominent in our own day in the various historical manifestations of the perennial temptation on humanity's part "to turn his gaze away from the living and true God."[13] With his eyes turned away from God and toward the pantheon of idols which humanity makes for himself, "man's capacity to know the truth is . . . darkened, and his will to submit to it is weakened."[14] In lieu of handing itself over to the truth of God his all-loving Creator, humanity is ever prone to give itself over to any number of idolatrous alternatives. JP2 perceived that in his own day, this temptation manifested itself in a number of ways. And the allure of relativism was prominent among these manifestations of the temptation of idolatry.

Relativism, JP2 warned, condemns humanity to go "off in search of an illusory freedom apart from truth itself."[15] Nonetheless, as JP2 found even in the midst of Soviet domination for the youth of Poland, so it is under the subsequent regime of relativism: humanity has a persistent, innate drive to seek out the splendor of the Creator in the beauty of creation. It was JP2's conviction that "no darkness of error or of sin can totally take away from man the light of God the Creator."[16] Indeed, "in the depths of his heart there always remains a yearning for absolute truth and a thirst to attain full knowledge of it."[17]

A key aspect of the perennial existential tension experienced by humanity—that tension between a yearning for truth and a refusal of it—is a yearning for the truth about *the good*. Part and parcel with this yearning for the truth about the good is a yearning for the truth about *the good that we must do*, which is a yearning for *the truth about justice*, which includes *the truth about the good due to my neighbor* as well as the

---

12. *VS*, prefatory blessing, quoting Ps 4:6.

13. *VS*, sec. 1.

14. *VS*, sec. 1.

15. *VS*, sec. 1.

16. *VS*, sec. 1. As the *Compendium* puts it, citing St. Augustine's *Confessions*, "The natural law, which is the law of God, cannot be annulled by human sinfulness" (*Compendium*, sec. 142).

17. *VS*, sec. 1.

truth about the good due to me. According to JP2's anthropology, this truth about justice is something that we likewise, to our own detriment, have a tendency, by dint of concupiscence, to refuse. But if we refuse the truth about what the good is and what good is due to whom, which is to say, if we refuse *the truth about justice*, we refuse justice, we refuse the good, we refuse truth, and we refuse the God-given hope of human flourishing on an individual and communal level. Against such a refusal of truth, goodness, and justice, JP2's song of cosmic chastity offers us a robust notion of truth over and against relativism's refusal of it. Against the cacophony of relativism, JP2 sings according to the musical structure of truth.

The Truth about Justice and Freedom

In the body of social doctrine that JP2 left behind as a significant aspect of his legacy, he presents the integral place of truth in the cause of social justice. JP2 was adamant—in *VS* and elsewhere—that the pursuit of social justice is contingent upon a commitment to the truth. JP2 adamantly articulates, according to the same rationale, the ways in which an impoverished notion of truth or ambivalence toward it necessarily compromises the pursuit of justice. Given the degree to which the cause of justice is integrally bound up with the cause of authentic human freedom and the cause of human dignity (along with the rights and duties proper to that dignity), any authentic advocacy for justice—JP2 repeatedly underscores—presupposes a robust vision of human freedom rooted in truth.

As is proper to the field of integral human development,[18] the cause of social justice involves an advocacy for freedom and rights. JP2 provides an integral vision of truth upon which an authentic notion of freedom and rights depends. He likewise provides a detailed account of how the pursuit of social justice is undermined when, in the pursuit of freedom and rights, an authentic notion of truth is forgotten. For JP2, neglecting an authentic notion of truth inevitably results in misunderstanding the meaning of human freedom and the meaning of the rights proper to human dignity. An authentic advocacy for justice likewise presupposes, for JP2, *a robust account of the meaning* of human existence

18. See *PP*, secs. 59–63; *CV*, secs. 25, 40, 567, 570–71. See Schindler, "Habits of Presence," 575.

and the implications of the dignity proper to that meaning, according to the truth of the human person, the truth of human community, and the truth of creation.

It is by this same token that any notion of freedom and rights emptied of their integral relation to truth are thereby falsified and end up *compromising* and *undermining* the struggle for social justice.[19] Likewise, an authentic notion of rights and duties, as well as a robust understanding of the notion of justice, are all preconditions for an authentic struggle for justice. As a tireless warrior for the cause of social justice, JP2 sees it as absolutely necessary to conserve the notions upon which an authentic understanding of justice depends. What all this means is that in JP2's view, a robust moral vision, accompanied by a robust understanding of freedom and rights, empowers an authentic struggle for social justice, as social justice concerns itself with the moral life of society. In JP2's body of moral teaching, the rationale of moral doctrine and the rationale of social justice are one and the same. And for him, elucidating the meaning of authentic human freedom and elucidating an authentic notion of human rights lays the groundwork for authentic social doctrine and is an integral aspect of an authentic moral theology.

In his adamant insistence upon integral human freedom's intimate relationship with *truth*, JP2 follows closely the rationale of his predecessor Leo XIII. In *Centesimus annus*, JP2 recalls that Pope Leo "called attention to the essential bond between human freedom and truth, so that freedom which refused to be bound to the truth would fall into arbitrariness and end up submitting itself to the vilest of passions, to the point of self-destruction."[20] JP2 rhetorically asks in *Centesimus annus*, "what is the origin of all the evils to which *Rerum novarum* wished to respond, if not a kind of freedom which, in the area of economic and social activity, cuts itself off from the truth about man?"[21] According to JP2, the injustices that manifested themselves in the industrial capitalism of Leo's day, as well as in the inhumanity endorsed by the atheistic socialist ideologies of the same era, had at their core a shared falsifying divorce between the notion of freedom and the notion of truth.[22] An authentic public morality, i.e., an

---

19. See *Compendium*, secs. 137–38, which cites *Catechism*, paras. 1749–56.

20. *CA*, sec. 4.

21. *CA*, sec. 4.

22. *Compendium*, para. 142, citing *EV*, secs. 19–20.

authentic vision of social justice, is built upon the truth about humanity, inherent to which is the notion of a shared human nature.

The truth about humanity and its shared nature is integrally linked, then, to the truth about social justice, over and against relativism's abhorrence of moral standards. The truth about social justice, then, is found in the truth of a human nature held in common by all of us. The truth about social justice is not determined by the individual; it does not arise from the individual subject as its source. The truth about social justice necessarily precedes the individual, makes demands upon the individual, upon communities, upon states, and upon society as a whole. The truth about social justice is integrally bound up with what is *good for the individual*, good for human community, good for society at large, and good for our common home.[23]

Because of the propensity on the part of the human heart to abuse the freedom proper to it by nature, human freedom itself needs "*to be liberated*,"[24] according to the Church's social teaching. It is Christ who, "by the power of his Paschal Mystery, frees man from his disordered love of self"[25]—a lustful, self-indulgent, distorted love for self that is a key expression of our bondage to sin. For JP2, the authentic concern for economic justice proper to the tradition of Catholic social teaching speaks out against false notions of freedom, and seeks to facilitate the liberation of the human heart from disordered self-love. Economic justice was the concern of Pope Leo's heart when he wrote *Rerum novarm*, and it is the concern from which the tradition of Catholic social teaching properly speaking initially sprang forth, beginning with Leo. And economic injustice, at its root, is part of humanity's distorted and disordered self-love. An authentically Catholic concern for economic justice speaks out against false notions of freedom and guards against the ways in which these false notions of freedom threaten society's capacity to make large-scale moral discernments at the collective and individual level according to the demands of truth, justice, and charity. "Freedom" to act from mere self-interest according to the interests of a self-indulgent heart is not in reality freedom. Indeed, such a notion of freedom only further distorts the human heart, furthering the disorder of its already disordered

---

23. To appropriate Francis's term "common home," which he uses throughout *LS*. *Compendium*, sec. 143.

24. *Compendium*, para. 143.

25. *Compendium*, sec. 143, citing *Catechism*, para. 1741.

appetites in lieu of authentic freedom's inherent altruism and impulse toward the good.

An authentically Catholic concern for economic justice perceives a shared social responsibility to set up safeguards against the ways in which false notions of freedom threaten the capacity of individuals, smaller communities, municipalities, and larger political bodies to make just and loving moral discernments. False notions of freedom disempower members of society from being able to respond to the demands of truth and justice. These false notions of freedom set "freedom" up against a notion of universal truth, and weaken individuals and communities in their capacity to set limits according to what truth and justice demand. The demands of truth and justice pertain to economics, ecology, sexuality, foreign policy, and to the public as well as the private realm. No sphere of life is external to the purview of truth and justice.

Summarizing the historical setting of Pope Leo's social teaching, JP2 recounts that "the Pope and the Church with him were confronted, as was the civil community, by a society which was torn by a conflict all the more harsh and inhumane because it knew no rule or regulation."[26] The conflict to which JP2 here refers, with which Leo was confronted and which was made more harsh and inhumane given the unlimited and unregulated character of the capitalist market in Leo's day—not entirely unlike our own—"is the conflict between capital and labour."[27] Here, JP2 sets himself apart from economic libertarianism. This sets JP2 in strong opposition to what he describes as "currents of thought which end by detaching human freedom from its essential and constitutive relationship to truth."[28]

Freedom, JP2 persistently insists in his writings on moral theology in general and in his writings on social doctrine in particular, does not consist of freedom *from* a moral standard of the truth about the good, but consists of *a freedom to abide by precisely this standard*, a freedom that is cultivated by communal formation and that is fundamentally possible thanks only to the redeeming work of Christ by way of the paschal mystery.[29]

26. *CA*, sec. 5.

27. *Compendium*, sec. 139.

28. *CA*, sec. 4.

29 *Compendium*, sec. 139.

But there's a great deal that stands in the way of transmitting a Catholic vision of authentic freedom according to an integral notion of moral truth, given the state of our own hearts, and the state of the society in which our hearts are formed and deformed. There's a great deal of unmusical discord in society and in our hearts. A prominent aspect of this discord goes by the name of *relativism*.

Benedict's Concern for Moral Truth vs. Relativism: The Son of God as the Measure of True Humanism

As dean of the College of Cardinals, Joseph Ratzinger preached the homily at the "Mass for the Election of the Roman Pontiff" in April of 2005, kicking off, in a sacramental-liturgical context, the conclave which would ultimately choose him as the shepherd of the universal Church to succeed JP2, who had died just a few days previous. The second Scripture reading for that Mass was taken from St. Paul's letter to the Ephesians, chapter 4. One of the aspects of that reading upon which Ratzinger dwelt in his homily was what he called the "journey" toward the "'measure of the fullness of Christ' . . . which we are called to reach in order to be true adults in the faith."[30] If, as St. Paul puts it, "we should not remain infants in faith," then "what does it mean," Ratzinger asks, "to be an infant in faith?"[31] Ratzinger finds the answer in the same passage of Paul: to be an infant in the faith is to be "tossed by waves and swept along by every wind of teaching arising from human trickery."[32]

It is in this context that Ratzinger's famous phrase "the dictatorship of relativism"[33] appeared on the world stage. Reflecting on St. Paul's warning against being "tossed by waves and swept along by every wind of teaching arising from human trickery," Ratzinger engaged the passage in the context of the circumstances of our own day.[34] The soon-to-be-pope, gearing up his fellow cardinals to discern God's chosen universal shepherd at the dawn of the new millennium, proceeded to ask, rhetorically,

---

30. Ratzinger, "Election," 22.
31. Ratzinger, "Election," 22.
32. Ratzinger, "Election," 22, quoting Eph 4:14.
33. Ratzinger, "Election," 22.
34. Ratzinger, "Election," 22.

"How many winds of doctrine we have known in recent decades, how many ideological currents, how many ways of thinking?"[35]

Ratzinger went on to identify some of the many "winds" that toss "the small boat of thought,"[36] such that the "many Christians" aboard the ship of society-wide inquiry can hardly keep afloat.[37] This "small boat" of poorly equipped, unseasoned sailors "has often been tossed about by these waves, thrown from one extreme to the other: from Marxism to liberalism, even to libertinism; from collectivism to radical individualism; from atheism to a vague religious mysticism; from agnosticism to syncretism; and so forth."[38]

For Ratzinger—at the threshold of his own election as pontiff—the warning of St. Paul against "every wind of teaching arising from human trickery"[39] was a warning with particular import for the present historical moment. The call to journey toward the "maturity of Christ," toward the "measure of the fullness of Christ" was, for him, a journey we *must* take.[40] Indeed, "every day new sects are created and what St. Paul says about human trickery comes true, with cunning that tries to draw those" whom it will "into error."[41] In this context, however, "having a clear faith, based on the Creed of the Church, is often labeled today as a fundamentalism."[42] Relativism, "which is letting oneself be tossed and 'swept along by every wind of teaching,' looks like the only attitude (acceptable) to today's standards."[43] Such a dichotomy in our societal context, between the perceived fundamentalism assigned to those with a clarity of faith in the Creed on the one hand and the alleged open-mindedness of relativism on the other, moves society "toward a dictatorship of relativism, which does not recognize anything as certain and which has as its highest goal one's own ego and one's own desires," Ratzinger related.[44] This relativism forbids external standards of morality as a part of its reaction against fundamentalism, seeking in moral relativism fundamentalism's alternative.

35. Ratzinger, "Election," 22.
36. Ratzinger, "Election," 22.
37. Ratzinger, "Election," 22.
38. Ratzinger, "Election," 22.
39. Ratzinger, "Election," 22, citing Eph 4:14.
40. Ratzinger, "Election," 22.
41. Ratzinger, "Election," 22.
42. Ratzinger, "Election," 22.
43. Ratzinger, "Election," 22.
44. Ratzinger, "Election," 22.

It is not difficult to see, then, how the dictatorship of relativism sets itself up in opposition to a notion of moral truth. By the same token, it is not difficult to see that a commitment to moral truth stands in direct opposition to a dictatorship of relativism.[45] If there's no universal truth, no moral law, then there's no such thing as rights, no such thing as duties, and there's no grounding for a notion of social justice.

The alternative that Ratzinger presented to the College of Cardinals—the alternative to pursuing the goal of one's own ego and one's own desires (as is proper to the dictatorship of relativism)—is to pursue a very "different goal," namely, to pursue "the Son of God," who, according to Ratzinger, "is the measure of true humanism."[46] In Ratzinger's thinking, the void of teleological content—a void inherent to relativism's claims—is filled by my own ego and my own desires, such that these goals, inherently antithetical to an authentic humanism, become for me my *highest* goals, and likely, my *only* goals. Journeying toward maturity in Christ on the other hand, is, for Ratzinger, *the* alternative to relativism's inherent fickleness of heart, which, at the end of the day, is a dictatorship because it forbids me from rendering allegiance to *anything* external to my arbitrary desires. And under the reign of relativism's dictatorship, an allegiance to the measure of true humanism, namely, the Son of God, is certainly forbidden.

An authentic humanism is antithetical to the relativistic outlook, because relativism forbids *any* measure of moral truth, *any* standard of behavior. And without these, authentic justice and authentic freedom cannot be upheld, the dignity of humanity cannot be safeguarded, and human society cannot flourish.

Authentic humanism, for Ratzinger, is integrally dependent upon a robust vision of morality, according to a notion of the natural law, and according to an anthropology confident in the God-given human capacity to perceive moral truth by the light of that law.[47] For Ratzinger, when the Son of God is my goal, rather than my own ego and desires, we journey toward "the maturity of Christ," toward "the fullness of Christ," toward a fulfillment in Christ.[48] "Being an 'adult'" in the sense that St. Paul speaks of in Ephesians means pursuing Christ as the goal, with a "faith

---

45. See *Compendium*, sec. 140, citing *VS*, sec. 50.

46. Ratzinger, "Election," 23.

47. *Compendium*, sec. 140.

48. Ratzinger, "Election," 22.

that does not follow the waves of today's fashions or the latest novelties."[49] An integral aspect of being an adult in this Pauline manner is *adhering* to a moral standard that can stand up against these same "waves of today's fashions" and "the latest novelties."[50] Faith, "deeply rooted in friendship with Christ . . . opens us up to all that is good and gives us the knowledge to judge true from false, and deceit from truth."[51] Faith plays an important role then, for Ratzinger, in humanity's capacity to hear the music of the cosmos, according to its inherent structure. Equally important for becoming equipped to stand up against the waves of today's fashions, and to discern between truth and falsehood, is authentic charity, which stands in integral relation to the good, to justice, and to truth.

Benedict's Concern for the Truth about Justice and Charity

In his 2009 encyclical *CV*, Benedict XVI identifies *caritas in veritate*— charity in truth—as "*the* principle around which the Church's social doctrine turns."[52] According to Benedict, "charity is at the heart of the Church's social doctrine."[53] However, "charity has been and continues to be misconstrued and emptied of meaning, with the consequent risk of being misinterpreted, detached from ethical living and, in any event, undervalued."[54] In the context of "the social, juridical, cultural, political and economic fields," which "are most exposed to this danger" of misunderstanding the meaning of charity, charity "is easily dismissed as irrelevant for interpreting and giving direction to moral responsibility."[55] It is in the face of this danger arising from the misunderstanding of the meaning of charity that Benedict perceives "the need to link charity with truth," and to do so "not only in the sequence, pointed out by Saint Paul, of *veritas in caritate* (Eph 4:15), but also in the inverse and complementary sequence of *caritas in veritate*."[56] For indeed, "truth needs to be

49. Ratzinger, "Election," 23.
50. Ratzinger, "Election," 23.
51. Ratzinger, "Election," 23.
52. *CV*, sec. 6 (emphasis added).
53. *CV*, sec. 2.
54. *CV*, sec. 2.
55. *CV*, sec. 2.
56. *CV*, sec. 2.

sought, found and expressed within the 'economy' of charity, but charity in its turn needs to be understood, confirmed and practiced in the light of truth."[57] Just as, according to St. Paul's wording, an authentic notion of truth is rooted in charity, so, according to Benedict's inversion of St. Paul's dictum, an authentic notion of charity is rooted in truth. In contemplating charity's integral rootedness in truth, "not only do we do a service to charity enlightened by truth, but we also help give credibility to truth, demonstrating its persuasive and authenticating power in the practical setting of social living."[58] Benedict, then, has an ontological basis as well as a rhetorical, apologetic, catechetical, evangelistic, mystagogical, and social basis for exploring the meaning of charity in the light of truth, as well as truth in the light of charity. Giving credibility to the notion of truth "is a matter of no small account today," Benedict reflects, "in a social and cultural context which relativizes truth, often paying little heed to it and showing increasing reluctance to acknowledge its existence."[59] If we are not to be swept away by every wind of doctrine arising from human trickery, a perception of charity in the light of truth is in order. Elucidating the integral relationship between charity and truth in this way gives credence to the notion of truth, which, Ratzinger perceived, is very much under attack.

For Benedict, charity in truth, which concerns itself with justice and the common good, "takes on practical form in the criteria that govern moral action."[60] Justice and the common good are criteria "of special relevance to the commitment to development in an increasingly globalized society."[61] Justice "prompts us to give the other what is 'his,' what is due to him by reason of his being or his acting."[62] As Benedict points out, "every society draws up its own system of justice,"[63] a system that facilitates this granting of the good that is due to whom it is due. According to Benedict, charity stands in relation to justice as that which "goes beyond justice, because to love is to give, to offer what is '*mine*' to the *other*."[64] As Bene-

57. *CV*, sec. 2.

58. *CV*, sec. 2.

59. *CV*, sec. 2.

60. *CV*, sec. 6.

61. *CV*, sec. 7.

62. *CV*, sec. 6.

63. *CV*, sec. 6.

64. *CV*, sec. 6 (emphasis added).

dict recounts, charity "never lacks justice."[65] While by dint of justice I am prompted to give to another what is already due to them, charity goes beyond that in that it prompts me to go so far as to give what is *mine* to another, not only what I already owe to another by dint of justice. Charity gives *more* good than what I as an individual owe to another. As Benedict explains, justice is *foundational* for charity, because "I cannot 'give' what is mine to the other, without first giving him what pertains to him in justice."[66] No justice, no love.

Justice, as the foundation of charity, is seen for what it is—with all the demands it makes upon individuals and upon society—in the light of truth. Only in the light of truth can justice direct our action, and overflow into charity in opposition to the "war, violence, oppression, injustice and moral decay"[67] against which Benedict cried out and against which JP2 cried out prior to him, persistently raising his prophetic voice throughout his pastoral career.

The Triad of Harmony in JP2's Theology of Justice

"If we cast a glance at the world and its history, at first sight the banner of war, violence, oppression, injustice and moral decay seems to predominate," JP2 reflected in a catechesis at the beginning of 2001.[68] We are "faced with the tragedies of history and rampant immorality."[69] With such tragedy before our eyes—with the characteristic plagues of "war, violence, oppression, injustice and moral decay, we feel like repeating the question posed to God by the prophet Jeremiah, giving voice to so many suffering and oppressed people . . . 'Why does the way of the wicked prosper? Why do all who are treacherous thrive?'"[70] For an explanation of the tragic state of affairs that gives rise to these perennial questions of the human heart, JP2 turned to St. Irenaeus, who, according to JP2's summary, identified the root cause for the prevalence of injustice in the world: "instead of following the divine plan of peaceful harmony,"

---

65. *CV*, sec. 6.
66. *CV*, sec. 6.
67. "FMW," sec. 1.
68. "FMW," sec. 1.
69. "FMW," sec. 1.
70. "FMW," sec. 1.

Irenaeus proposed (according to JP2's summary paraphrase), man "severed his relationship with God, with man and with the world."[71]

As an antidote to this disharmony of severed relationships on humanity's part within the human family, in relation to the rest of creation and to the Creator, "a continuous effort of conversion is needed to straighten humanity's course, so that it may freely choose to follow" what JP2, with Irenaeus, calls "God's art."[72] It is in following the way of "God's art" that authentic human freedom is found. And conversion is needed—individually and collectively—in order for this freedom to be found on the part of the human family. God's art, JP2 says, is God's "plan of peace and love, of truth and justice."[73]

The ongoing call to conversion is a call to adopt a "love for humanity, for its material and spiritual well-being, for its authentic progress."[74] Such love, JP2 insists, "must stir all believers," for "everything done to create a better future, a more habitable land and a more fraternal society participates, even if indirectly, in building up God's kingdom."[75] These relationships among ourselves, with the rest of creation, and with God— relationships which are meant by God to be harmonious but which we in sin have severed—are integrally related with each other. Disharmony in relation to my neighbor means disharmony in relation to God; disharmony in relation to creation at large means disharmony in relation to my neighbor and to God, and so forth. The human vocation according to a vision of God's art involves the cultivation of harmony in what Benedict calls "the earthly city."[76]

Charity in Building up the Earthly City: The Justice and Charity of Cosmic Chastity in Benedict's Song of Integral Human Development

Key to the musical structure of what we're referring to as B16's song of cosmic chastity is his insistence that charity "strives to build the earthly

71. "FMW," sec. 1. See also *Compendium*, para. 143, citing Second Vatican Council, *Gaudium et spes*, para. 13.

72. "FMW," sec. 2.

73. "FMW," sec. 2.

74. "FMW," sec. 4.

75. "FMW," sec. 4.

76. *CV*, sec. 6.

city."[77] B16, citing JP2, says that charity "transcends justice and completes it in the logic of giving and forgiving."[78] B16 goes on to say that "the earthly city is promoted not merely by relationships of rights and duties, but to an even greater and more fundamental extent by relationships of gratuitousness, mercy and communion."[79] If we're to revere the dignity of people and things in a posture of chaste love as opposed to possessive lust, we need to know a bit about the social role of love, and its relationship to justice, the good, and truth. And that's precisely what Benedict helps us to see in *CV*.

There are two essential aspects of justice in the human heart in Benedict's vision that we must keep in mind to understand the structure of his thought: First, justice has a rightful place in the human heart. For Benedict, the human heart is built to cultivate within itself an urge to see justice met, as each human heart is called to make its own contribution to the building up of the earthly city "according to law and justice."[80] What that means is that the human heart is built to cultivate the inborn urge to see the good due granted to those to whom it is due. And for Benedict, it is charity that animates this urge. We are drawn by love to render the good that is due to whom it is due. Love impels us to execute justice. Second, human hearts and human communities are called by God to cultivate within the earthly city on micro and macro levels "relationships of gratuitousness, mercy and communion," which, according to the very meaning of charity integral to gratuitousness, mercy, and communion, go *beyond* mere justice.[81] By way of relationships characterized by gratuitousness, mercy, and communion, I render *more* good to my neighbors than I as an individual owe them (by way of charity) and perhaps I render more good than is even due to them by any one (according to a notion of mercy). That is, I give to my neighbors what in justice belongs to me. By way of charity I render to my neighbor what is authentically good for my neighbor in a manner that exceeds the bare minimum of what justice requires of me. It is rendering not only what I owe (which would be to render what isn't rightfully mine anyway) to another to whom it is due; it is rendering what is in all justice mine to another out of sheer love, sheer

77. *CV*, sec. 6.

78. *CV*, sec. 6, which cites JP2, "No Peace Without Justice."

79. *CV*, sec. 6.

80. *CV*, sec. 6.

81. *CV*, sec. 6.

gratuity, a sheer drive for communion, in sheer gratitude for God and his freely given gifts. It is the communion motive over and against the profit motive, the will to communion over and against the will to power, the humility of life proper to creaturely realism, over and against the false and self-deification of the pride of life.

What we are to be guided by in our dealings in the earthly city, for Benedict, is something far deeper than a superficial vision of "freedom" to choose this or that consumer item, the "freedom" of corporations and individuals from government regulation. We're to be guided by something far deeper than the freedom to maximize the "bottom line," something far more fundamental than the profit motive. What we are to be guided by fundamentally, Benedict insists, is the standard of charity, which is a standard that bids us to render the good I owe and more to my neighbor. What we are to be guided by is the standard of divine gratuity.

Benedict on the Posture of Charity in the Earthly City within the Cosmos: Integral Sociology and Cosmology

This posture of justice and charity in relation to the earthly city is constitutive for what I'm calling a posture of cosmic chastity according to B16's social teaching. Integral to the earthly city are its ecological and economic dimensions. The earthly city, from a Catholic perspective, is an integral part of the cosmos. To stand within the earthly city is to stand within the cosmos, with all its ecological, anthropological, and societal dimensions. To inhabit the cosmos according to a posture of *justice* is to abide within the earthly city according to what Benedict following the rationale of Paul VI calls "the primary way of charity."[82] Standing within the earthly city according to a posture of chastity requires that we stand within the earthly city according to a posture of justice. What this means is that we are to act within the earthly city according to charity's "minimum measure."[83] It likewise means that we are called higher still—to stand within the earthly city according to a posture of charity, by which we manifest "God's love in human relationships,"[84] *beyond* love's minimum measure, beyond justice.

82. *CV*, sec. 6.
83. *CV*, sec. 6, citing Paul VI, "Day of Development."
84. *CV*, sec. 6.

Manifesting God's love in human relationships within the complex systems of the earthly city, for B16, is an inherently economic and ecological task. The task of manifesting God's love in human relationships as a part of an interconnected society, i.e., within the earthly city—is a task that makes enormous demands upon our hearts. This task of manifesting God's love in human relationships within the complex systems of the earthly city—with all its economic and ecological aspects as a singular household (all of society within creation) made up of many domestic households—is integral to the human vocation. Acting with charity within the interconnected web of the earthly city, requiring a posture inclusive of justice and transcending justice, is what I'm identifying as Benedict's notion of cosmic chastity on the societal level. Charity in the earthly city gives "theological and salvific value to all commitment for justice in the world," Benedict details.[85]

Another integral aspect of what I'm calling Benedict's notion of cosmic chastity and the place of justice within that notion is *the common good*. "To love someone is to desire that person's good and to take effective steps to secure it," Benedict says.[86] "Besides the good of the individual, there is a good that is linked to living in society: the common good."[87] A pursuit of the common good requires a chaste love that honors the meaning of humanity according to its inherently communal and ecological dimensions. Our ecological context is a key aspect of the communal dimension of human living. Chaste love is called for by the very interrelatedness of each human person to the other, and each in relation to its creaturely context at large. While this chaste love always pertains to the individual, it never pertains exclusively to the individual, at the exclusion of others. It always pertains to my behavior as an inherently social creature within a community, within a dwelling place. For the cultivation of authentic chaste love, which by its very nature has a regard for the common good and never bypasses the common good, individuals cannot be conceived of as little atoms isolated from their societal and cosmo-ecological context. According to the viewpoint of an integrally chaste social love, individuals are bound to other individuals by way of social relationships, in a web of interdependence that entails a call to cooperation inclusive of and far beyond the individual's most immediate

---

85. *CV*, sec. 6.

86. *CV*, sec. 7.

87. *CV*, sec. 7.

associates. This is Benedict's political piety, which is a key facet of his vision of cosmic chastity.

Cosmic chastity according to Benedict's rationale is a chaste love that seeks out the common good, particularly as that good pertains to our common home, which is to say, our common context, the reality of creation with its own intrinsic truth, a truth that is held in common by all. The common good, Benedict says, "is the good of 'all of us.'"[88] It's the good of this singular social entity known as the earthly city, "made up of individuals, families and intermediate groups who together constitute society," as Benedict puts it, citing *Gaudium et spes*.[89]

Human Freedom and the Truth of Nature in Relation to Justice in JP2's Theology of Cosmic Chastity

As we have seen, justice concerns itself with rendering the good due to whom it is due, which means the notion of social justice and the common good are inextricably and intimately bound. As we've begun to see in our earlier discussion of JP2's commitment to the integral relationship between freedom and truth, a fundamental barrier to understanding justice in our own times, according to JP2, is the widespread misunderstanding of human nature and human freedom, and the widespread misunderstanding of the relationship between nature and freedom. This loss is the culprit, to a great extent, for our loss of a true sense of the common good, which means it's the culprit responsible for our loss of solidarity. Such a loss constitutes a significant barrier to building communities and societal structures that are characterized by chaste love, inherent to which is justice as love's minimum measure.

JP2 gives a compelling account of the disconnect between popular uses of the term *justice* and popular uses of the term *freedom*, each of which are highly prized in much of the popular imagination, in both liberal and conservative circles alike. But the inherent interrelation between justice and freedom and their inherent relationship to the nature of reality—the nature of the cosmos—is largely unknown and therefore largely unappreciated. Citing *Gaudium et spes*, JP2 says that the natural law "refers to man's proper and primordial nature, the 'nature of the human

88. *CV*, sec. 7.
89. *CV*, sec. 7.

person."[90] It is by way of perceiving the natural law that we are informed of what nature demands of us, what human nature and the nature of all creation demands of our hearts.

Characterizing a number of the falsifying moral theologies against which JP2 warns in *VS* is the prominent tendency to "conceive of freedom as somehow in opposition to or in conflict with material and biological nature, over which it must progressively assert itself."[91] It is this false notion of freedom that underlies the technocratic paradigm's underlying posture of technologically empowered lust over and against a cosmically chaste love. What such a divorce between freedom and nature overlooks is "the created dimension of nature" and "its integrity"[92] within the cosmic order. Among the schools of thought that divorce freedom from nature—a divorce against which JP2 adamantly warns—there is the perspective according to which "'nature' becomes reduced to raw material for human activity and for its power."[93]

This is the misperception that underlies and seeks to justify a posture of *technocratic lust* and the relativism of the market as we know it, which forbids the imposition of moral standards from outside its own internal rationale. According to the popular false view of nature detailed by JP2 in *VS*, the sphere of nature is perceived as merely useful for and at the disposal of humanity's own expression of power.[94] According to this misunderstanding of the relationship between nature and freedom, the limitations set by nature (the nature of the human person as well as the nature of all created things) need to be overcome by man for man to be free. This perspective lacks any sense of reverence for the way things are

90. *VS*, sec. 50, citing Second Vatican Council, *Gaudium et spes*, sec. 51. The *Compendium* explains that the natural law is called "'natural' because the reason that promulgates it is proper to human nature. It is universal, it extends to all people insofar as it is established by reason. In its principle precepts, the divine and natural law is presented in the Decalogue and indicates the primary and essential norms regulating moral life" (*Compendium*, sec. 140). The *Compendium*, quoting the *Catechism*, goes on to explain that "the natural law expresses the dignity of the person and lays the foundations of the person's fundamental duties" (*Compendium*, sec. 140).

91. *VS*, sec. 46. We will return in chapter 4 to Guardini's rejection of this opposition between nature and freedom.

92. *VS*, sec. 46.

93. *VS*, sec. 46.

94. *VS*, sec. 46. In Pope Francis's Guardinian account, this is the understanding of nature according to a technocratic paradigm, as we shall explore.

according to nature, and assumes an inherently antagonistic relationship toward the demands of the nature of people and things.

The nature of a person or thing, from this perspective, is something that "needs to be profoundly transformed, and indeed overcome by freedom, inasmuch as it represents a limitation and denial of freedom."[95] An insistence upon something having a nature with a meaning and dignity inherent to it is an insistence that stands in opposition to my alleged "freedom" or "right" to obtain what I might want to extract from the thing. If I am to be free, according to this outlook, I must be free to conquer and manipulate things according to my desires. The nature of myself, another person, or thing cannot come into the equation of discerning how to act or not act, for such a notion would be a barrier to my freedom to act in relation to myself, a given person, or thing as I wish.

If I am to be "free" to get from a person or thing just whatever I might want from him, her, or it, I do not stand in relation to that entity with a posture of chaste reverence, but with a posture of domination, of lust, as a mere consumer, a manipulator. My freedom is contingent, from this perspective, upon my power to manipulate things according to what I, in my alleged freedom, want from them. The nature of something, from this perspective, makes no demand upon me to appreciate it for what it is, according to a meaning inherent to it as a gift given by the Creator. Rather, I am "free" to subdue objects of my desire, so that they might fulfill not a purpose inherent to them, but the purposes determined by my own desires in my "freedom" to get what I desire from the world around me, according to my own lusts, wielding the power of technology at my disposal to this end.

According to one such school of thought that divorces freedom from nature, "it is in the untrammeled advancement of man's power, or of his freedom, that economic, cultural, social and even moral values are established: nature would thus come to mean everything found in man and the world apart from freedom," JP2 relates. This antagonism between "freedom" and nature, we can see, stands in close relationship to relativism and underlies the technocratic paradigm.[96] This false notion of power and freedom identified by JP2 is among the primary ideological roots of what I'm calling technocratic lust, and is the basis for an outlook contrary to chaste love in social life.

95. *VS*, sec. 46. As we shall see in chapter 4, it is this modern notion of freedom and nature to which Guardini, and following him, Francis, seeks an alternative.

96. *VS*, sec. 46.

Prominent among the failures in globalized society today that arise from modernity's false notion of freedom is what Pope Francis criticizes as *neocolonialism*.[97] We'll see in the upcoming chapters how Francis contributes to the song of cosmic chastity his critique of neocolonialism, as a part of his overall protest against the tyranny of technocratic lust. Francis critiques the neocolonialism proper to technocratic lust by drawing upon the strength of JP2's challenge to the logic of the global market as we know it. Francis, following JP2, perceives the destruction that the global market has wrought upon the world's cultures, particularly the destruction wrought upon traditions that have a built-in reverence for sexuality, marriage, and family proper to a diversity of the world's cultures. In his critique of neocolonialism, Francis continues JP2's and Benedict's war on the dictatorship of relativism, offering a paradigm of charity in truth.

Let's begin to listen, then, for the structure of Francis's tenor line.

---

97. For example, Francis, "Meeting with Indigenous People of Amazonia," para. 13; Francis, "Message to Organisers," para. 1. Francis, "Participation," sec. 3.2. Francis, "Letter of His Holiness," para. 4.

2

· · · · ·

Pope Francis on the Crisis of Communal Commitment

Moral Truth and the Truth about Family Life
against the Regime of Relativism

THE FOUNDATIONAL NOTIONS OF Catholic social teaching upon which JP2 and Benedict built are the foundations upon which Pope Francis builds his social commentary as well. Catholic doctrine, not political correctness, is at the root of Francis's call for young people to take the "risk of fruitfulness and life" by marrying and starting families.[1] Catholic doctrine, not political correctness, is at the root of Francis's vision of the family as the nexus of Church and creation. Catholic doctrine, not political correctness, is at the root of Francis's advocacy for authentic freedom and solidarity over and against moral relativism's false notions of freedom and its indifference to the common good. Catholic doctrine, not political correctness, is at the root of Francis's critique of the liberal market as one of the main governing arms of the dictatorship of relativism. Each of these key facets of the Francis message in the framework of Francis's social teaching belongs to an ontology of creation-as-gift and an anthropology of humanity-as-gift, which is what I'm advocating throughout this book as the underlying basis of the shared social message of Francis and the two previous popes.

1. "WMF," para. 14.

The melody of Catholic social teaching manifests itself especially in Francis's vision of family and marriage, which we explore in this chapter and to which we will return in chapter 8 as an integral part of JP2's and Francis's shared vision of moral truth and in chapter 9 as an integral part of the papal trio's theology of marriage within an ecological framework. Let's listen, in this chapter's exposition of the key structural features of the social teaching of Pope Francis, for his ontology of creation-as-gift, which is a fundamental feature that unites Francis's message with the teaching of the two previous popes.

Francis on Marriage and Family: "The Risk of Fruitfulness and Life"

When Pope Francis met with the bishops gathered for the 2015 World Meeting of Families in Philadelphia, he gave his fellow pastors a snapshot of the crippling fear that paralyzed many of the young adults he had pastored as their archbishop in Argentina. Francis recounted to his episcopal collaborators that during his time as shepherd of the flock in Buenos Aires, many parents used to share with him their grievance that "their children who were 30, 32 or 34 years old" were "still single."[2] These bewildered parents would say to their archbishop, "I don't know what to do."[3] Archbishop Bergoglio had a radical strategy for them as they navigated their adult children's perpetuated bachelorhood and unending adolescence: "Well"—Bergoglio used to say to these perplexed parents—"stop ironing their shirts!"[4]

The crippling distaste for permanent commitment that prevents young Argentinians from taking steps toward marriage and child-rearing, Francis suggested, paralyzes young people the world over in society today. It's not just a problem for the archbishop of Buenos Aires. Francis explained to the shepherds gathered in Philly that "young people have to be encouraged to take" the "risk" of starting a family.[5] This risk—which Francis identified as "a risk of fruitfulness and life"[6]—is a risk that young adults need to be *emboldened* to take.

2. "WMF," para. 14.
3. "WMF," para. 14.
4. "WMF," para. 14.
5. "WMF," para. 14.
6. "WMF," para. 14.

Starting a family is indeed a countercultural move that today's culture directly opposes. Reflecting upon his visit to the US capital, which he made a few days previous, Francis recounted that "addressing Congress, a few days ago, I said that we are living in a culture which pressures some young people not to start a family."[7] Francis proceeded to identify the reasons that this pressure is applied, having to do with a societal dearth of generosity and solidarity. Young people today are discouraged from starting a family on the grounds that they "lack the material means to do so."[8] And this same culture that urges many young people not to start a family on the basis that they can't afford to do so likewise urges well-to-do young people not to start a family on the grounds that "they are so well off that they are happy as they are,"[9] such that they ought not disturb their "happiness" by introducing into their smooth lives the instability of child-rearing.

"Should we blame our young people for having grown up in this kind of society?" Francis asks his fellow pastors. There are, as we shall be exploring, enormous sociological pressures that militate against family life, such as lack of stable work and lack of social and psychological support for struggling families.[10] Francis asks the world's shepherds, concerned for the young adults of their flock, "Should we condemn them for living in this kind of a world? Should they hear their pastors saying that 'it was all better back then,' 'the world is falling apart and if things go on this way, who knows where we will end up?'"[11] Francis concludes that no, this is not the way.[12] Francis isn't accusing young adults of refraining from starting families due to some unfounded fear. He doesn't accuse them of lacking the courage that previous generations had. The fear of marital commitment isn't simply a matter of men and women today being weaker and more self-indulgent than men and women in the past. Young people today have been placed by society upon a track that is largely incompatible with family life. Thus, Francis suggests to the bishops in Philly, "As shepherds following in the footsteps of the Good Shepherd, we are asked to seek out, to accompany, to lift up, to bind up the wounds of our time,"

7. "WMF," para. 13.

8. "WMF," para. 13.

9. "WMF," para. 13.

10. Thanks to Sara Matthews for helping me to identify and articulate this point and to develop the subsequent points of this paragraph.

11. "WMF," para. 10.

12. "WMF," para. 10.

in particular, the wounds within a society in which even the most faithful and well-intentioned Catholic family can crumble without adequate
communal support.[13] What Francis is addressing here is a societal failing
to provide culturally robust social structures and norms that help the
weak and wounded make and live out their permanent commitments; its
not so much a matter of unprecedented personal failings and weaknesses
on the part of young adults today. Francis isn't calling for a rugged individualism, but for a robust communal culture capable of forming hearts
to grow in their capacity to take the risk of fruitfulness and life. In the
face of circumstances today, in which our communal structures tend to
be weak, enormous courage is indeed called for on the part of individuals
in making the bold countercultural move of starting a family and taking
the risk of permanent commitment. At the same time, it's on the Church
and society to do all they can to build up communal structures that allow
families to flourish.[14]

    "Many young people, in the context of this culture of discourage-
ment have yielded to a form of unconscious acquiescence."[15] Indeed,
"they are afraid, deep down, paralyzed before the beautiful, noble and
truly necessary challenges" of life.[16] "Many put off marriage while waiting for ideal conditions, when everything can be perfect. Meanwhile,
life goes on, without really being lived to the full,"[17] Francis lamented.
In these circumstances, many young people miss out on what Francis
identified as "life's true pleasures,"[18] found in bringing to fruition their
existence-as-gift.

    For Pope Francis, life's true pleasures, proper to a fullness of life,
are found precisely in taking the "risk" of commitment. Taking this risk
enables us to pour ourselves out in service to others, Francis proposed.
"For knowledge of life's true pleasures only comes as the fruit of a long-
term, generous investment of our intelligence, enthusiasm and passion."[19]
To promote the countercultural challenge of child-rearing among young
adults, Francis said to his fellow pastors, "we need to invest our energies

---

13. "WMF," para. 10.
14. See West and George, "Politics of the Gospel," 19–23.
15. "WMF," para. 12.
16. "WMF," para. 12.
17. "WMF," para. 12.
18. "WMF," para. 12.
19. "WMF," para. 12.

. . . in extending a sincere invitation to young people to be brave and to opt for marriage and the family."[20] In this context, "we need a bit of holy *parrhesia* on the part of bishops."[21] Bold speech on the part of pastors is in order, to counteract the societal pressure *not* to marry. Francis went on to rehearse, ad lib, a conversation between a bishop and an unmarried young adult: Bishop: "Why aren't you married?"[22] Young adult: "Yes, I have a fiancée, but we don't know . . . maybe yes, maybe no . . . We're saving some money for the party, for this or that . . ."[23]

Precisely in a societal context in which any sort of definitive commitment is discouraged, pastors need to accompany young adults with a holy boldness of speech, Francis said. He exhorted the bishops to embolden young people to "grow towards the commitment of marriage."[24] For Francis is convinced that in truth, the demands of family life must be proclaimed as good news in our age of self-indulgence.

In Francis's social vision, the demands of family life serve as light in the darkness of a culture of self-service. The demands of family life constitute a message of *give* in a culture of *get*.[25] Today, then, "a pastor must show that the 'Gospel of the family' is truly 'good news' in a world where self-concern seems to reign supreme!"[26] For Francis, the demands of family life—the costs of family life—do not constitute an unfortunate side effect of having a family; such challenges, like the cost of Christian discipleship at large,[27] are precisely where family life's deepest joy is found.

In speaking of marriage and family, Francis said, "we are not speaking about some romantic dream."[28] Far from it, "the perseverance which is called for in having a family and raising it transforms the world and human history."[29] It is precisely the *perseverance* required by family life that gives families the evangelical capacity to "transform the world and

20. "WMF," para. 14.
21. "WMF," para. 15.
22. "WMF," para. 15.
23. "WMF," para. 15.
24. "WMF," para. 15.
25. See Maurin, "Personalist Communitarian," lines 2–3.
26. "WMF," para. 16.
27. See Bonhoeffer, *Cost of Discipleship*, 47–48.
28. "WMF," para. 16.
29. "WMF," para. 16.

history."[30] The evangelical self-divestment proper to perseverance in family life serves as an ecclesial leaven in society.

The Good News of Family Life against the Reign of Self-Concern: The Family as the Nexus of Church and Creation

On that morning in Philadelphia, the Pope discussed with his fellow pastors what he identified as "*the* foremost pastoral challenge of our changing times."[31] That foremost pastoral challenge, according to Francis, is the challenge before the Church's pastors to help society "move decisively towards recognizing" the gift of the family.[32] This is *the* countercultural, rhetorical, and evangelistic project of the Church today, in Francis's view. As things stand, society does not recognize the family for what it is. "For the Church," Francis said, the family is "the joyous confirmation of God's blessing upon the masterpiece of creation."[33] Francis went on to propose that "the family is the fundamental locus of the covenant between the Church and God's creation, with that creation which God blessed on the last day with a family."[34]

The family stands in a peculiar relationship with the rest of creation. The family, according to Francis, is the meeting point of that Church-cosmos relationship. According to Francis's hermeneutic, cosmology and ecclesiology find their meeting point in *the family*. For at the same time that the family is the crown of God's creation and is the confirmation of God's blessing upon creation, the Church depends upon the family for its existence. "Without the family, not even the Church would exist,"[35] Francis proposed, alluding to the contingency of the existence of the mystical body of Christ upon the biological realities of the nuptial embrace and the fruit this embrace orients itself toward by its very nature and the Church's constitution as a family made of many families.[36] Such is the

30. "WMF," para. 16.

31. "WMF," para. 4 (emphasis added).

32. "WMF," para. 4.

33. The masterpiece of creation being man and woman in the marriage covenant."WMF," para. 3.

34. "WMF," para. 4.

35. "WMF," para. 4.

36. Adrian Walker gets at this meeting point of biology and mystery

outlook of Francis's cosmologically rooted ecclesiology, according to the meaning of creation and the meaning of the family unit as the confirmation of God's blessing upon humanity within creation. Parallel to Lubac's dictum that the Eucharist makes the Church and the Church makes the Eucharist, for Francis, the sacrament of matrimony and the family life that springs forth from it *finds its source* in the Church and *is* the source of the Church. The Church makes marriage and family; marriage and family make the Church.[37]

Apart from the family, the Church could not "be what she is called to be, namely 'a sign and instrument of communion with God and of the unity of the entire human race,'" said Francis, appealing to *Lumen gentium*'s characterization of the Church.[38] According to Francis's ecclesial hermeneutic of the family and familial hermeneutic of the Church, "the Church's understanding" is "shaped by the interplay of ecclesial faith and the conjugal experience of sacramental grace."[39] This interplay between ecclesial faith and the conjugal experience of sacramental grace takes place in the family, that nexus between the Church and the rest of God's creation. Ecclesial faith meets the conjugal experience of sacramental grace precisely where the Church meets the cosmos: in the family. In family and marriage, as a singular biological and sacramental reality, the cosmos—God's creation—becomes imbued with sacramental grace. This is true in the case of all the sacraments, but in a particularly biologically contingent way in the sacrament of matrimony. The family, as a part of the rest of creation—with all its biological and physiological phenomenon—is from an ecclesial perspective a *sacramental* reality. In the family, biological realities—which humanity shares with the rest of the biological world—are sacramentalized. These biological phenomena are incorporated into the sacramental economy, and indeed, become a constitutive aspect of the sacramental economy. For Francis, sacramental grace and the biological aspects of creation meet in marriage and family. What in the natural world is mere mating is in the Church's sacramental theology elevated to the throne of God.[40] As Pope, Francis has continually

---

(sacramentology) quite eloquently. Walker, "What God Has Conjoined."

37. Marriage and family is not source of the Church in the very same way that the Eucharist is the source of the Church; nonetheless, it does have a role as source of the Church.

38. "WMF," para. 4, citing *Lumen gentium*, sec. 1.

39. "WMF," para. 5.

40. On the meaning of the love between Dante and Beatrice, see Balthasar, *Glory*

directed attention to this nexus between the Church's sacramental grace and creation at large.

In this visit with the bishops gathered in Philly, Francis identified the ailment that leaves society—and in particular, the family—vulnerable to disintegration today. At a time when characteristics of "the civil institution of marriage and the Christian sacrament" are no longer shared, Francis offers an outlook that reintegrates the civil, sacramental, as well as biological-cosmic aspects of family and marriage.[41] In the context of "today's culture" that "seems to encourage people not to bond with anything or anyone, not to trust," it seems, Francis said, that "the most important thing" from the impoverished and relativistic perspective of popular culture today is to "follow the latest trend or activity."[42] A singular ailment in today's society cripples any capacity for the kind of fidelity required for the type of bonding and responsibility integral to human flourishing, and Francis puts his finger on that ailment. This singular ailment—which bends our hearts double in a singular consumptive posture—defines even our posture toward one another, toward religion, and toward existence at large. It's an all-encompassing deformity on the part of the human heart in relation to that before which we are called to stand as fellow creatures, as gifts of God among the gifts of God. In this all-encompassing consumptive posture, we contradict the very nature of what we are as gift, and the very nature of the many gifts that the Creator has lavished upon humanity.

In having assumed this consumptive posture, the standard according to which we conduct our relationships, then, is not according to bonds of trust, but according to "the latest trend or activity," Francis said.[43] Today, "consumption seems to determine what is important. Consuming relationships, consuming friendships, consuming religions, consuming, consuming . . . Whatever the cost or consequences."[44] This all-encompassing consumptive posture denigrates the bonds proper to social life. It engenders "a consumption which does not favor bonding, a consumption which has little to do with human relationships."[45] This

---

of the Lord, 3:31–32.

41. "WMF," para. 6.

42. "WMF," para. 8. Such is the dictatorship of relativism, as identified by Cardinal Ratzinger at the threshold of his own pontificate (see chapter 1, 25–28.).

43. "WMF," para. 8.

44. "WMF," para. 8.

45. "WMF," para. 8.

fickleness of societal trends, in Francis's diagnosis, greatly distorts our religious and moral outlook.

Solidarity vs. Relativism: Truth and the Fickle-Heartedness of a Consumeristic Society

The fickle-heartedness of societal trends is part of a singular fickle-heartedness prevalent in society today that turns "social bonds" into "a mere 'means' for the satisfaction of 'my needs,'" according to Francis.[46] When social bonds are perceived as merely useful for satisfying my alleged needs, social relationships are emptied of their inherent and most fundamental meaning. Relationships as perceived in such a utilitarian and merely self-serving fashion are lacking in any sense of human solidarity. The inherent import of my neighbor as a gift of God, before whom I am called to stand as one gift beholding another, is lost to us. A vision of marriage and family as merely useful for the satisfaction of needs obliterates any sense of the dignity of my neighbor "with his or her familiar face, story and personality."[47] That is, a consumeristic notion of marriage is deeply connected with a consumeristic notion of relationships in general. The distortion of marriage as merely a useful contract for the fulfillment of my emotional needs stands in an antithetical relationship to the principle of solidarity. To opt for marriage and family according to an ontology of creation-as-gift, in contrast, is to opt for the way of solidarity. It's to opt for a posture of concern for the other's good as my very own, rather than viewing my neighbor as a mere means to the end of satisfying my alleged needs.

The utilitarian, consumeristic view of marriage stands in contrast to Francis's integral view of marriage and family as the crown God places upon creation. For Francis, we have seen, marriage is the coronation of creation that confirms God's blessing upon creation. Precisely by way of formation in an authentic and robust understanding of the "interplay of ecclesial faith and the conjugal experience of sacramental grace,"[48] we are empowered with the capacity to engage head-on—rather than turn a

---

46. "WMF," para. 8.

47. "WMF," para. 8.

48. That is to say, the interplay of the Church's faith as a singular mystery containing a myriad of facets on the one hand and one key facet of ecclesial faith lived out in society, namely, marriage. "WMF," para. 5.

blind eye to—"the unprecedented changes taking place in contemporary society, with their social, cultural—and, sadly, also legal—effects on family bonds."[49] The *Obergefell* ruling, in which the US Supreme Court ruled that states had to include within its notion of marriage certain civil legal arrangements made between two people of the same sex, was made three months prior to Francis's Philly visit. For Catholics in the US and the world over, as for the Pope, the "unprecedented changes"[50] pressed upon the faithful from every side.

At the root of the crisis of family and sexuality in society today is what Francis identified as a "widespread indifference and relativism."[51] In his first apostolic exhortation, *EG*, which hit the press on the Feast of Christ the King 2013, Francis presented this widespread indifference and relativism as first among the cultural challenges to the task of evangelization today. This indifference and relativism, Francis said, is "linked to disillusionment . . . which has come about as a reaction to anything which might appear totalitarian."[52] An insistence upon truths with universal pertinence has come to be popularly rejected as "totalitarian."[53] Such a reactionary rejection of a notion of *truth*, however, "not only harms the Church but the fabric of society as a whole."[54] Relativism, as an impediment to evangelization, is a prominent aspect of what Francis identifies in *EG* as the "crisis of communal commitment."[55] Relativism strikes a destructive blow upon the communal fabric of society. For, "in a culture where each person wants to be bearer of his or her own subjective truth, it becomes difficult to devise a common plan which transcends individual gain and personal ambitions."[56] For Francis, the void left behind by the rejection of truth is easily filled with "individual gain and personal ambitions" as the driving force for large-scale and small-scale

49. "WMF," para. 5.

50. "WMF," para. 5.

51. *EG*, sec. 61.

52. *EG*, sec. 61.

53. *EG*, sec. 61. This parallels Ratzinger's observation that anything advocating universal truths is dismissed as fundamentalist in his homily for the election of the Roman Pontiff. See page 26.

54. *EG*, sec. 61.

55. The title of *EG*'s second chapter is "Amid the Crisis of Communal Commitment," secs. 50–109, esp. sec. 106.

56. *EG*, sec. 61.

decision-making.[57] The logic of the market in the dictatorship of relativism provides a new standard of decision-making, according to the criteria of individual gain and personal ambition—the will to power, a.k.a., the pride of life, along with the lust of the eyes and the lust of the flesh. The logic of the market today prominently includes the logic of consumerism, and specifically, the logic of sexual identity and orientation as a consumer product.[58]

Francis does not mince words in his critique of the effects of relativism on the prevailing culture.[59] In an ontologically shallow society without a shared commitment to what is true and good, and without a shared sense of the meaning of these notions, "priority is given to the outward, the immediate, the visible, the quick, the superficial and the provisional."[60] In this context, with no shared sense of reality, "what is real gives way to appearances."[61] Without the depth of a communally shared sense of what is true and good, without a shared basis upon which to determine what is true and good, and without logical structures for navigating the meaning of these words, society is left to make its discernments based exclusively upon surface-level appearances. The current lack of communal commitment prevalent in society has to do with the ways in which we have become alienated from our communal origins. "In many countries," Francis said, "globalization has meant a hastened deterioration of their own cultural roots and the invasion of ways of thinking and acting proper to other cultures which are economically advanced but ethically debilitated."[62] A shared standard governing our actions as a society, then, has become what can be regarded as economically "advanced" but is deficient on an ethical level. When the market-driven rules of alleged economic advancement fill the void of a shared ethics and a shared sense of what is true, whole countries and people groups are robbed of their dignity.

In this context of lamenting today's crisis of communal commitment for which relativism is chiefly responsible, Francis appeals to a conversation that JP2 had with the bishops of Africa. In this conversation,

---

57. *EG*, sec., 61. Paralleling Ratzinger's identification of the aggrandizement of my own ego as filling the void left by relativism's rejection of the notion of truth.

58. See Cary, "Gender as Consumer Choice," paras. 1–5.

59. *EG*, sec. 62.

60. *EG*, sec. 62.

61. *EG*, sec. 62.

62. *EG*, sec. 62.

Francis recounts, the African bishops "pointed out . . . that there have been frequent attempts" in the context of the global market "to make the African countries 'parts of a machine, cogs on a gigantic wheel.'"[63] Francis, in relaying JP2's engagement with the African bishops, joins in JP2's lamentation that the attempt at making countries "cogs on a gigantic wheel" manifests itself in particular "in the field of social communications which, being run by centres mostly in the northern hemisphere, do not always give due consideration to the priorities and problems of" the African countries "or respect their cultural make-up."[64]

The same relativistic outlook—in which forces of alleged economic advancement inevitably replace a shared sense of what is true and good—has taken its toll on Asian countries as well, Francis recounts. Appealing to JP2's engagement with the Asian bishops, he reiterates the Asian bishops' concern about "the external influences being brought to bear on Asian cultures."[65] Francis highlights in this context the "new patterns of behavior" that "are emerging as a result of over-exposure to the mass media."[66] These patterns of behavior, imported from the commercial world of the secular West, have taken their toll on the flock over which the bishops of Asia keep guard. The cultural deformation affected by the ontologically impoverished media and entertainment industry of the West threatens many aspects of non-European cultures that had previously passed on "traditional values" that included a sense of "the sacredness of marriage" according to a holistic vision of sexuality and a sense of "the stability of the family" complementary with a Christian vision of marriage.[67]

Francis against the Injustices of Secularization: A Call for Communal Commitment

Communal commitment is far from intuitive in this aggressively secular, consumeristic context. Individualism, according to Francis, reigns supreme in society today. Unfortunately, within the context of the regime of relativism—which opposes standards of universally pertinent truths

63. *EG*, sec. 62.

64. *EG*, sec. 62. This is what Francis refers to as "neocolonialism," as we shall see especially in chapter 3.

65. *EG*, sec. 62.

66. *EG*, sec. 62.

67. *EG*, sec. 62.

as "totalitarian"—the Church is popularly perceived as a primary culprit responsible for imposing unjust moral standards that make demands upon individuals contrary to their alleged "freedom" and "rights." Yes, the Church makes social demands upon the hearts of individuals, ever insisting upon the social implications of individual decisions, and the social responsibility inherent to individual agency. The Church is thus identified on a popular level as the totalitarian culprit responsible for imposing certain prohibitions in a way that infringes upon basic human rights. Appealing to the US bishops, Francis observes that "while the Church insists on the existence of objective moral norms which are valid for everyone, there are those in our culture who portray this teaching as unjust, that is, as opposed to basic human rights."[68] Precisely the very notion of truth—which Francis presents as a fundamental safeguard for justice and basic human rights—much of American culture has come to reject as a *threat* to justice and human rights. Echoing the US bishops, Francis perceives that these accusations (that the Church's insistence on the existence of objective moral norms is antithetical to justice and human rights) are charges which "usually follow from a form of moral relativism that is joined, not without inconsistency, to a belief in the absolute rights of individuals."[69]

This is what makes relativism a crisis of communal commitment. It pits the "rights" of individuals against any communally shared standard of truth and justice. This is why, according to Francis, relativism cripples a sense of common commitment. Rights are conceived of in this relativistic and consumeristic context in an extremely individualistic manner. This false notion of rights opposes any sense of authentic solidarity and duty proper to an authentic notion of rights. In this widespread individualistic misunderstanding of human rights, the insistence upon the existence of objective moral norms is perceived as a *threat* to human rights, a threat to my freedom to consume in just any way I wish, without any reference to the nature of that which I seek to consume and without any regard for the demands of my own nature and with no standard of justice.

Francis, speaking for the Church as a whole, insists upon objective moral norms precisely in view of safeguarding universal human dignity. From Francis's perspective, it is only by way of a robust notion of *morality* that *human rights* can be safeguarded. In an age in which human

68. *EG*, sec. 62.
69. *EG*, sec. 62.

rights are advocated on a popular level, the very guarantee of those rights—namely, a moral norm—is widely rejected as contrary to the notion of rights. And this is because of a widespread misunderstanding of the meaning of *freedom*. Given the reflections from Benedict and JP2 we rehearsed in chapter 1, this widespread contradiction should come as no surprise. From the perspective of relativism's incoherent embrace of a notion of human rights and rejection of moral norms, "the Church is perceived as promoting a particular prejudice and as interfering with individual freedom," Francis observed, citing the US bishops.[70] For Francis, our society displays "a remarkable superficiality in the area of moral discernment."[71] Essential to the Church's task of evangelization in this societal context, Francis says, is the task of providing for society "an education which teaches critical thinking and encourages the development of mature moral values."[72]

In this context, Francis identifies a peculiar aspect of the popular perception of the Church in our current context: even as "the tide of secularism . . . has swept our societies," aspects of what the Catholic Church represents in the popular imagination maintains a great deal of credibility, trusted as she is "for her solidarity and concern for those in greatest need."[73] The Church continues to be called upon "as a mediator in finding solutions to problems affecting peace, social harmony, the land, the defense of life, human and civil rights, and so forth."[74] The Church, then, in the popular progressive imagination, has all sorts of positive aspects that render her an ally in the struggle for progress in society today. Yet, according to a widespread conceit, the Church retains all sorts of archaic—even bigoted—sets of commitments. Our challenge, then, is to help "people see that when we raise other questions less palatable to public opinion, we are doing so out of fidelity to precisely the same convictions about human dignity and the common good."[75]

It is within the larger crisis of communal commitment—in which "all communities and social bonds" are "experiencing a profound cultural crisis"—that "the family is experiencing" a "profound cultural crisis" in

70. *EG*, sec. 62.

71. *EG*, sec. 62.

72. *EG*, sec. 64.

73. *EG*, sec. 65.

74. *EG*, sec. 62.

75. *EG*, sec. 65.

a particular way.[76] As Francis suggested in Philadelphia and in *Evangelii gaudium*, relativism is at the root of the crisis of the family today. "In the case of the family, the weakening of these" communal and social bonds "is particularly serious because the family is the fundamental cell of society."[77] It is in the family that "we learn to live with others despite our differences."[78] In the family, we learn "to belong to one another."[79] Family is the fundamental school of solidarity and the fundamental human realization of solidarity, in that it is in the family that our belonging to one another is most concretely and intensively realized as human beings.

The Family and Its Indispensable Contribution to Society

The integral relationship between solidarity in society on the one hand and marriage and family on the other contains within it, for Francis, an integral relationship to the Church's task of evangelization. The family is "the place where parents pass on the faith to their children."[80] But if emotional satisfaction is the exclusive purpose of marriage, as it is popularly viewed to be, if it contains within it no other inherent meaning, if it contains no integral truth, no demands of justice or charity, then *nothing* stands in the way of my manipulation of it, my reconstruction and modification of it according to my raw will to emotional satisfaction. Marriage, like any other consumer product aimed at satisfying my emotional needs or desires, is at my disposal, to serve *me*—its master, its maker, its consumer, its stockholder, its CEO, its technocratic despot, its all-powerful manipulator. It is subject to my genetic engineering. It can undergo a reconstructive surgery, according to my emotional impulses.

Here we see at play society's false notion of freedom that sets itself up in opposition to nature, as identified by JP2.[81] Francis, following JP2, advocates for a vision of family life according to an authentic vision of freedom in harmony with nature, not in opposition to it. When we miss the meaning of marriage—when we miss the ways in which its meaning

76. *EG*, sec. 66.

77. *EG*, sec., 66.

78. *EG*, sec. 66.

79. *EG*, sec. 66.

80. *EG*, sec. 66.

81. *VS*, secs. 32–33. This point is big for the papal trio's precursor Guardini, as we'll see in chapter 4.

transcends the mere satisfaction of my emotional needs and desires—we miss its "indispensable contribution" to society.[82] Francis insists that "the indispensable contribution of marriage to society transcends the feelings and momentary needs of the couple."[83] Marriage's indispensable contribution to society, Francis says (quoting the bishops of France), arises "from the depth of obligation assumed by the spouses who accept to enter a total communion of life."[84] Marriage, for Francis, doesn't contribute to society as a commodity in the marketplace of emotional satisfaction.[85] Marriage is "a total communion of life"[86] that contains within it the most profound bond of mutual obligation. This, for Francis, is what makes marriage— according to its authentic understanding—a uniquely powerful force of evangelization and cultural renewal, as well as foundational for the implementation of social justice. When we perceive marriage's inherent meaning as a total communion of life, we can perceive that marriage and family is the fundamental realization in society of solidarity, justice, and charity.[87] A sound vision of marriage and family, then, is integral to Francis's vision of social justice as well as his vision of gospel proclamation and the Church's articulation of the demands the gospel makes upon our hearts, as it contains within itself the demands of justice, the demands of charity, the demands of moral truth, the demands of ethics.

The bond of marriage, by its very nature, makes demands upon those whom it binds. Indeed, it demands their entire selves. This demand of radical interpersonal solidarity, justice, and charity inherent to marriage (in the interspousal relationship and in the relationship between parents and children) stands in striking contrast to "the individualism of our postmodern and globalized era," which "favours a lifestyle which" seriously "weakens the development and stability of personal

---

82. *EG*, sec. 66.

83. *EG*, sec. 66.

84. *EG*, sec. 66.

85. See West and George, "Politics of the Gospel," 22, where West critiques what he calls "the commodification of the family." West states that "raising children is, or should be, a non-market activity—just like falling in love and having a healthy marriage." The challenge posed to us today, according to West, is that "we do these things within a market culture" (West, "Politics of the Gospel," 22).

86. *EG*, sec. 66.

87. Solidarity, justice, and charity in marriage and family as society's basic building block are preconditions for the same in society at large.

relationships."[88] Individualism as it manifests itself in our postmodern and globalized context "distorts family bonds."[89] But "our relationship with" God the Father "demands and encourages a communion which heals, promotes and reinforces interpersonal bonds."[90] Our very relationship with God the Father is for us an imperative call to communion and solidarity. Our relationship with God the Father contains within itself an imperative call to a communion that by its very nature heals, strengthens, safeguards, and promotes the bonds of interpersonal love. It is the triune bond of Father and Son—that is, it is the bond of the Spirit—that serves as the source of all solidarity, justice, and charity in society.

Antithetical to the meaning of these relationships to which the love of God the Father calls us are the "forms of war and conflict"[91] that do violence to the bonds of human solidarity, Francis insists. These are an offense to the bond of Father and Son, which is to say, an offense to the Holy Spirit. The love of God the Father—to which Francis will return in a similar manner in his reflections on St. Joseph in December of 2020[92]— demands of Christians a steadfastness "in our intention to respect others, to heal wounds, to build bridges" that transcend the enmities and rivalries characteristic of society today, and "to strengthen relationships," to strengthen the bonds of solidarity integral to social life.[93] The love of God the Father calls us to *bear one another's burdens,"* Francis declares, citing St. Paul's Letter to the Galatians as a canticle of solidarity.[94] It is upon this dogmatic and scriptural basis that Francis allies himself with "various associations for the defense of rights and the pursuit of noble goals" today.[95] It is from this dogmatic, trinitarian basis that Francis perceives in today's "defense of rights" on a popular level "a sign" of the noble "desire to contribute to social and cultural progress."[96] At its core, any authentic desire for social and cultural progress is fundamentally a desire to respond to the demands of the love of God the Father.

88. *EG*, sec. 67.
89. *EG*, sec. 67.
90. *EG*, sec. 67.
91. *EG*, sec. 67.
92. *PC*, sec. 7.
93. *EG*, sec. 67.
94. *EG*, sec. 67.
95. *EG*, sec. 67.
96. *EG*, sec. 67.

Individualism over and against solidarity is what Francis identifies as primary among the challenges faced by the family today, "in
all its complexity, with both its lights and shadows."[97] That shadow of
what Francis, in *AL*, identifies as "the growing danger" of "an extreme
individualism which weakens family bonds and ends up considering
each member of a family as an isolated unit"[98] is among "the principle
tendencies in" the "anthropological-cultural changes" found in society
today that render "social structures" less supportive "than in the past."[99]
These significant cultural and anthropological "changes in our times
influence all aspects of life."[100] Individualism takes an all-pervasive toll
upon society. Among these devastating effects of individualism is that
it leads to the false notion "that one's personality is shaped by his or her
desires, which are considered absolute,"[101] as is proper to the logic of the
free market as we know it, facilitating as it does precisely this absolute
primacy of individuals to construct their own personalities by way of
access to an infinity of consumer options.[102] In our "overly individualistic
culture," we are easily "caught up with possessions and pleasures."[103] Far
from facilitating a respect for the individual dignity of the human person,
"an overly individualistic culture" produces an atmosphere of "intoler-
ance and hostility in families."

What is lost in an "individualistic culture"[104]—characterized by an
individualism that undermines the kind of patience, tolerance, and cohesion inherent to family life—is, as we have already suggested, the principle
of solidarity. A loss of solidarity at the fundamental societal level of the
family unit deals a devastating blow upon human existence individually,
communally, and society at large. As much as the Church *makes* marriage
and family, and as much as marriage and family *make* the Church, individualism *breaks* family, and a consumeristically individualistic vision of
sexuality *breaks* society and undermines the Church's ministry.

97. *AL*, sec. 32. Francis here is employing the imagery of JP2's *FC*, secs. 4–10.

98. *AL*, sec. 33.

99. *AL*, sec. 32.

100. *AL*, sec. 32.

101. *AL*, sec. 33.

102. See Cary, "Gender as Consumer Choice," paras. 1–5.

103. *AL*, sec. 33.

104. *AL*, sec. 33.

Our capacity to respond to the call to the kind of solidarity proper to family life is threatened by "today's fast pace of life, stress and the organization of society and labour,"[105] which is part and parcel with this individualism. What each of these inhumane aspects of society today "militate against" is the notion of "*permanent decisions*,"[106] Francis observes—as we've already seen he would later observe in Philadelphia. This has a crippling effect upon the capacity of families to flourish and upon society as a whole to flourish. Indeed, it has a crippling effect upon the capacity of individuals to even begin to embark upon the task of starting a family. This incapacity for permanent decisions is among the primary "changes taking place in contemporary society" that "affect all of us, believers and non-believers alike."[107] This widespread incapacity for commitment is among the changes in society today which we must not "disregard."[108]

It is precisely in this context and in these circumstances, in "this concrete world, with all its many problems and possibilities," that "we must live, believe and proclaim,"[109] Francis said to the bishops gathered for the World Meeting of Families in Philadelphia. Indeed, the Church is called upon by God to respond to this individualism with all the ingenuity bestowed upon her by God. It is this extreme individualism that Francis identifies as *the* culprit in developing an unfortunate discrepancy of meaning "between the civil institution of marriage and the Christian sacrament."[110] It is this extreme individualism to which we must offer a radical alternative.

The Supermarket Mentality: A Parable of the Desacralization of Marriage

"The similarities between the civil institution of marriage and the Christian sacrament" which were once "considerable and shared," such that the two notions "were interrelated and mutually supportive"[111]—as a

105. *AL*, sec. 33.
106. *AL*, sec. 33.
107. *AL*, sec. 33.
108. *AL*, sec. 33.
109. "WMF," sec. 2.
110. "WMF," sec. 2.
111. "WMF," sec. 2.

singular, integral notion with civil, sacramental, and cosmo-biological aspects—have eroded in the context of the extreme individualistic outlook characteristic of society today, Francis observed. It is in this context that Francis described the state of the family today, for his episcopal audience, with "two familiar images: our neighborhood stores and our large supermarkets."[112]

Francis proceeded to recount, for his fellow pastors at the World Meeting of Families, the story of the development of endemic individualism, which is part and parcel with the story of the desacralization of marriage. Civil society once upon a time perceived the civic aspects of the singular reality of marriage in a manner that stood in complementary relationship with the Church's perception of marriage according to its civic, biological, and sacramental dimensions. Now civil society has adopted a notion of marriage altogether different from the Church's sacramental understanding of it. Making this observation at the close of that strange, hot summer of 2015, in the wake of *Obergefell*,[113] Francis proceeded to tell his episcopal audience a parable, as his global audience, and particularly, his audience in the United States, listened in.

Huge jumbotrons broadcasted Francis's message in Spanish and simultaneously translated into English on loudspeakers every few hundred yards between the Philadelphia Art Museum with its statue of Rocky Balboa at its base and the Basilica of St. Peter and St. Paul on the famed Ben Franklin Parkway. In the parable that Francis proceeded to tell in that context, he told the story of the degeneration of society's understanding of the civil institution of marriage. In that short parable, Francis recounted, in symbols, how the civil institution referred to today by the name of *marriage* has established a relationship of antagonism and incompatibility with the Church's understanding of marriage. Francis told this story of the degeneration of the meaning of marriage in society with the imagery of the transformation of the local neighborhood market into the enormous big-box supermarket. "To describe our situation today"[114]—in which "the civil institution of marriage and the Christian sacrament"[115] are at odds—Francis told the parable of "our neighborhood

112. "WMF," sec. 2.
113. See Snell, "Feverish Summer," paras. 12–13.
114. "WMF," 2.
115. "WMF," 2.

stores and our large supermarkets"[116] to the bishops at the seminary as it was simultaneously broadcasted live on the Parkway and on screens worldwide:

> There was a time when one neighborhood store had everything one needed for personal and family life. The products may not have been cleverly displayed, or offered much choice, but there was a personal bond between the shopkeeper and his custom-ers. Business was done on the basis of trust, people knew one another, they were all neighbors. They trusted one another. They built up trust. These stores were often simply known as "the lo-cal market."
>
> Then a different kind of store grew up: the supermarket. Huge spaces with a great selection of merchandise. The world seems to have become one of these great supermarkets; our culture has become more and more competitive. Business is no longer conducted on the basis of trust; others can no longer be trusted. There are no longer close personal relationships.[117]

Civil society no longer bases its notion of marriage upon a vision of soli-darity, justice, charity, and truth, which is what is required for relation-ships of trust. Its notion of marriage no longer honors the human bonds proper to authentic social justice. It is in this context, having told this parable, that Francis proceeded to observe, as we've already noted, that "Today's culture seems to encourage people not to bond with anything or anyone, not to trust."[118] As a society, we've turned marriage into just one more commodity in the big-box store of consumer desire.[119]

What Francis is primarily commenting upon here—he himself had made clear—is civil society's distortion of the meaning of marriage, which, as we have said, is no longer supportive of or in a complementary rela-tionship with the Church's sacrament of matrimony. Civil society's notion of marriage today is no longer based upon an authentic understanding of human bonds or upon interpersonal trust. This is parallel to the ways in which we no longer can regard the local mom and pop store as sufficient for providing "everything one needed for personal and family life."[120] For Francis, just as the supermarket or big-box store is antithetical to the

116. "WMF," para. 2.

117. "WMF," para. 2.

118. "WMF," para. 2.

119. See Snell, *Acedia*, 1–2, and Reno, "Empire of Desire," para. 6.

120. Francis, "WMF," para. 2.

trust and sense of sufficiency and satisfaction within limits—facilitated in the context of the little mom-and-pop store—so today's distorted outlook on the meaning of marriage and sexuality militates against the trust and sense of sufficiency and satisfaction within limits facilitated by an integral view of marriage. In the supermarket of sexuality and so-called marriage as we know it in society today, we are faced with plenty of options that militate against the fidelity proper to a sense of permanence.[121] In this consumeristic context, as I the consumer go from aisle to aisle, seeing bargain after bargain, item after item calling out to me to make use of it just as I wish according to my own demands, "needs," and desires, we "encounter widespread uncertainty and ambiguity."[122] Today's civil institution of marriage offers "huge spaces with a great selection of merchandise,"[123] leaving consumers across the globe in a posture of uncertainty and ambiguity concerning just *which* disposable product can meet their desires and needs at *this* given moment.[124] In Francis's social critique, it is this relativistic rationale of the market—of Wall Street and Walmart—that has come to dictate the rules of marriage and sex, filling the void left behind by society's rejection of an integral vision of human sexuality built upon the values of truth, justice, freedom, charity, and the principles of solidarity and the common good.

According to Francis's critique of a consumeristic society's commodification of marriage, "the world seems to have become one of these great supermarkets,"[125] fostering "fear of commitment" and "self-centredness."[126] Our culture—governed according to the rules of a big-box store mentality, ruled according to the dictates of a Wall Street/Walmart/Amazon.com/Koch brothers ambition for profit—"has become one of these great supermarkets,"[127] ever "more and more competitive,"[128] the one product competing with the next, one consumer item after the other competing for a claim upon my heart's momentary allegiance, only to be used and disposed of according to an unholy alliance between the

121. See *AL*, sec. 33.

122. See *AL*, sec. 33.

123. "WMF," para. 2.

124. See Cary, "Gender as Consumer Choice," para. 2.

125. "WMF," para. 8.

126. *AL*, sec. 33.

127. "WMF," para. 2.

128. "WMF," para. 2.

market and my own propensity toward self-indulgence. In our big-box store of a society, which Francis describes as a supermarket that has rendered marriage, family, and everything else in God's creation a mere consumer product, only to be used and disposed of according to the alliance between the market and the cacophony of disordered desires screaming within our hearts, as is proper to the relativistic rules of a relativistic market in a world under the thumb of relativism's dictatorship.

It is within the context of his parable of the supermarket as an image for the distortion of marriage in society today that Francis laments that such dehumanizing consumerism has formed "a culture which discards everything that is no longer 'useful' or 'satisfying' for the tastes of the consumer."[129] Commenting directly upon the alienation between the Church's notion of marriage on the one hand and civil society's current notion of marriage on the other, Francis laments that society has turned itself "into a huge multicultural showcase tied only to the tastes of certain 'consumers,' while so many others only 'eat the crumbs which fall from their masters' table.'"[130]

The supermarket of consumer options in the realm of marriage and sexuality today is often justified and indeed promoted as progressive on the basis of an impulse to "value a personalism that opts for authenticity as opposed to mere conformity,"[131] Francis observed in *AL*. There is in the supermarket of options a delusional sense that it is in this market of consumer options that "spontaneity and a better use of people's talents"[132] can have their source and grow. But in reality—according to Francis's critique—the big-box store mentality misdirects and distorts authentic spontaneity, and misleads us in our efforts to make "better use of people's talents."[133] When these efforts are misdirected, what is fostered is an attitude of "constant suspicion, fear of commitment, self-centrednesss and arrogance."[134]

The supermarket mentality has sought to place that which is inherently about self-emptying self-gift—namely, sexuality and marriage—as a commodity on the shelf of consumer desire, stripped of its inherent

129. "WMF," para. 3.
130. "WMF," para. 3, citing Matt 15:27.
131. *AL*, sec. 33.
132. *AL*, sec. 33.
133. *AL*, sec. 33.
134. *AL*, sec. 33.

meaning as gift and stripped of its character as a call to kenotic dispossession. Authentic freedom is not found in the big-box store mentality.
"Freedom of choice makes it possible to plan our lives and to make
the most of ourselves. Yet if this freedom lacks noble goals or personal
discipline, it degenerates into an inability to give oneself generously to
others."[135] Indeed, the big-box store is designed to facilitate our impulse to
get for ourselves as much as we can; it's not designed to develop human
freedom according to freedom's integral meaning. And this, for Francis,
is a crisis that strikes a mortal blow at the core of our capacity for fidelity
in marriage and family life. "Indeed, in many countries where the number of marriages is decreasing, more and more people are choosing to live
alone or simply to spend time together without cohabiting."[136] The current
crisis is one of men and women no longer making homes together. Given
the consumer options at our disposal on the shelves of the big-box store
of society today, our hearts are in need of a reformation for the self-giving
charity integral to human society's flourishing. Our hearts are in need
of a mature understanding of the meaning of the family as it stands in
integral relation to the meaning of the human person and the meaning
of human society.

By way of a popular misunderstanding of justice and solidarity in our
consumeristic society today, citizens are turned "into clients interested
solely in the provision of services."[137] Citizens become mere consumers,
and the state, in bed with corporate power, provides these consumable
and disposable services, catering to individualistic and arbitrary whims
unguided by any authentic notions of truth, justice, or freedom. By way of
a false notion of freedom that "lacks noble goals or personal discipline,"
this alleged freedom degenerates "into an inability to give oneself generously to others."[138] According to this pseudo-freedom, which is part and
parcel with an indifference to truth, "each individual can act arbitrarily,
as if there were no truths, values and principles to provide guidance,
and everything were possible and permissible."[139] These false notions of
justice and freedom and this indifference toward truth affect "our understanding of the family" such that the family "can come to be seen as a way

135. *AL*, sec. 33.
136. *AL*, sec. 33.
137. *AL*, sec. 33.
138. *AL*, sec. 33.
139. *AL*, sec. 34.

station, helpful when convenient."[140] The family, from this perspective, becomes "a setting in which rights can be asserted while relationships are left to the changing winds of personal desire and circumstances."[141] Francis laments that in this consumeristic, relativistic context, "the ideal of marriage, marked by a commitment to exclusivity and stability, is swept aside whenever it proves inconvenient or tiresome."[142]

While on the one hand, "the fear of loneliness and the desire for stability and fidelity" is a palpable reality in society today, there is at the same time "a growing fear of entrapment in a relationship that could hamper the achievement of one's personal goals."[143] The very antidote to the loneliness that so many of us fear is an antidote we have a propensity to refuse in society today, insofar as we are crippled by the fear of any commitment to another—an *other* who might stand in the way of my achieving my own "personal goals," to which our individualistic society today urges each of us to render all our allegiance in the name of our individualistic notions of "freedom," "rights," and "dignity."

In this context Francis insists that Christians must not give up on advocating for marriage, however unpopular these efforts may be. We may be tempted to retreat from these efforts, in order "to avoid countering contemporary sensibilities, or out of a desire to be fashionable or a sense of helplessness in the face of human and moral failings."[144] But if we did stop advocating for marriage, Francis warns, "we would be depriving the world of values that we can and must offer."[145] While Francis admits that "there is no sense in simply decrying present-day evils, as if this could change things,"[146] he insists that the task of Christians to follow Christ's example in expressing "compassion and closeness to the frailty of individuals"[147] does not mean "that we cease warning against a cultural decline that fails to promote love or self-giving."[148]

Francis's fight for marriage and family and his fight for an ontology and anthropology of givenness against the market mentality and the

140. *AL*, sec. 34.
141. *AL*, sec. 34.
142. *AL*, sec. 34.
143. *AL*, sec. 34.
144. *AL*, sec. 34.
145. *AL*, sec. 34.
146. *AL*, sec. 35.
147. *AL*, sec. 38.
148. *AL*, sec. 38.

throwaway culture is a singular fight. Characteristic of the symptoms of what Francis identifies as the "culture of the ephemeral"—symptoms that deform the human heart according to the dictates of relativism and consumerism—is "the speed with which people move from one affective relationship to another."[149] An interpersonal relationship, unmoored from the bonds of justice, solidarity, truth, and charity, is simply one more item to be delivered in a cardboard box from Amazon.com, as it were, and to be disposed of when I've made use of it. Our hearts are formed "along the lines of social networks" to perceive love as something that "can be connected or disconnected at the whim of the consumer, and the relationship quickly 'blocked.'"[150]

In the crisis of communal commitment, relativism displaces any of the integral cultural values of many of the world's traditions, including the cultural values proper to or compatible with a Christian vision of marriage. This crisis of communal commitment is part and parcel with "the process of secularization," which "tends to reduce the faith of the Church to the sphere of the private and personal."[151] The Church is to a great extent forbidden on a popular level from proposing universally pertinent truths and standards of the good. This leaves the market-driven media free to set its own rules, according to an ontologically emptied standard of economic "advancement," which, as we have already said, consistently sets itself up in direct opposition to the moral values of Christianity and the moral values proper to many cultural traditions, especially those pertaining directly to sexuality, marriage, and family. As the West establishes its paradigm of market liberalism across the globe, the alleged freedom of the market and the alleged freedom of corporations becomes *the* absolute priority and law of the land—feeding as it does upon the perennial lusts and temptations of the human heart, feeding these lusts in an unprecedentedly powerful manner, as the profit motive plows over all other loves and allegiances, at the expense of all previously established cultural priorities and collectively cherished and esteemed moral truths. As the West establishes its paradigm of market liberalism, it likewise establishes its paradigm of sexual liberalism, which has proven to be extremely "profitable."

149. *AL*, sec. 39.
150. *AL*, sec. 39.
151. *EG*, sec. 64.

The moral indifference proper to secularization sets itself up in a particularly aggressive posture of opposition to the sanctity of marriage and family, Francis continually reminds us. We've seen earlier in this chapter that for Francis—in his reiteration of the discussions between JP2 and the shepherds of both Africa and Asia—marriage and family is what has taken the primary hit in the spread of secularization's singular consumeristic rationale underlying the logic of the market as we know it. Filling the void of universally pertinent truths, we've seen, is the media and entertainment industry's desacralization of marriage and family and its all-encompassing antagonism toward ethics. The assault on marriage and family comes not exclusively or even primarily from state power, from government and "liberal" politicians and Supreme Court judges and public school sex education curriculums, but just as powerfully—or far more powerfully, rather—from a liberal market's forces of corporate power, which has a near monopoly on the formation (or deformation, rather) of our imaginations and habits of consumption and of relating to each other. This all-encompassing "process of secularization"—"by completely rejecting the transcendent"—"has produced a growing deterioration of ethics, a weakening of the sense of personal and collective sin, and the steady increase of relativism," Francis laments.[152] Intentionally rejecting any basis for truth or any standard of goodness, consumeristic secularization has "led to a general sense of disorientation, especially in the periods of adolescence and young adulthood which are so vulnerable."[153]

As we set out in the coming chapter to present cosmic chastity's concern for an authentic vision of freedom and moral truth in the desert of relativism, and as we set out to explicate the theological roots of Catholic social teaching by way of Francis's cultural commentary in view of the theological framework of JP2 and Benedict, we shall continue exploring JP2's and Benedict's vision of social justice. Chapter 3's presentation of Francis in the inheritance of a JP2-B16 social teaching will thus conclude part 1's introductory exploration of the musical structure of the song of cosmic chastity sung by Francis and the two previous popes.

152. *EG*, sec. 64.
153. *EG*, sec. 64.

3

. . . . .

A Canticle of Praise against
the Logic of Babel

*The Papal Trio's Liturgical Ontology over
and against the Culture Wars*

INSTEAD OF LINING UP with the battle lines of conservatives versus liberals, Pope Francis's position on the cultural battlefield is defined by the *liturgical ontology of praise* that defined the location of JP2 and Benedict in their fight for truth, justice, and love against *the exploitative logic of Babel*, as we'll begin exploring in this chapter. Francis criticizes market liberalism and sexual liberalism in the same breath, because he sees these two ideological distortions of reality as two expressions of the same problem. Indeed, he regards the mentality of market liberalism as largely responsible for the spread of sexual liberalism globally, in what he criticizes as neocolonialism. Liberal capitalism and sexual liberalism are deeply connected, for Francis, as part of the technocratic paradigm and throwaway culture. The liberal market has been the main force contributing to the disintegration of family households throughout the global household. It has played a key role in deforming hearts, severely weakening their capacity for developing a sense of commitment, solidarity, responsibility, and stewardship. It forms our hearts according to the market's own rules—rules that take little interest in the laws written into the fabric of human nature and the nature of the cosmos.

Francis's singular advocacy for human ecology—a singular and deep pro-family environmentalism—bursts through the confines of the

66

categories of the culture wars. Francis's critique of neoliberal capitalism and neocolonialism, which the radical left likewise critiques, are integral to his high view of sexuality, marriage, and family.

Against the Logic of Babel

Pope Francis's alternative to market liberalism and sexual liberalism is found in his call to the reverential awe and wonder that characterized St. Francis's posture before the mystery of creation as *a gift of the outstretched hand of God*.[1] This is what Pope Francis has on offer as an alternative to the culture wars, playing by the rules of neither left nor right.

We see this singular "Francis option" at play in the last third of his book *LUD*, where the Pope makes reference to a "twelfth-century midrash, or commentary, on the story of the Tower of Babel in chapter 11 of the Book of Genesis."[2] According to the medieval rabbi who authored this commentary, "If a brick fell it was" perceived to be "a great tragedy," Francis recounts. "Work stopped and the negligent worker was beaten severely as an example. But if a worker fell to his death? The work went on. One of the surplus laborers—slaves waiting in line for work—stepped forward to take his place so that the tower could continue to rise." Here arises the key question for Francis and for the JP2-B16 inheritance of social teaching: "Which was more valuable, the brick or the worker?" Thus Francis articulates the fundamental rhetorical economic query asked of society by the Church-as-gadfly since Leo XIII: "Which was considered an expendable surplus in the pursuit of endless growth?"[3]

The worker, in the logic of Babel, was expendable, whereas the brick was highly prized as a means to an inhumane end. Francis proceeds then to bring the question home to our present era: "And nowadays? When shares of major corporations fall a few percent, the news makes headlines. Experts endlessly discuss what it might mean. But when a homeless person is found frozen in the streets behind empty hotels, or a whole population goes hungry, few notice; and if it makes the news at all, we just shake our heads sadly and carry on, believing there is no solution."[4] Francis employs the rabbinic reading of the Babel story as an image for

1. *LS*, sec. 76.
2. *LUD*, 116. See also Francis, "Healing the World," paras. 5–6.
3. *LUD*, 117.
4. *LUD*, 117.

development gone wrong from the perspective of the Church's inheritance
of theological reflection on social justice.[5]

The papal trio's critique of the logic of the market focuses on the
ways in which the logic of the market misidentifies the *means* and *ends*
in economic life. For JP2, as he recounts in the opening sentence of *SRS*,
"the social concern of the Church" is "directed towards an authentic
development of man and society which would respect and promote
all the dimensions of the human person,"[6] especially those dimensions
having to do with labor and sexuality—perennial human concerns that
are front, center, and intertwined in the human drama since Eden. The
well-being of the human person, communities, and society as a whole
is the end of all development, including economic development, and of
the economy itself. The economy is called by the demands of justice and
charity to honor human dignity.[7]

Babel and the Question of St. James Today

Ours is a society to which JP2 addresses the biting question posed by St.
James: "What causes wars, and what causes fighting among you? Is it not
your passions that are at war in your members? You desire and do not
have."[8] Is this not what Johannine language calls *lust in its three forms*,
by which our hearts become obsessively set upon possessing what is not
ours to possess, or possessing in a manner in which we are not meant to
possess? For the hope-filled JP2, "in a different world, ruled by concern
for the common good of all humanity, or by concern for the 'spiritual and
human development of all' instead of by the quest for individual profit,
peace would be possible as the result of a 'more perfect justice among

---

5. For JP2, authentic development is not about "merely satisfying material necessities through an increase of goods, while ignoring the sufferings of the many and
making the selfishness of individuals and nations the principal motivation" for development (*SRS*, sec. 10).

6. *SRS*, sec. 1.

7. All integral development is directed toward this end. Development does not
have the amassment of capital as its end, nor does it have production as its end. Rather,
any humanely made profit or any humane method of production needs to be a means
to the end of human flourishing on a collective and individual level, and can never
come at its expense.

8. *SRS*, sec. 10, citing Jas 4:1–2.

people."[9] JP2's appropriation of St. James's prophetic query is at the core of his economic critique. JP2 roots his economic critique of the logic of the market in a deep theological anthropology that takes seriously the reality of our captivity to sin—in particular, our lust, avarice, and hunger for power—the reality of our desires for what we "do not have."[10]

Francis offers a diagnosis of what's *off* in society today similar to that offered by JP2. It's what's off in our economics, in our household management practices as a society. Its what's off in historical humanity since the fall. As Francis observes, "in our lives, just as in our societies, if you put money at the center, you enter the pattern of" idolatrous "sacrifice: whatever the human cost or the damage to the environment, the tower" of Babel "must go higher and higher. But when you put people's dignity at the center, you create a new logic of mercy and of care. Then what is truly of value is restored to its rightful place."[11] Here, Francis urges us to choose what is at the center, people or capital, "people or bricks," "the triumph of the fittest and the throwaway culture" or "mercy and care."[12] Here Francis builds explicitly upon the social critique proper to JP2 and Benedict. As Francis recounts,

> When the accumulation of wealth becomes our chief goal, whether as individuals or as an economy, we practice a form of idolatry that puts us in chains. It is inconceivable that so many women and children are being exploited for power, pleasure, or profit. Our brothers and sisters are being enslaved in clandestine warehouses, exploited as undocumented migrants in prostitution rings, and the situation is even worse when it is children subject to such injustices, all for profit and the greed of a few.[13]

For Francis, Catholic social commentary is not a matter of checking off all the hot-button issues, from one disconnected issue to the next, akin to establishing a campaign platform that might gain a popular vote. Nor is Francis's approach a matter of bipartisan collaboration, as though he were reaching "across the aisle" in savvy political attempts to arrive at compromises we can all agree on. For Francis, Catholic social commentary is a matter of identifying where the end has been mistaken as

---

9. *SRS*, sec. 10, citing *PP*, sec. 76.
10. *SRS*, sec. 10, citing Jas 4:2.
11. *LUD*, 116–17.
12. *LUD*, 117.
13. *LUD*, 113–14.

a means, and vice versa. *Where in our social life have human beings been treated as mere capital, and where has amassing capital been treated as an end, to which human persons are subjected as a means?* That is the crux of the matter, in the social commentary of Francis. These questions are to be applied at the level of the global household and the micro domestic household, and at every level between. The culprit for Francis is what he identifies as "the neo-Darwinist ideology of the survival of the fittest, underpinned by an unfettered market obsessed with profit and individual sovereignty" that has "penetrated our culture and hardened our hearts."[14]

The Pope Francis body of social commentary—particularly by way of its critique of technocracy and its articulation of its positive alternative, namely, an integral human development that honors the human person whole and entire, each person and humanity-at-large as a social entity—is true to the heritage of JP2 and Benedict in its adherence to the intellectual framework of Paul VI's *HV*, in its critique of technocracy, particularly its critique of contraception. As Francis observes, "Paul VI warned in his 1968 encyclical *HV* of the temptation to view human life as one more object over which the powerful and educated should exercise mastery. How prophetic his message now looks!"[15] Technocracy manifests itself today in myriad ways, offending the meaning of human life at its core. Francis identifies some key examples in addition to that of contraception: "These days prenatal diagnosis is commonly used to filter out those deemed weak or inferior, while at the other end of life, euthanasia is becoming normal: either overtly, through assisted suicide laws in some countries or states, or covertly, through neglect of the elderly."[16]

What Francis identifies as the "causes of this erosion of the value of life"—causes which "have to be faced"—is the exclusion "from public policymaking any consideration of the common good," such that we end up "promoting individual autonomy to the exclusion of all other values and reference points," for, "without a vision for society rooted in the dignity of all people, the logic of the unfettered market ends up turning life from a gift into a product."[17] Here, we see how Francis, by way of the rationale of JP2 and Benedict, pushes back against the logic of the

14. *LUD*, 116.
15. *LUD*, 116.
16. *LUD*, 116.
17. *LUD*, 116.

market[18] on the basis of a theology of givenness. It is in the context of this discussion that Francis states, "While many will be irritated to hear a pope return to the topic, I cannot stay silent over 30 to 40 million unborn lives cast aside every year through abortion. It is painful to behold how in many regions that see themselves as developed the practice is often urged because the children to come are disabled, or unplanned."[19]

The papal trio pushes back against the liberal market's culture of death, condemning its commodification of human lives, and condemning how it renders human life disposable. The papal trio's integral pro-life, pro-family logic is the alternative to the logic of so-called economic "freedom" in our technocratic context.

For Francis, because human life and human flourishing constitute the end, and human beings are not meant to be a mere means to other ends, "human life is never" to be considered merely as "a burden."[20] Rather, human life

> demands we make space for it, not cast it off. Of course the arrival of a new human life in need—whether the unborn child in the womb or the migrant at our border—challenges and changes our priorities. With abortion and closed borders we refuse that readjustment of our priorities, sacrificing human life to defend our economic security or to assuage our fear that parenthood will upend our lives. Abortion is a grave injustice. It can never be a legitimate expression of autonomy and power. If our autonomy demands the death of another, it is none other than an iron cage.[21]

Francis, as a global Socrates in the shoes of the fisherman, asks his audience, in view of the controversial issue of abortion: "Is it right to eliminate a human life to resolve a problem? Is it right to hire an assassin to resolve a problem?"[22] There's no mincing of words here. For this postmodern papal Socrates corrupting the youth of a global Athens, a physician who performs abortions is a hired assassin. This global Socrates has indeed committed a crime of impiety against the city's gods—particularly the

---

18. See West, "Politics of the Gospel," 17, and *LUD*, 116, for Francis's critique of "the logic of the unfettered market," parallel to that of West.

19. *LUD*, 115.

20. *LUD*, 115.

21. *LUD*, 115.

22. *LUD*, 115.

god of freedom, individualistically conceived and divorced from a notion of responsibility.

Safeguarding the Dignity of Human Life against Development Gone Wrong

In the papal trio's alternative to the culture wars, advocating for the sanctity of human life in a culture of death, and taking responsibility as individuals and collectively for the stewardship of life, is a concern of economics. In his review of economic circumstances as they've developed since the publication of *PP*, Benedict expressed the concern that "from the social point of view, systems of protection and welfare, already present in many countries in Paul VI's day, are finding it hard and could find it even harder in the future to pursue their goals of true social justice in today's profoundly changed environment."[23] What has transpired, in Benedict's account, is that

> the global market has stimulated first and foremost, on the part of rich countries, a search for areas in which to outsource production at low cost with a view to reducing the prices of many goods, increasing purchasing power and thus accelerating the rate of development in terms of greater availability of consumer goods for the domestic market.[24]

The result of this is that "the market has prompted new forms of competition between States as they seek to attract foreign businesses to set up production centres, by means of a variety of instruments, including favourable fiscal regimes and deregulation of the labour market."[25] Unfortunately, as B16 recounts, "these processes have led to a downsizing of social security systems as the price to be paid for seeking greater competitive advantage in the global market, with consequent grave danger for the rights of workers, for fundamental human rights and for the solidarity associated with the traditional forms of the social State."[26] In these circumstances,

23. *CV*, sec. 25.
24. *CV*, sec. 25.
25. *CV*, sec. 25.
26. *CV*, sec. 25.

Systems of social security can lose the capacity to carry out their task, both in emerging countries and in those that were among the earliest to develop, as well as in poor countries. Here budgetary policies, with cuts in social spending often made under pressure from international financial institutions, can leave citizens powerless in the face of old and new risks; such powerlessness is increased by the lack of effective protection on the part of workers' associations. Through the combination of social and economic change, trade union organizations experience greater difficulty in carrying out their task of representing the interests of workers, partly because Governments, for reasons of economic utility, often limit the freedom or the negotiating capacity of labour unions.[27]

The State, then, is in today's context of market liberalism motivated to prioritize the utilitarian "thriving" of corporations over and against the humane thriving of workers, their families, and their communities, upon whom production depends—the very human lives and communities that production is actually meant to serve. The good of human lives and communities is never to be commoditized in an economy that honors the truth of social justice. We see then that for Benedict, as for Francis after him (as we saw in Francis's commentary on the Babel narrative), social justice demands that society safeguards the truth of human dignity—in this case, safeguarded by the protection of workers, by way of strong social security systems, safeguards against the deregulation of corporate activity, and safeguards protecting the right of workers to organize so that they themselves can exercise their God-given leverage to defend their own rights against any profit-obsessed wielders of corporate power who may threaten their dignity in the name of economic "freedom."

The prioritization of economic utility in a regime of alleged economic freedom, which is characteristic of our liberal capitalist economy today, in Benedict's account, has a tendency to place limits on the freedom of labor unions, whose purpose is to safeguard the dignity of workers. But again, the economic "freedom" of corporations by way of deregulation is prone to jeopardize the authentic freedom of workers to effectively organize as stewards of their own collective welfare and the welfare of their families and communities. Just as for Francis the dignity of the newborn baby and the dignity of the newly arrived immigrant makes a demand upon us—a demand inherent to human dignity—so here for

27. *CV*, sec. 25.

Benedict, the worker's dignity makes a demand upon all of society, and in a particular way, it makes demands upon governing political powers and those who wield corporate power—all those who have a portion of control over the means of production—*to safeguard the dignity of human life* on behalf of society's members, and particularly, on behalf of workers. We are all called, according to this rationale of stewardship and solidarity in society, to advocate a culture of life in a context of development gone severely wrong, in a culture otherwise unequipped to safeguard and prioritize the dignity of human life. The right of workers to organize in order to stand up for their rights, a right which keeps in check the power of corporations to simply minimize labor costs, is, for Benedict, a primary concern at the heart of integral human development. It's part and parcel with any culture that safeguards the dignity of human life. It cannot be compromised without compromising human dignity itself.

Cain, Abel, and the Good Samaritan: Fraternal Enmity and Harmony in Francis's Social Teaching

In the JP2-B16 inheritance of Catholic social doctrine taken up by Francis, the primary categories of discussion are defined not by party platforms, ideologies, and the battle lines of the culture wars, but by the lives of the saints and the theology of sacred Scripture. Signing off at the conclusion of *FT* on the Feast of St. Francis at the *poverello*'s tomb in Assisi, Pope Francis drew the attention of his audience to the figure of Charles de Foucauld, whom he placed alongside the figure of St. Francis as a model of fraternal love. Charles "directed his ideal of total surrender to God towards an identification with the poor, abandoned in the depths of the African desert."[28] Francis went on to recount that "in that setting" Charles "expressed his desire to feel himself a brother to every human being, and asked a friend to 'pray to God that I truly be the brother of all.' He wanted to be, in the end, 'the universal brother.'"[29] It was precisely by way of "identifying with the least" in poverty that Charles came "at last to be the brother of all"[30]—by way of an expansion of his own limited

28. *FT*, sec. 287.

29. *FT*, sec. 287. Francis cites a Foucault letter as the source of this title, and cites Paul VI's use of "these words in praising his [Foucault's] commitment" as found in *PP*, sec. 12. The official English translation of *PP* renders it "everyone's brother."

30. *FT*, sec. 287.

human heart to Christlike proportions, well beyond its own individual capacity and narrow confines. In the encyclical's closing sentence, Pope Francis prays God would inspire "in each one of us"[31] the same dream that Foucault had—that of becoming a brother to all.

Francis's insistence upon solidarity, which involves for him an insistence upon identifying the means and the end in economic life, becomes particularly controversial in the social climate dominated by the allied "enlightened" "orthodoxies" of market liberalism and sexual liberalism that have colonized the hearts of so many cultures across the globe today. Economic liberalism cannot tolerate when the truth of social morality is applied to questions of economics, and in particular, questions concerning the truth about the meaning of work in relation to the meaning of the human person. Sexual liberalism cannot tolerate the application of the truth of social morality to questions concerning the truth about the meaning of sexuality and marriage in relation to the meaning of the human person.

Recounting Christ's parable of the Good Samaritan, Pope Francis locates the story within the context of humanity's own impoverishment in its capacity for fraternal love and propensity toward enmity—an enmity that rages today and manifests itself in a myriad of technocratic forms. After the manner of Lubac's patristic-medieval retrieval of an integral theological anthropology and soteriology, Francis narrates the human drama of *failure in fraternity* and *propensity toward enmity* in terms of the Gospel parable of the Good Samaritan. In Francis's presentation, all of humanity travels on the Jericho road. All of us are characters in this unfolding drama of injustice, this drama of humankind destined to at last be won over by the kind of cruciform self-giving love that we see in the figure of the Good Samaritan, which can propel the human family toward embracing an ethos of authentic social justice.

In Francis's telling, the parable's beginning is a portrayal of a world in which the call to familial love goes unheeded. In locating the parable within the context of human history, and in locating human history within the narrative context of the parable, Francis locates *society today* in a particular way within this narrative context, with all the immediacy of the present, characterized as it is by the primal and perennial problem of *sin*. "This parable has to do with an age-old problem,"[32] the Pope said,

---

31. *FT*, sec. 287.

32. *FT*, sec. 57.

alluding to Scripture's telling of the history of humanity as a story of humanity *at enmity with itself.*[33] "Shortly after its account of the creation of the world and of man, the Bible takes up the issue of human relationships," Francis recounts early in his second social encyclical which focuses upon the *polis*, following upon his first social encyclical, which focused on the *cosmos.*[34] The Scripture turns quickly from its portrait of the creation of the cosmos and humanity within the cosmos to what we could call *a disaster in the polis*, which is at heart *a disaster in the family*, a disaster for the fundamental building block of society, and therefore, a disaster for all society, all of humanity. "Cain kills his brother Abel and then hears God ask: 'Where is your brother Abel?' (Gen 4:9)."[35] Cain's answer, the Pope says, "is one that we ourselves all too often give: 'Am I my brother's keeper?'"[36]

In the question that God asks Cain, God offers to humanity his own divine hermeneutic of humanity, a hermeneutic which perceives humanity's meaning as rooted in the divine call to fraternity, which stands in contrast to our characteristic inhumane indifference toward our brother's welfare, or worse, our efforts to work against our brother's welfare, and perhaps even to take his life. Francis thus gets at the heart of what we're up against, what the Church's social teaching is up against. Far from rendering to our brother what is his due, we have a terrible propensity to offend his dignity in the worst of ways, namely, by taking his life—taking the gift of life which God has given to him. In taking the life of a brother, we abhor the gift that our brother's life is to him, to us, and to all society.

"By the very question he asks, God leaves no room for an appeal to determinism or fatalism as a justification for our own indifference,"[37] Francis explains in a manner proper to an authentic Catholic anthropology of freedom, agency, and responsibility. God holds Cain responsible, and in so doing, appeals to our inherent freedom. This is the divine appeal to our freedom—a freedom that lies buried within our hearts as our hearts are distorted by its lusts. This fundamental freedom of the

33. Which of course, in the cosmo-anthropology of Francis and the two previous popes, is inherently a history of humanity also at enmity with God and with the rest of creation. As we shall explore in chapter 4, this is central to Lubac's cosmo-anthropological theology.

34. *FT*, sec. 57.

35. *FT*, sec. 57.

36. *FT*, sec. 57.

37. *FT*, sec. 237.

human heart, containing within itself an inherent call to responsibility, is what JP2 constantly directed our attention to throughout his catechesis on the theology of the human body.

Francis's scriptural hermeneutic of reality is a hermeneutic of humanity's call to cultivate its God-given freedom—freedom that flowers when the human heart perceives the good and acts in a manner true to the good. Resolving conflict, caring for one another: these terms, in the Pope Francis lexicon, are no mere goals of superficial civility.[38] They are for him fundamental alternatives to fatalism, determinism, and self-justified indifference,[39] and are building blocks for the restoration of the earthly city, anticipating the advent of the new Jerusalem. The Word of God, in the question God poses to Cain, itself poses *a question to us* and encourages "us to create a different culture,"[40] a counterculture, "in which we resolve our conflicts and care for one another."[41] Resolving conflict and caring for one another is the alternative to fratricide, the alternative to a murderous spirit arising from what St. James identifies as a covetous grasping for what we do not have[42] and inextricably bound with what St. John identifies as lust, in each of its three forms.[43]

Perceiving the Givenness of All That Is and Opposing the Myth of Self-Sufficiency

The resolution to resolve conflict and to care for one another in fraternal love in the *polis* of the human family arises from a perception of the givenness of all that is. As Francis puts it in *LUD*,

> We are born, beloved creatures of our Creator, God of love, into a world that has lived long before us. We belong to God and to one another, and we are part of creation. And from this understanding, grasped by the heart, must flow our love for each other, a love not earned or bought because all we are and have is unearned gift.

38. See Reno, "Civility Trap," paras. 15–17.

39. *FT*, sec. 57.

40. *FT*, sec. 57.

41. *FT*, sec. 57.

42. Jas 4:2.

43. 1 John 2:16.

How are we persuaded otherwise?[44]

Rendering the good due to one another, which is a requirement for the implementation of justice, arises from hearts informed by love, inspired by love, hearts that perceive that the goods of creation rendered to humanity are an utter gift from God, as Benedict helped us to see in *Caritas in veritate*.[45] It is the truth of the gratuity of God's gifts that is the ultimate indictment upon social injustice. I have no right to steal what God has given to my brother, and I have no right to fall short of generosity in sharing the gifts that God has lavishly bestowed upon me. To grasp tightly to the gifts of God as merely "mine" at the expense of the welfare of my brother is to miss the truth of the gratuity of creation. Following this hermeneutic of gratuity as the underlying basis for an ethos of social justice, Francis asks, as a new Socrates in the Chair of Peter,

> How did we become blind to the preciousness of creation and the fragility of humanity? How did we forget the gifts of God and of each other? How to explain that we live in a world where nature is suffocated . . . where heartbreaking poverty coexists with inconceivable wealth, where entire peoples like the Rohingya are consigned to the dustheap?[46]

Francis then describes the twisted basis of what we're calling the logic of *technocratic lust*. The logic of technocratic lust, Francis helps us to see, is based on the myth of self-sufficiency. "I believe that what has persuaded us" that we aren't gift and that all that we have isn't gift "is the myth of self-sufficiency" (as the antithesis of solidarity)—"that whispering in our ears that the earth exists to be plundered; that others exist to meet our needs; that what we have earned or what we lack is what we deserve; that my reward is riches, even if that means that the fate of others will be poverty."[47] As Francis recounted at the 2015 World Meeting of Families in Philadelphia and in *Evangelii gaudium* (so we've seen in chapter 2), this false perception of my neighbor as existing merely to meet my needs has greatly distorted the popular perception of the meaning of marriage and the meaning of a spouse as merely at the service of meeting my emotional "needs" and desires. In this context in *LUD*, Francis goes on to suggest that "if . . . we repent, and look back to our Creator and to each other, we

44. *LUD*, 13–14.
45. *CV*, sec. 48.
46. *LUD*, 14.
47. *LUD*, 14.

might remember the truth that God put in our hearts: that we belong to Him and to each other,"[48] in a shared home. What Francis calls for is that the world "be organized differently, to reflect" the truth that we belong to each other and to God, over and against the falsehood of "the selfishness of the culture in which we are immersed," a culture that "denies the best of who we are,"[49] having "neglected and mistreated our ties with our Creator, with creation, and with our fellow creatures,"[50] denying what JP2 and Irenaeus call God's art, God's plan of harmony with God, with each other, and with the rest of Creation.[51] Francis calls us to assume a new posture, a singular posture informed by an ethos of cosmic chastity, an ethos of harmony.

With the evangelical backdrop of the parable of the Good Samaritan as recounted in Luke's Gospel, and with the historical-scriptural consciousness of humanity's propensity to fraternal *indifference* at its best and *spite* at its worst (typified in the story of Cain and Abel), in *FT*, Pope Francis states the simple truth loud and clear: "in today's world, many forms of injustice persist, fed by reductive anthropological visions and by a profit-based economic model that does not hesitate to exploit, discard and even kill human beings."[52] A dearth of clairvoyance concerning *anthropological truth*, accompanied by the toxins of a profit-based economic model with all its inherent falsehood clouding our vision, according to Francis's diagnosis, contributes to the dearth of justice in society at large today. "While one part of humanity lives in opulence, another part sees its own dignity denied, scorned or trampled upon, and its fundamental rights discarded or violated."[53] As in the case of Cain's murder of Abel in the early pages of the story of human history, so in society today, *injustice* is front and center in the human drama.

Appealing to the same story of Cain and Abel in *LS* as paradigmatic for humanity at enmity with the Creator, with itself, and with the rest of Creation and therefore as paradigmatic for what a justice-deprived society is like, Pope Francis observed that "in the story of Cain and Abel, we see how envy led Cain to commit the ultimate injustice against his

48. *LUD*, 14.

49. *LUD*, 14.

50. *LUD*, 14.

51. "FMW," sec. 2.

52. *FT*, sec. 22.

53. *FT*, sec. 22.

brother, which in turn ruptured the relationship between Cain and God, and between Cain and the earth from which he was banished."[54]

The great social-political and spiritual problem identified by Francis and the two previous popes is this very rupture in the relationship among human beings, between humans and the earth, and between humanity and God. This is the very rupture that we saw in chapter 1—the rupture of harmony identified by Irenaeus and JP2. The social-political platform of Francis is a restoration of the harmony between humanity, all creation, and God, a restoration of the triad of harmony.

A Liturgically Based Call to Ecological Conversion

Francis's social platform is informed by JP2's call to a global ecological conversion, to which Francis made explicit appeal in *Laudato si'*. In the Catechesis in which JP2 articulated this particular call to conversion quoted by Francis in *Laudato si'*, JP2 described humanity's universal priestly calling to fulfill its role as "the shepherd of being."[55] This means— JP2 explains—that the believer "leads all beings to God, inviting them to sing an 'alleluia' of praise."[56] Commenting upon Psalm 148, JP2 proposes that "the Psalm brings us into a sort of cosmic church, whose apse is the heavens and whose aisles are the regions of the world, in which the choir of God's creatures sings his praise."[57] The social platform of JP2—to which Francis makes direct appeal in *LS*—is based upon this liturgical-ecclesial reading of creation and of humanity within creation. JP2's cosmology and anthropology, upon which Francis directly builds, is in turn built upon Scripture's liturgical ontology. At the heart of humanity's being—in the scriptural-liturgical ontology of JP2—is humanity's role as psalmist and liturgist, singing a hymn of praise.

"The world is God's gift to us," Pope Francis wrote in *LUD*.[58] "The biblical story of creation has a constant refrain: 'And God saw that it was good' (Genesis 1:12). 'Good' means bountiful," Francis reflects. It means "life-giving, and beautiful."[59] It is precisely this goodness that is portrayed

54. Francis, *LS*, sec. 70.
55. JP2, "God Made Man," sec. 1.
56. JP2, "God Made Man," sec. 1.
57. JP2, "God Made Man," sec. 1.
58. *LUD*, 30.
59. *LUD*, 30.

by the image of the pregnant mother featured as an icon of the theological and ontological heart of the Amazon Synod, as an icon of cosmic chastity, an icon of creation as perceived by the eyes of chaste love, an icon capable, we can hope, of restoring eyes infected by lust. She is a personification of the goodness, the bounty, the beauty and fruitfulness of creation.

At the heart of the meaning of the universe is the hymn of praise that humanity leads all creation in singing, convicted as humanity is by belief in the truth of the Creator and in the truth of the meaning of creation. It is the hymn that humanity sings when humanity responds to its fundamental calling, awestruck as it is by creation's beauty. Such beauty is "the entryway to ecological awareness," Francis says. On this score, Pope Francis reflected that when he listens "to Hadyn's *The Creation*," he is "transported into the glory of God and the beauty of created things." Francis goes on to recount that "at the end" of the piece, "in the long duet of Adam and Eve, you meet a man and woman enraptured by the beauty they have been given. "Beauty, like creation itself"—in humanity in particular and in creation at large—"is pure gift, a sign of the God who overflows with love for us."[60]

A Scripturally Rooted Economic and Ecological Commentary: The Cosmic Church

It is from a place of awe before the truth of the beauty and goodness of creation that many of the songs in the Psalter arise, shaping much of the Church's posture in liturgical prayer. And it was precisely in such a liturgical context of song—a liturgical context in which a Psalm is sung—that JP2 addressed his catechesis on humanity's role as steward within creation, and in that context, sounded forth his call to a global ecological conversion that Pope Francis has made his own. It is a conversion to recognize the gift given, a recognition that inspires a posture of reverence, liturgical reverence, of a chaste love for the gift of the cosmos in opposition to the technocratic lust that has deformed our hearts and their relationship with the cosmos. With this conviction, Pope Francis asks, "If someone who loves you gives you a beautiful and valuable gift, how do you handle it?"[61] He responds, declaring, "To treat it with contempt is to treat the giver with contempt. If you value it, you admire it, look after it.

60. *LUD*, 30.
61. *LUD*, 30.

You do not disdain it; you respect it and are grateful. The damage to our planet stems from the loss of this awareness of gratitude. We have grown used to owning, but too little to thanking."[62] But thanking—in a posture of *eucharistia*—is the fundamental posture proper to human existence within the cosmos, within the home given to us. It is a posture which precedes and which is presupposed by any authentic and humane notion of ownership, stewardship, responsibility, and receptivity to gifts.

With a liturgical point of departure, JP2 presented an ontology of praise as the basis for apprehending the nature and meaning of existence in the universe. Liturgical ontology is not the concern of the culture wars. But it is the fundamental concern of JP2 and the two successive popes. This is where the culture wars and the popes diverge. While it is all too easy for us—in the context of the culture wars—to reduce the message of Christianity to the sound bites expedient for success on the battlefield of cyber-politics and electoral politics, Francis, explicitly citing this very rationale of JP2, calls us into a liturgical reading of the universe, in which all of humanity's endeavors and each creature we encounter contains within itself a liturgical meaning, and at base is liturgically defined.

On this score, Francis recounts his own story of developing what he calls an "ecological awareness"[63] that transcends the knee-jerk reactions proper to both sides of the culture wars. Francis's own awareness of the truth of the place of gratitude before the gift of creation in all its beauty and goodness "began to take root," he recounts, "during a meeting of the bishops of Latin America at the shrine of Aparecida, Brazil, in May 2007."[64] As Bergoglio was "on the committee drafting the concluding document of the meeting" he was "at first . . . a bit annoyed that the Brazilians and bishops of other countries wanted so much in there on Amazonia. It struck me as excessive."[65] In contrast to his reaction back in 2007, Francis recounts that in 2019, "I called a special synod on Amazonia."[66] Something "had happened between these two moments"—something that changed Francis's perspective on how to talk about Amazonia and ecological stewardship at large. With various encounters and stories of specific regions of the globe suffering the effects of environmental

62. *LUD*, 30.
63. *LUD*, 31.
64. *LUD*, 30.
65. *LUD*, 30.
66. *LUD*, 31.

deterioration, as well as engaging Patriarch Bartholomew's concern for ecological stewardship, Bergoglio "started to see the harmonious unity of humanity and nature, and how humanity's fate is inseparably bound up with that of our common home."[67] Fundamentally, that unity characterizing the meaning of humanity and our common home is a unity rooted in the liturgical meaning of humanity within a liturgically defined cosmos.

The catechesis in which JP2 sounded his call to a global ecological conversion was a catechetical commentary on Psalm 148. In this context, JP2 recounts that in that Psalm, "the Psalmist summons all creatures, calling them by name."[68] In this liturgical act, a stupendous proposition is asserted. It is a proposition made by an ancient Hebraic hymnwriter, remade throughout history in the liturgical prayer of Israel and Judah, and made yet again in our own day by Jewish and Christian worshippers the world over. It is a proposition about the fundamental meaning of all creation as destined to bow in adoration before the Creator.

This statement was made simply by way of this Psalm being prayed by those pilgrims gathered in Rome to hear the Polish pontiff teach on January 17, 2001. The proposition made by the liturgical recitation of Psalm 148 in any and every time is this: *humanity's task is to summon all creatures of heaven and earth to sing praises to their Creator*. According to this vision of liturgical harmony, this vision of thanksgiving—the ecological vision that Pope Francis shares with the two previous popes— bursts through the confines of the culture wars, and tells us what our common household is all about. It tells us that the laws of the household are fundamentally laws of the cosmic liturgy within the cosmic church.

Having presented his *liturgical hermeneutic of being* in his catechesis on humanity's task of ecological stewardship on January 17, 2001, the following week JP2 turned to the topic of strife within human society. As Francis seamlessly zoomed in from his birds-eye view of the whole cosmos to the polis in his turn from *Laudato si'* to *Fratelli tutti*, so in those two weeks of late January, JP2 turned seamlessly from the cosmos to the polis, from cosmology to social anthropology.[69] Francis and JP2

67. *LUD*, 31.

68. JP2, "God Made Man," 1.

69. In his foreword to Caldecott's *Not as the World Gives*, Walker characterizes that volume along with Caldecott's preceding volume *The Radiance of Being* as "twin panels of a diptych that share a common motif," in that "the two books join to display the Trinitarian communion illuminating cosmos and society" (Walker, foreword to *Not as the World Gives*, xv). Francis's *LS* and *FT* form the same diptych of cosmos and polis.

can do this because they perceive the integral relationship between humanity and humanity's common home. In his turn to the polis, explicating aspects of a Catholic understanding of the meaning of justice, JP2 observed that "against a horizon that is often marked by discouragement, pessimism, choices of death, inertia and superficiality, Christians must be open to the hope that springs from faith."[70] In this context of a polis in distress, Francis alongside the Grand Imam Ahmed Al-Tayyeb observed that "we see 'outbreaks of tension and a buildup of arms and ammunition in a global context dominated by uncertainty, disillusionment, fear of the future, and controlled by narrow economic interests.' We can also point to 'major political crises, situations of injustice and the lack of an equitable distribution of natural resources.'"[71] Informed by the liturgical ontology of Scripture, the papal trio's body of social teaching breaks the rules set by both the left and the right. It is on the basis of this liturgical ontology that the papal trio sounds forth its impassioned words of political protest—protest against the inequitable distribution of resources, the tyranny of inhumane economic interests, and the build-up of armaments.

Francis in the Papal Tradition of Protest and Praise

Making this form of political protest his own—a form of protest that arises from divine praise and gives way to divine praise—Pope Francis in the encyclical *LS* locates his social teaching and call to political conversion within the context of St. Francis's song of cosmic praise.[72] "In the words of this beautiful canticle, Saint Francis of Assisi reminds us that our common home is like a sister with whom we share our life and a beautiful mother who opens her arms to embrace us," Pope Francis

---

This is the trajectory of the canticle of the three young men in Daniel 3, which begins with a cosmic scanning of all creatures and begins to zero in on the polis of the Judean people with its liturgical cult, which is inherently cosmically located. The three young men turn from the first panel of the diptych to the second over the course of the song. Or, to change imagery, Caldecott, Francis, and the three young men begin with the birds-eye view of the cosmic whole and then zero in on the polis within the cosmos. At the summit of both polis and cosmos, we will see in chapter 9, is the marriage alliance between man and woman.

70. "FMW," sec. 3.

71. *FT*, sec. 29, citing Francis and Al-Tayyeb, *Document on Human Fraternity for World Peace and Living Together*, 6.

72. See Francis, "Prayer of the Psalms," para. 3–6.

recounts.[73] However, "this sister now cries out to us because of the harm we have inflicted on her by our irresponsible use and abuse of the goods with which God has endowed her. We have come to see ourselves as her lords and masters, entitled to plunder her at will."[74] Sister earth, herself made in order to praise her Creator, also, by dint of her task of praise, must cry out against injustice. Not all is well concerning our relationship with the rest of creation. Indeed, as Pope Francis proposes, "the violence present in our hearts, wounded by sin, is also reflected in the symptoms of sickness evident in the soil, in the water, in the air and in all forms of life."[75] We have fallen gravely short in our task as cosmic liturgists, and have become cosmic abusers. And in our abuse, we wound our fellow humans and our fellow creatures in general, in an all-encompassing posture of sacrilege against the Creator.

The ecological vision that Francis began to assume as his own following the 2007 episcopal gathering in Aparecida is "an awareness, not an ideology," Francis maintains.[76] As he explains, "there are green movements that turn the ecological experience into ideology, but" authentic and humane "ecological awareness is . . . just that: awareness, not ideology. It's being conscious of what's at stake in the fate of humanity."[77] According to Francis, "*Laudato Si'* is not a green encyclical. It's a social encyclical. The green and the social go hand in hand. The fate of creation is tied to the fate of all humanity."[78] We see this integral relationship between cosmological welfare and social welfare played out today in concrete ways. Francis laments, for example, that "you can't eat an apple these days without peeling it first in case it does you harm. Doctors advise mothers not to give their kids chicken from factory farms until they're four years old, because the chickens have been fattened with hormones that can make the kids unbalanced."[79] These are social realities that affect human beings, which is to say, they affect the common good and offend the truth of human dignity.

73. *LS*, sec 1.

74. *LS*, sec. 2.

75. *LS*, sec. 2.

76. *LUD*, 31.

77. *LUD*, 32.

78. *LUD*, 32.

79. *LUD*, 33.

As Francis recounts, "Saint John Paul II became increasingly concerned about"[80] the impending "ecological catastrophe under the effective explosion of industrial civilization"[81] of which Paul VI warned. While in the context of the culture wars, language of ecological catastrophe is proper to the agenda of the left, in the context of Catholic social teaching's liturgical hermeneutic of the cosmos, warnings concerning the ecological catastrophe are proper to the biblical tradition of prophetic outcry. In this tradition, Francis recounts, "Paul VI referred to the ecological concern as 'a tragic consequence' of unchecked human activity."[82] Paul VI's and Francis's shared assessment of society's economic-ecological situation is this: "humanity runs the risk of destroying" nature "and becoming in turn a victim of this degradation." This is attributed by Pope Paul and Francis after him to "an ill-considered exploitation of nature."[83] Paul VI stressed, as Francis recounts, "the urgent need for a radical change in the conduct of humanity."[84] Pope Paul warns society that "the most extraordinary scientific advances, the most amazing technical abilities, the most astonishing economic growth, unless they are accompanied by authentic social and moral progress, will definitively turn against man,"[85] as Francis reiterated verbatim in *LS*.

As Francis recounts, Benedict called for an elimination of "the structural causes of the dysfunctions of the world economy" and perceived the great need for "correcting models of growth which have proved incapable of ensuring respect for the environment."[86] Benedict, Francis relates, "observed that the world cannot be analyzed by isolating only one of its aspects, since 'the book of nature is one and indivisible,' and includes the environment, life, sexuality, the family, social relations, and so forth."[87]

Five years after the publication of *LS*, Francis reflected: "*LS* links the scientific consensus on the destruction of the environment with

---

80. *LS*, sec. 5.

81. *LS*, sec. 4.

82. *LS*, sec. 4.

83. *LS*, sec. 4, quoting *OA*, sec. 21.

84. *LS*, sec. 4, quoting Paul VI. Unlike Weigel, I do not distinguish between red and gold quotes from Paul VI or Benedict. For Weigel's source-critical theory and his rejection of allegedly leftist and incoherent aspects of *PP* and *CV*, see Weigel, "Gold and Red," paras. 4–5, and Weigel, "Charity in Truth," para. 10.

85. *LS*, sec. 4, citing Paul VI, "F.A.O. 25th Anniversary," sec. 4.

86. *LS*, sec. 6, citing Benedict, "Diplomatic Corps," para. 4.

87. *LS*, sec. 6, citing *CV*, sec. 51.

our self-forgetting, our rejection of who we are as creatures of a loving Creator, living inside His creation but at odds with it. It's the sadness of a humanity rich in know-how but lacking the inner security of knowing ourselves as creatures of God's love."[88] When we know ourselves as creatures of God's love, however, this knowledge expresses itself "in our simultaneous respect for God, for each other, and for creation,"[89] according to the cosmic harmony of which JP2, following Irenaeus, spoke. For Francis, "our sin lies in failing to recognize value, in wanting to possess and exploit that which we do not value as a gift."[90] In other words, our sin, in an all-encompassing exploitative posture, is that of possessive lust, over and against the posture of chaste love. "Sin always has this same root of possessiveness,"[91] Francis says, manifesting itself today in our willingness to seek "enrichment at the expense of other people and creation itself"[92] in a singular antagonistic relationship with the cosmos and the polis. Francis identifies this as "the sinful mindset" of abuse.[93] "The sin is in exploiting what must not be exploited, in extracting wealth (power or satisfaction) from where it should not be taken," by way of lustful desires that we feed by means of technological power. The sins in which we engage by way of technocratic lust is like all human sin. As Francis puts it, "sin is a rejection of the limits that love requires."[94] Sin is the opposite of the chastity that safeguards the dignity of the gifts of God.

Francis observes that "the Psalms frequently exhort us to praise God the Creator" for the greatness of his work—which is understood as a sign and manifestation of his steadfast love—to praise the one "'who spread out the earth on the waters, for his steadfast love endures for ever.'"[95] This Psalter-formed ontology of Francis roots itself in our meaning as creatures. This is why, in discussing the ecological crisis, *LS* seeks to root the ecological discussion both in science and in the deepest theological meaning of humanity, inclusive of a recognition of the reality of human brokenness and sin.

88. *LUD*, 33.
89. *LUD*, 33.
90. *LUD*, 34.
91. *LUD*, 34.
92. *LUD*, 34.
93. *LUD*, 34.
94. *LUD*, 34.
95. *LS*, sec. 72, quoting Ps 136:6.

Fundamentally, humanity's and all creation's liturgical meaning is the basis for a right ordering of means and ends in social life, and particularly, in economic life. The papal trio's ontology of praise is the foundation of their economic and ecological vision, undergirding their alternative approach to the culture wars.

PART II

. . . . .

Another Song, Other Singers;
Another War, Other Warriors

*A Fight for the Heart of Culture, the Meaning of Work,
and Vocational Commitment*

4
. . . . .

Benedict and Francis
in the Fiery Furnace

A Fight for the Heart of Culture

IN PART II OF THIS BOOK, we explore the social teaching of the papal trio as a form of social commentary independent of the shallow categories proper to today's culture wars. We show that Francis, true to the JP2-B16 tradition, (1) directs our attention to the fundamental meaning of human society and (2) continues to transmit the same social ethic as that of the two previous popes, with the same theological and spiritual basis. The social teaching of Francis is part of the papal trio's song whose features come across loud and clear when we pay attention to their notions of truth, justice, and charity (which we have spelled out in part I). Romano Guardini and Henri de Lubac, whom we shall place alongside the papal trio in this chapter, are two primary heralds of what we can call a *liturgical reading of the universe* within the societal circumstances peculiar to our own epoch in history.

Prophets in the Furnace of a Technocratic Babylon

The three young men in the book of Daniel sing a song of political protest and cosmic praise, like the three popes who sing their song even as the fires of technocratic lust rage in society at large. Society today has become such a furnace of technocracy's empire of lust, and it is in the midst of this society-wide fire that the amphitheater of Catholic social teaching where the popes sing stands as a monument to an all-encompassing chaste love. Guardini and Lubac—two of the twentieth century's most prominent theological social commentators—speak at a point in history where the modern world becomes conscious of its own implosion, to use Cornel West's terminology.[1] Or, to use Guardini's language, they speak at a point when the modern world starts to become conscious of the "end of the modern world,"[2] when modernity perceives its own demise and downfall. They speak at a point when society begins searching for what comes *after* modernity, for the new things that shall arise in the midst of modernity's fallout.

In a homily entitled "The Courage of Definitive Choices," Francis commented upon the scriptural narrative of the captivity of the prophet Daniel and his three companions in the service of the Babylonian king, highlighting the precarious place in which Daniel and the three young men found themselves, in their position of servitude in a pagan empire. The pope made the point that the young Judeans in Babylon could have sought out "an emergency exit from their situation. They could have said: 'We are slaves, we cannot fulfil the law here'"—the law of God—"'we need to preserve our lives, not get too thin, not fall ill . . . let's eat!'"[3] As opposed to exiting by way of capitulating to the demands of the pagan empire and surrendering in the fight to live according to the divine precepts of the people of God, "they said no," Francis recounts.[4] "They made their choice: the Lord. And they found a way to remain faithful, even under very difficult circumstances."[5] The young men "took a risk . . . and in their risk they chose the Lord."[6] As the pope suggested, "they acted from the heart, with no personal interest and not so as to attract attention to themselves, but rather,"[7] as he put it, "because they knew that the Lord is faithful."[8] On this basis "they entrusted themselves to his eternal faithfulness."[9] Indeed, "the Lord is always faithful, for he cannot deny himself."[10]

1. See West and Taylor, "America's Moment of Reckoning," para. 9.

2. The title of Guardini's mid-century book.

3. Francis, "Courage," para. 5.

4. Francis, "Courage," para. 5.

5. Francis, "Courage," para. 5.

6. Francis, "Courage," para. 6.

7. Francis, "Courage," para. 6.

8. Francis, "Courage," para. 6.

9. Francis, "Courage," para. 6.

10. Francis, "Courage," para. 6.

What Francis urges us toward—in his reflections upon the young Judean men working in Nebuchadnezzar's court—is an entrustment of ourselves "to the Lord's faithfulness."[11] Such entrustment, Francis says, "is a choice"[12] that involves *putting everything on the line*. This is a choice we "have the opportunity to make in our Christian lives,"[13] involving "great and difficult decisions."[14] In today's Babylonian landscape the truth of the gospel calls us to take the risk of commitment over and against the fickle-heartedness characteristic of the throwaway culture—commitments of marriage, child-rearing, consecrated life, and holy orders—in a manner true to the moral demands of justice and charity. The truth of the gospel calls us to take the risk of commitment, born of entrustment to the Lord.

According to Francis, the young men who were drafted into the service of the empire were called to remain faithful to God in the context of the empire's attempts to utterly "Babylonianize" them. This, for Francis, is very much our own situation today. To remain faithful to the truth of social justice in a context of secularization—a context which in many ways directly opposes the very notion of truth—is no easy task. Francis sees in the quandaries of Daniel and his three companions a parable of our own circumstances. We find ourselves in an empire of technocracy, relativism, and consumerism, drafted into the service of the Babylon of secularization and relativism, and thrown into a fiery furnace of technocratic lust. In this very context we are called to assume a posture of chaste love, a love that makes rigorous and costly demands on how we act.

Identifying the Problem of Modernity: The Problem of Technocracy as the Problem of Sin

For the papal trio, we're in a singular ecological and anthropological crisis of stewardship. Our failure as stewards of our common household is a key aspect of what Francis calls the crisis of communal commitment, which is part and parcel with the technocratic rationale to which our hearts are too easily conformed in contemporary societal circumstances. In his own critique of modernity's fundamental illnesses, Francis consistently appeals to Guardini for guidance.

11. Francis, "Courage," para. 7.
12. Francis, "Courage," para. 7 (according to the Vatican's paraphrase).
13. Francis, "Courage," para. 7.
14. Francis, "Courage," para. 7.

The crisis of communal commitment, for Francis, is part of the same perennial crisis of sin characterizing the entirety of the human drama since the fall. The crisis of communal commitment in our age of technocracy is simply a modern manifestation of this same age-old problem of humanity at enmity with itself, with the rest of creation, and with God. The enmity between peoples inherent to historical humanity is what lies at the heart of the crisis of communal commitment. The social vision which Francis espouses, along with Benedict, JP2, Lubac, and Guardini, is a social vision that calls for an adherence to the demands of truth and justice in order to make the kinds of commitments proper to humanity according to humanity's inherently communal meaning. If we can rightly think of the Benedict and Francis pontificates as forming a singular pontificate of "Pope Guardini" (given Guardini's enormous influence upon the commentary and outlook of these two papacies), the JP2, Benedict, and Francis pontificates can rightly be referred to as a singular "Lubac pontificate," given Lubac's place as a main theological reference point for all three papacies. What Lubac refuses—so he made clear at the outset of his book *Catholicism*—is a pseudo-spirituality according to which I, as an individual, can find *my* joy apart from the rest of the human community—that I can find salvation as a mere individual, indifferent to the strife of my neighbors.[15] For Lubac, my neighbor's well-being is my own well-being, and apart from my neighbor's well-being and salvation, I have not arrived at well-being or salvation. Lubac refuses a pseudo-Christianity according to which I can, as an individual, find an exclusively personal blessedness by which I can pass "through the battlefields with a rose" in my hand.[16] Lubac poses a challenge to a soteriology that "is uninterested in our terrestrial future and in human fellowship."[17] What Lubac seeks to present, in his turn to the deep collectivism of the church fathers and the medieval monastics—deeper than Marxism's shallow collectivism—is an authentic Christian vision convinced that "fundamentally the Gospel is obsessed with the idea of the unity of human society."[18]

In his encyclical *Spe salvi*, Benedict presents Lubac's communal soteriology, which conceives of salvation as an inherently communal

---

15. Lubac, *Catholicism*, 13.

16. Lubac, *Catholicism*, 13.

17. Lubac, *Catholicism*, 13–14.

18. Lubac, *Catholicism*, 13–14.

reality.[19] In that context, Benedict points out that in the soteriology of the Letter to the Hebrews, salvation is portrayed as a *city*. This eschatological rationale underlies Benedict's vision of social justice, with the goal of safeguarding the common good in society *today* and advocating the *humane* development of the earthly city. The "metropolitan" portrayal of salvation found in Hebrews and throughout Scripture alludes, Benedict suggests, to the inherently communal character of salvation in integral relation to the earthly city.

"Sin is understood by the Fathers as the destruction of the unity of the human race, as fragmentation and division," Benedict writes, expounding upon Lubac's social soteriology. The confusion of language and the subsequent scattering of humanity in the story of Babel, Benedict and Lubac suggest, signifies the separation that "is seen to be an expression of what sin fundamentally is."[20] In Benedict's account, which explicitly follows Lubac's dogmatic rationale, the lines of separation that divide humanity—one faction against another—are manifest in and represented by the division of humanity and its scattering across the face of the earth, one nation against another. "Hence, 'redemption,'" Benedict proposes, "appears as the reestablishment of unity, in which we come together once more in a union that begins to take shape in the world community of believers."[21] This is what makes Catholicism *catholic*. Its vision of salvation is inherently universal. Catholicism is universal to its spiritual and dogmatic core, Lubac insists—not just universal in terms of polity. Humanity is saved as a singular universal social entity, as a singular universal ecclesial bride united to her bridegroom.[22]

Following his explication of Lubac's patristic theology of salvation as a social reality—according to which humanity's unity has been destroyed in the fragmentation, division, and separation expressed in the narrative of Babel—Benedict proceeds to explicate the "community-oriented vision of the 'blessed life'" in medieval Benedictine monastic spirituality.[23] According to the prominent medieval Benedictine monastic abbot and preacher, Bernard of Clairvaux—so Pope Benedict recounts—"monks

---

19. *SS*, sec. 14.
20. *SS*, sec. 14.
21. *SS*, sec. 14.
22. See Lubac, *Catholicism*, 15.
23. *SS*, sec. 14.

perform a task for the whole Church and hence also for the world."[24] This *monastic task* serves as a template for Pope Benedict's vision of our social responsibility and call to solidarity (i.e., communal commitment) in contemporary circumstances, both locally and globally, on micro and macro levels.

Bernard, according to Pope Benedict's account, "uses many images to illustrate the responsibility that monks have towards the entire body of the Church, and indeed towards humanity."[25] For Bernard, Pope Benedict says, "contemplatives—*contemplantes*—must become agricultural labourers—*laborantes*," working as laborers on behalf of the universal body, for its welfare.[26] Commending to contemporary society Bernard's medieval Benedictine social vision of working toward eschatological restoration for the sake of the universal body of the Church in the immediate tasks of communal living in this material world, Pope Benedict explains that for Bernard, while monastic communities cannot "restore Paradise," they nonetheless "must prepare the new Paradise."[27] This is the very link between immanent and transcendent that we discussed in chapter 1 in this book, in terms of Pope Benedict's theological vision of integral human development and eschatology, his perception of the intimate link between development in the earthly city and the building up of the eschatological city of God, all according to a vision of truth, justice, and love.

Indeed, from Bernard's monastic Benedictine perspective (as presented by Pope Benedict), the monastic community is "a place of practical and spiritual 'tilling the soil."[28] The monastic community, for Pope Benedict, is a template for the task of society at large and for every member of society. Bernard's vision of the monastic task is archetypical for the Catholic social vision of humanity on its way to salvation, building the earthly city in integral relation to the city of God, which the earthly city is called to approximate and usher in.

In a singular communal life of labor and contemplation is found the singular spiritual-material task of preparing the new paradise, restoring the unity of humanity that, as we see in the Babel account, was shattered in humanity's sin. In the monastic vision of contemplation and labor as a

24. *SS*, sec. 15.
25. *SS*, sec. 15.
26. *SS*, sec. 15.
27. *SS*, sec. 15.
28. *SS*, sec. 15.

singular task of restoring the new paradise (as Pope Benedict recounts in his gloss on Bernard), we see that "a wild plot of forest land is rendered fertile—and in the process, the trees of pride are felled, whatever weeds may be growing inside souls are pulled up, and the ground is thereby prepared so that bread for body and soul can flourish."[29]

Manual labor provides a paradigmatic image for Pope Benedict's understanding of humanity's task of development at large. It has likewise been a central concern in the entire tradition of Catholic social teaching since Leo XIII. Historically speaking, the truth of the dignity of manual labor and of the manual laborer has been foundational for Catholic social teaching since its inception in Leo XIII's *RN* up to and including the Pope Francis body of social teaching. Manual labor stands in integral relation to every aspect of social teaching, and it has an integral place in all that pertains to economics and ecology. For Pope Benedict, following Bernard, manual labor, as an inherent aspect of integral development and an icon of it, contains within itself a great spiritual and eschatological significance. Manual labor itself contains a theologically significant spiritual meaning and at the same time illustrates spiritual realities with theological meaning—realities like conversion, redemption, restoration, and purgation.

Pope Benedict, employing Bernard's imagery taken from the forestry and agricultural work of the Benedictine tradition, asks as a new Socratic John the Baptist crying out in the wilderness of modernity: "Are we not perhaps seeing once again, in the light of current history, that no positive world order can prosper where souls are overgrown?"[30] For Pope Benedict, the unity which we see lost in the Babel narrative is a unity and world order that is *restored by way of humanity's perennial and primal vocation of stewardship*—as a tiller of the soil, the soil of the earth and the soil of human hearts. Such is the singular spiritual, economic, and ecological task of humanity as a society, according to Pope Benedict's social vision, following the medieval monastic template described by Bernard.

29. *SS*, sec. 15.
30. *SS*, sec. 15.

The Bernard Option against Baconian Modernity: Pope Benedict's Medieval Monastic Antidote to Modernity's Ills

Bernard's imagery, appropriated by Pope Benedict in his teaching on the dogmatic-spiritual basis for the principle of solidarity, explicates the integral relation between the cultivation of the human soul and the cultivation of the land in the economic ordering of a human community—in Bernard's case, a monastery. The monastic community—though with its own distinctive charismatic character peculiar to consecrated life in the cloister—is in many ways paradigmatic for human society at large, for Pope Benedict. In Pope Benedict's own appropriation of Bernard's communitarian vision of labor, the raising of food, the harvesting of trees, and communal sustenance at large as integrally related to humanity's communal destiny for salvation—inclusive of the salvation of individual souls integrally rooted in their collective ecclesial identity—Pope Benedict opposes the same spiritual individualism that Lubac opposed. Standing before the specter of individualistic modern spirituality, Pope Benedict, a new Socrates on the streets of a new global Athens, asks his students in the streets: "How could the idea have developed that Jesus's message is narrowly individualistic and aimed only at each person singly? How did we arrive at this interpretation of the 'salvation of the soul' as a flight from responsibility for the whole . . . ?"[31] For Benedict's soteriology, which he inherited from Lubac's retrieval of patristic and medieval ecclesiology, the salvation of the individual is inseparable from the well-being of the *whole* of humanity. "How" then—this papal Socrates asks us—"did we come to conceive the Christian project as a selfish search for salvation which rejects the idea of serving others?"[32]

Benedict proposes, in the fashion of his teacher, Guardini, that "in order to find an answer to this we must take a look at the foundations of the modern age."[33] Pope Benedict holds modernity responsible for the development of individualistic faith. It is modernity that invented such a distorted, a-communal version of the Christian faith. It is the age of imperialism, the age of colonialism, the age of modernity, that relegates faith and spirituality to the merely private, individual, and isolated

31. *SS*, sec. 16.

32. *SS*, sec. 16.

33. *SS*, sec. 16.

"spiritual" realm, rendering it indifferent to public life, forbidding it from having a prophetic voice in the public square, emptying it of any concern for the common good, removing from it the social demands of truth, justice, and charity.

Modernity, in Benedict's account, doesn't do away with the notion of faith. Modernity simply forces faith and spirituality out of its inherently communal context, and divests it of any place in the sphere of shared space, shared life, shared work. "That a new era emerged—through the discovery of America and the new technical achievements that had made this development possible—is undeniable," Pope Benedict recognizes.[34] "But what," asks this new Socrates on the streets of an imploding modern Athens[35]—"is the basis of this new era?" These foundational ways of thinking for modernity appear with particular clarity in the writings of Francis Bacon, icon of European imperialism in the New World, Benedict suggests. In Benedict's account, scientific progress—with its impressive discoveries—empowers humanity "finally to achieve 'the triumph of art over nature' (*victoria cursusartis super naturam*),"[36] which, in a modernistic anthropological teleology, is the fundamental God-given goal of humanity. In a Christian vision of integral human development, scientific discovery, the scientific method, and scientific experimentation, are each called to serve the authentic welfare of humanity according to humanity's nature and according to the truth of the nature of all creatures, the truth of the nature of the cosmos, the truth of social justice and cosmic chastity. But in the modernistic distortion of Christianity, scientific discovery, the scientific method, and scientific experimentation are used to exploit creatures according to a vision of conquest and exploitation in view of utility and the will to raw power, which in turn tend to be harnessed for the amassment of capital, and vice versa, in that the amassment of capital is employed for utility and the achievement of power.

For modernity, art and human ingenuity at large stand in opposition to nature. In a more integral Christian vision, by way of artisanship, humanity is called to work in harmony with nature. Here, we see a close connection with what JP2 diagnosed as modernity's opposition between freedom and nature in *VS*.[37] This opposition, as JP2 recounted, manifests

---

34. *SS*, sec. 16.

35. To use the same imagery from West, "Reckoning," para. 9.

36. *SS*, sec. 16.

37. *VS*, secs. 4, 32.

itself in liberal moral theology. The opposition between truth and freedom lamented by JP2 and Benedict together, as recounted in chapter 1, is integrally connected with this opposition between freedom and artisanship on the one hand and nature and truth (and the truth about nature) on the other. As we saw in chapter 1, a fundamental flaw of atheistic socialism and capitalism for JP2 is precisely this flawed view of freedom in opposition to any notion of truth, which is inherently an opposition to a classical notion of nature, a notion according to which all created things are bearers of a built-in truth concerning their being and meaning.[38]

Modernity, JP2 helped us to see, sets freedom up against nature, such that nature is perceived as an enemy of freedom, an enemy that must be conquered to safeguard freedom. Benedict helps us to see that in the same way, modernity sets art (all that humanity does by way of his capacity for design) against nature. Whereas in JP2's and Irenaeus's vision of *God's art*, according to which humans exercise their freedom as artisans in harmony with the designs of God, in modernity—with its false conceptions of freedom and art—humans wield the power of art and the power of freedom *against* nature to conquer it. For JP2, however, humanity is indeed inherently an artistic animal, called to be an artisan, called to apply his ingenuity by way of building, constructing, designing—but called to do so in a manner that honors the truth of the nature of the material with which humanity works, and in a manner that honors the truth of humanity's own nature.

A modernistic hermeneutics of art, ingenuity, and technology—as standing in inherent opposition to nature, not in harmonious collaboration with it—serves as the ideological basis for our characteristically modern refusal of the truth of a classical notion of the *nature of things*. Our refusal of the truth of the nature of things enables and justifies our pursuit of an alleged freedom unrestrained by the limits of nature. It's a freedom that, by way of technological power, overcomes nature. Our refusal of the nature of things—our refusal of the very notion of something containing within itself a nature and meaning inherent to it—is part and parcel with our modernistic refusal of *existence as a gift from God*, which is the fundamental meaning of all that exists.[39] In a Christian vision of the integral relation between human ingenuity, art, and technology on the one hand and nature on the other, art and nature do not stand

---

38. *VS*, secs. 32.

39. See Schindler, *Ordering Love*, 4.

in opposition to one another. Rather, human artisanship and technology—guided by a chaste ingenuity—are most fully what they are meant to be when they honor the nature of the things in relation to which they are used.

The stuff of nature contains within itself a meaning that pertains to the good of humanity in relation to the Creator, according to the design of the Creator. Things contain within their own being, then, an invitation to chaste ingenuity and collaboration (as opposed to the lustful, utilitarian, profit-obsessed cunning and exploitation proper to technocracy). We are poised—by the hermeneutics characteristic of what Benedict calls *modernity*—to reject the nature of a thing, such that we must dominate it, conquer it, manipulate it, in order to put it to the service of "progress." This distorts not only our economic practices, but our theological outlook as well. For our economic illnesses and our theological illnesses are deeply related; indeed, they are the same. Theological liberalism and market liberalism are distorted by the very same divorce of nature and freedom, which is at root a divorce between truth and freedom.

In modernistically distorted theology, human progress pits itself against nature, justified by the conviction that "dominion over creation—given to man by God and lost through original sin—would be reestablished."[40] Western Baconian modernity, in Benedict's account, invented a new modernistic theology according to this distorted notion of dominion, a new technocratic eschatology. It refashioned a deity in modernity's own image, a deity who mandates technological prowess. In Baconian modernity's account of fall and redemption—so Benedict details—humanity in its fall loses its dominion over creation, but reestablishes that dominion by way of technological control that stands in opposition to nature, not in harmony with it. Hence, what Pope Francis calls technocracy plays a fundamental theological role in the theology of the new religion of Baconian modernity. For it is by way of technological rule that humanity overcomes its fallen state. It is, we could say, society's salvation by technological prowess alone.

What of faith and the practice of religion, then, if—in Baconian modernity—externally and socially, the consequences of humanity's fall are overcome by way of humanity's dominion over nature? The realm of spirituality, worship, faith, and the salvation of the individual soul in the afterlife is relegated to the exclusively personal, individual, and

40. *SS*, sec. 16.

private sphere in the new religion of Baconian modernity. As Benedict tells the story, in modernity, "a disturbing step has been taken."[41] Until the modern era, "the recovery of what man had lost through the expulsion from Paradise was expected from faith in Jesus Christ: herein lay 'redemption.'"[42] According to the authentic Christian outlook advocated by Benedict, redemption as initiated by Christ consists of the reestablishment of the Creator's intended harmony between himself, humanity, and the whole of Creation. Not so in the enlightened West's twisting of Christian eschatology. In Western enlightened "eschatology," the notion of "redemption," i.e., the notion of "the restoration of the lost 'Paradise,' is no longer expected from faith."[43] The restoration of humanity as a social community is not a concern of faith, from this modernist perspective, but a concern of scientific progress with the goal of a technological conquest of nature. Faith concerns itself exclusively with the salvation of the individual soul in the afterlife.

Classical Christianity's expectation of a restoration of harmony between God, humanity, and all creation is replaced in Baconian modernism by a confidence in "the newly discovered link between science and praxis,"[44] according to which science's empowerment of humanity is put to the service of a vision of "progress" directed toward mere utility—and all too often, a utility oriented toward the goal of amassing capital (and vice versa—the amassment of capital is sought in view of attaining merely utilitarian goals).[45] In this modern replacement of Christian eschatology, according to Benedict, "it is not that faith is simply denied; rather it is displaced and relegated to another level—that of purely private and other-worldly affairs—and at the same time it becomes somehow irrelevant for the world."[46] It is thus thought that humanity is meant to conquer nature—and this becomes the fundamental goal, understood as a recovery of humanity's proper place within the material world.

With respect to a modernistic utilitarian "teleology" of that which pertains to the temporal, material, social sphere, the modernist "eschaton" consists of material "progress" at all costs, with no regard for the

41. *SS*, sec. 17.

42. *SS*, sec. 17.

43. *SS*, sec. 17.

44. *SS*, sec. 17.

45. See *CV*, sec. 9.

46. *SS*, sec. 17.

meaning inherent to the stuff of existence, and with no regard to the integral relationship between creatures and their Creator.

An "ethics" of mere technocratic "progress" has replaced, in modernity, an ethics of nature, an ethics of the cosmos.

According to this distinctively modernistic and falsified theology, a false notion of nature criticized by Benedict in *SS* and by Francis in *LS*, humanity's technologically empowered dominion over creation—to which Scripture allegedly calls humanity—means a refusal of nature as it is presented to us, and a conquering manipulation and exploitation of it. This modernism has no notion of a God who gives gifts, and has no theology of creation as a sacred trust, but only a falsified vision of nature as an object to be plundered, manipulated, raped, re-engineered, contracepted, digitized, pornographized, enslaved, fracked, deforested, bought, numbered, packaged, stripped, slashed, burned, trafficked, sold, monetized, and prostituted according to its assigned market value, according to the laws of supply and demand. The challenge and call to honor the stuff of creation as containing within itself an integral meaning as *gift* isn't taken into consideration. The only meaning the stuff of nature has in Baconian modernity, as presented by Benedict, is *the meaning I assign to it by my conquest of it and by its reappropriation according to the goals of social "progress"*—understood in terms of *that which is expedient for utility*. Given our societal-economic context of the global liberal market, "utility" usually means *utility as defined by a market governed exclusively by the motive of profit, i.e., utility for financial profit, i.e., geared toward wealth creation for some and poverty for many*. In a modernistic distortion of Christianity, Benedict shows us, humanity's exploitative "dominion over creation is reestablished"—a dominion that was, according to the myth of modernity, "given to man by God and lost through original sin."[47]

The modernistic vision of restoring paradise by recovering humanity's alleged dominance over the rest of creation stands in marked contrast to Bernard's vision of the restoration of the world taking place by way of the communal management of a monastic farm, integrally linked with the restoration of the human soul, as work that prepares for the new paradise, which is to say, as work that prepares for humanity's integral *social and spiritual salvation*. The integral link between the immanent and the transcendent—the tasks of farming and the tasks of restoring souls

47. *SS*, sec. 16.

communally—proper to Bernard's integral spiritual theology of communal labor (as appropriated by Pope Benedict)—is lost to modernity.

As we suggested earlier in this chapter, it is a popular misconception that "monasteries were places of flight from the world (*contemptus mundi*) and of withdrawal from responsibility for the world, in search of private salvation," Pope Benedict recounts.[48] Bernard "had quite a different perspective on this," for, according to Bernard, "monks perform a task for the whole Church and hence also for the world."[49] In modernity, progress by way of the conquest of nature in view of technological usefulness (and usually driven by usefulness to make a profit) replaces, according to Benedict's account, an authentic Christian vision of humanity's relationship with the created order. In an authentically Christian eschatology, the goal of all our work, most fundamentally, is to restore harmony within the human family, on the part of humanity with God, and on the part of humanity with the rest of creation. Whereas a chasm is placed by modernity between salvation as it pertains to the realm of "faith" and "spirituality" on the one hand and our dealings with the material world on the other, in the world as Bernard perceived it according to his monastic ethos—as appropriated by Pope Benedict—the work of salvation and manual labor (i.e., agriculture, household management, communal sustenance) go hand in hand. According to the fissure that modernity places between the spiritual and the material, between faith and science, between religion and the public square,[50] there is a "redemption" as it pertains to spirituality and religion, and there is an altogether other "redemption" as it pertains to human progress in the world, which for modernity, means a co-opting of the things of nature, as opposed to a stewardship of them.

Modernity's task of manipulating nature "has determined the trajectory of modern time's progress," Benedict recounts.[51] The notion of faith in Christ is replaced with a notion of faith in progress. In Bacon's replacement of an integral Christian eschatology, "through the interplay of science and praxis, totally new discoveries will follow, a totally new

48. SS, sec. 15.

49. SS, sec. 15.

50. The public square, as conceived of in this book, consists of the market and politics within a common home, i.e., an environment with its own resources at humanity's disposal. That is to say, the public square consists of the polis integrally related to the cosmos at large.

51. SS, sec. 17.

world will emerge, the kingdom of man."[52] And unlike Pope Benedict's integral vision of the earthly city in intimate relation to the kingdom of God, Bacon's kingdom of man has little to do with the kingdom of God.

Bacon's kingdom of man has trampled upon the very notion and meaning of *nature*. "As the ideology of progress developed further, joy at visible advances in human potential remained a continuing confirmation of faith in progress as such," Benedict explains.[53] In the West, simultaneous with the development of an antagonism toward nature, "two categories become increasingly central to the idea of progress: reason and freedom. Progress is primarily associated with the growing dominion of reason, and this reason," modernistically conceived, is purported to be an infallible "force *of* good and a force *for* good."[54] Such progress by way of rational dominion over nature in a manner that empowers freedom from nature's constraints, in contrast to the Christian vision of development and progress humanely conceived, "is the overcoming of all forms of dependency—it is progress towards perfect freedom."[55] This modernist version of "progress" and "freedom" is not a progress and freedom in accord with the good inherent to the nature of things, but a good tied exclusively to mere progress in and of itself, a progress and a freedom that denies any notion of the demands of the good contained by the nature of the things with which we deal in social life, in work, in human development. This is a key aspect of the moral crisis identified by JP2 in *VS*—the divorce of freedom from a notion of the truth of the good in integral relation to nature, and the demands of justice that nature makes upon humanity.

The Prophetic Witness of JP2 in an Age of Destruction

As we've begun to see, within the order of the cosmos, "the human creature receives a mission to govern creation in order to make all its potential shine."[56] This is what JP2 proposed in his catechesis on Psalm 148. The task of cosmic governance "is a delegation granted at the very

52. *SS*, sec. 17.

53. *SS*, sec. 17.

54. *SS*, sec. 18 (emphasis added).

55. *SS*, sec. 18.

56. JP2, "God Made Man," sec. 2.

origins of creation, when man and woman, who are the 'image of God' (Gn 1: 27), receive the order to be fruitful and multiply, to fill the earth and subdue it, and to have dominion over the fish of the sea, the birds of the air," JP2 recounts.[57] Humanity has—to a cataclysmic extent—refused its task of shepherding its fellow beings toward God, and, at times, has blasted its fellow beings into oblivion.

God's vision for creation is often explicitly refused on the part of human society. As JP2 recounts, God's "plan was and is continually upset by human sin, which is inspired by an alternative plan depicted in the . . . Book of Genesis (chap. 3–11), which describes man's progressive conflictual tension with God, with his fellow human beings and even with nature."[58] The road upon which humanity set out in Genesis 3–11 indeed follows a plan other than that of God's intention for humanity and creation, according to their inherent meaning. We remain on this road of destruction with its plan in opposition to God's plan today. "Unfortunately, if we scan the regions of our planet, we immediately see that humanity has disappointed God's expectations," JP2 observes.[59] The fundamental failure of modernity, linked to human sin throughout the ages, is our fundamental denial of the doctrine of creation, our refusal to govern our lives—individually and collectively—in accordance with that doctrine, our refusal to heed the implications of that doctrine inherent to the meaning of the things with which we deal on a daily basis as inherently social creatures. For JP2, "man's harmony with his fellow beings, with creation and with God is the plan followed by the Creator."[60] This triad of harmony is the blueprint according to which God directs creation and guides history with his providential care. It is toward this goal of harmony that God directs the history of the cosmos.

Freedom and Responsibility in a Critique of the Technocratic Babylon

The significance of modernity's capacity for destruction did not escape Guardini's prophetic eye in the mid-twentieth century. Indeed, this is a significant focus of his social commentary. Like the prophet Daniel in

57. JP2, "God Made Man," sec. 2.
58. JP2, "God Made Man," sec. 1.
59. JP2, "God Made Man," sec. 3.
60. JP2, "God Made Man," sec. 1.

his own time, Guardini perceived apocalypse in his time. Indeed, in the words of the editor of the 1956 English edition of Guardini's *The End of the Modern World*, the text stands out as "the most somber book to come out of Germany since the Third Reich died in the bomb-pocked gardens of the Wilhelmstrasse."[61]

In contrast to the biblical vision of cosmic harmony, there has been a tendency since the dawn to the modern era "to believe that every increase in power means 'an increase of "progress" itself,' an advance in 'security, usefulness, welfare and vigour' . . . as if reality, goodness and truth automatically flow from technological and economic power as such," Guardini observed (as quoted by Francis in *LS*).[62] According to Francis, this tendency, indifferent as it is to the notion of harmony, is as alive today as it was in Guardini's era. To act in a manner that counteracts the modernistic approach, to act according to God's plan of harmony, is an inherently *ecological* task. Francis recounts, quoting Guardini, "contemporary man has not been trained to use power well."[63] This is because, Francis says, "our immense technological development has not been accompanied by a development in human responsibility, values and conscience,"[64] echoing Paul VI[65]—as we saw Benedict already echoed in the previous chapter.

The enormous technological developments that we have seen since the dawn of modernity stand out in the history of humanity. However, the problems that have accompanied this development are perennially human. As Francis observes, drawing directly from Guardini, "each age tends to have only a meager awareness of its own limitations."[66] For Francis, the technocratic rationale peculiar to our own epoch—a rationale that has accompanied and has served as the ideological basis for the rapid technological development which began at the dawn of modernity—is a manifestation of the larger and perennial problem of historical humanity's tendency to be blind to its own limits. As for our own day, Francis is concerned that "we do not grasp the gravity of the challenges now

---

61. Wilhelmsen, editor's introduction to *The End of the Modern World*, 3.

62. *LS*, sec. 105. Citing *End of the Modern World*.

63. *LS*, sec. 105.

64. *LS*, sec. 105.

65. For example, Paul VI, "Advertising in the Mass Media," paras. 4–14; Paul VI, "F.A.O. 25th Anniversary," secs. 2–3.

66. *LS*, sec. 105.

before us."[67] Francis thus reiterates Guardini's warning that "the risk is growing day by day that man will not use his power as he should."[68] Today, this is certainly not an overstatement. The line has indeed already been crossed—with or without nuclear warfare.

Yes, society's vulnerability to being *out of touch with its own limits* is perennial, but our vulnerability to the destructive use of technology and the degree to which our own agency has been handed over to techno-logical power has increased exponentially and continues to increase, as it has since the dawn of the industrial revolution.[69] We have lost a sense of the meaning of human freedom, power, and responsibility. When such a loss of understanding is accompanied by rapid, utilitarian development and technological empowerment motivated predominately by the lust for profit, we have a recipe for destruction. It's a recipe for human ingenuity to turn in upon itself—against humanity and against the cosmic order inte-gral to the truth of creaturely existence.[70] For, as Francis laments, again making Guardini's words his own, today "'power is never considered in terms of the responsibility of choice which is inherent in freedom' since its 'only norms are taken from alleged necessity, from either utility or security.'"[71] We need more than a mere removal of the HHS mandate and the removal of gender ideology in school curriculums. What's needed is a chaste outlook upon reality. The technocratic paradigm forms us to be concerned with mere expediency according to the demands of alleged security, necessity, and usefulness, and to ignore the authentic mean-ing of human freedom and responsibility for other people and things.[72] Against this technocratic mindset, Francis insists that "human beings are not completely autonomous,"[73] and warns that "our freedom fades when it is handed over to the blind forces of the unconscious, of immediate needs, of self-interest, and of violence," all of which are inherent to the technocratic logic of the market as we know it, which bids us to uncon-sciously reach for the contraceptive pill or to "swipe" our way through a

67. *LS*, sec. 105.

68. *LS*, sec. 105.

69. Contraception is the icon of this agency handed over to technology.

70. "The so-called sexual revolution . . . is most fundamentally the technological revolution turned on ourselves" (Hanby, "Gospel," 735). See also Hanby, "Technoc-racy," 1–3.

71. *LS*, sec. 105. Citing *End of the Modern World*.

72. See Ratzinger, "Europe's Crisis of Culture," 325–35.

73. *LS*, sec. 105.

virtual orgy of empty and solitary sexual "gratification" with our smart phones, to unconsciously acquiesce to the logic of neocolonialism and to unconsciously ride upon the backs of the oppressed worker to feed my many "needs" as a consumer. It is "in this sense" that as members of society today "we stand naked and exposed in the face of our ever-increasing power, lacking the wherewithal to control it," says Francis.[74] Though "we have certain superficial mechanisms," Francis continues, "we cannot claim to have a sound ethics, a culture and spirituality genuinely capable of setting limits and teaching clear-minded self-restraint."[75] Clear-minded self-restraint is what an ethos of cosmic chastity requires, cultivates, and facilitates.

What is needed as an antidote to technocratic lust is a theologically grounded spiritual hermeneutic capable of setting limits and cultivating self-restraint in view of the dignity of humanity and of the integrity of all created being according to its inherent meaning as gift. That's why Francis refuses to give bullets to conservative culture warriors. The ammo that conservative culture warriors want from the pontiff simply isn't enough. What's needed is a complete distancing from anything having to do with the bullet points of culture warriors. What is needed is an integral catechesis and mystagogy placed within the much larger context of a cosmic vision.

Un-cultivation and Cosmic Chastity: The Acoustics of an Integral Environmental Ethic against the Technocratic Exploitation of the Goods of Creation

In the midst of his apostolic journey to Sri Lanka and the Philippines prior to the publication of *LS*, Pope Francis, on his flight from Colombo to Manila, was asked a few questions by *America* magazine's Jerry O'Connell, who began his interview by observing that "in Sri Lanka we saw the beauty of nature but also how vulnerable that island is: from climate changes to the sea, etc. We are going to the Philippines and you will visit the area which has been hardest hit."[76] O'Connell proceeded to ask, "Is climate change mostly the effect of human causes, to our failure to

---

74. *LS*, sec. 105.

75. *LS*, sec. 105.

76. O'Connell, "CM," para. 4.

care of nature?" [*sic*]⁷⁷ Francis responded, "It is human beings who abuse nature, constantly. We have in some sense begun to lord it over nature, sister earth, mother earth. I remember . . . what an old farmer once told me: 'God always forgives, we men and women sometimes forgive, but nature never forgives.'"⁷⁸

Francis brings the question to the heart of the matter, namely, *humanity's refusal of its task as custodian and its assumption of a posture of irreverence and abuse.* In the context of expounding upon humanity's call to live according to the demands of justice, Francis draws attention to our propensity—particularly in our current socio-economic setting—to fall *far* short in our task as guardians, to fall *far* short in our calling as shepherds of being. Francis warns, alluding to the comment of a small farmer to whom he previously made reference, "If you abuse" mother earth, "she gives it back to you."⁷⁹ That is, our abuse of the earth will come back to haunt us. We will face the consequences of our abuse of her. Humanity's relationship with the earth—which is meant to be a relationship of gratitude, honor, and watchful care—has become a relationship of exploitation, and thus, of mutual enmity. "I believe that we have overly exploited nature," Francis said to O'Connell, identifying deforestation as a primary example.⁸⁰

Francis won't let us off the hook. He won't ease our consciences by dismissing the narrative of climate change as socialist propaganda. A ravenous technocratic neoliberal market logic has an effect on our approach to God's creatures with which we have been entrusted as stewards, and Francis won't mince words in communicating its threat to our perception of the truth—no matter how much some who perceive themselves as opponents of the Christian religion as they know it have a shared ecological concern. "Amazonia is one of the world's lungs," Francis recounted in his conversation with O'Connell.⁸¹ "I petitioned the Supreme Court of Argentina to halt, at least temporarily, a terrible deforestation taking place in the north of the country, in the zone north of Salta, Tartagal. This is one aspect."⁸² That is, this deforestation is one manifestation of humanity's

77. O'Connell, "CM," para. 4.
78. Francis, "CM," para. 5.
79. Francis, "CM," para. 5.
80. Francis, "CM," para. 5.
81. Francis, "CM," para. 5.
82. Francis, "CM," para. 5.

lording its power over nature in a violent manner. Another manifestation of humanity's failure as creaturely overseers that Francis identified on that flight to Manila is monocultural farming. Francis explains that "small farmers, for example, know that if you cultivate corn for three years, then you have to stop and plant something else for a couple of years in order to replenish nitrogen in the soil."[83] In some places "only soy is cultivated and you grow soy until the soil is exhausted."[84] "Not everybody does this, but it is one example" of humanity's misuse of natural resources, "and there are many others."[85] The problem is "that man has gone too far" in his manner of using the world's goods.[86]

In the context of this commentary on his way to Manila, Francis made reference to Guardini, who, according to Francis, identifies two forms of "non-cultivation."[87] The first form of non-cultivation is what we could call a *pre-cultivation*, referring to the state of a wild portion of the planet prior to human intervention. This is creation not touched by humanity. While there is a goodness and beauty peculiar to this positive form of uncultivated wilderness, neither Francis nor Guardini denounce cultivating the earth. Far from it, they celebrate humanity's cultivation of the earth. But integral cultivation, for them, involves honoring creation, working with it according to its nature, not overcoming its limits, but collaborating with it in what we can call a chaste encounter between humanity on the one hand and the land on the other, which we approach with loving reverence, honoring its limits. A humane form of cultivation honors the gift of the earth and its fruits. According to this cosmo-anthropological ethos of reverence, we must approach the land and its fruits with the fear of God.

The second form of non-cultivation "is the bad one," Francis went on to recount for O'Connell.[88] This is "when you go beyond" the meaning of creation "and become domineering," standing in opposition to the meaning of creation and therefore, in opposition to our own meaning within creation.[89] We render a part of creation *uncultivated* by way of pushing it

83. Francis, "CM," paras. 2–3.
84. Francis, "CM," para. 3.
85. Francis, "CM," para. 3.
86. Francis, "CM," para. 3.
87. Francis, "CM," para. 3.
88. Francis, "CM," para. 3.
89. Francis, "CM," para. 3.

beyond its capacity. We could call this post-cultivation. Pre-cultivation is a positive form of what Francis calls "non-cultivation," i.e., that which is uncultivated, while post-cultivation—a distorted form of cultivation by which we push the earth and its resources beyond nature's limits—is the form of un-cultivation or non-cultivation accompanying irresponsible human intervention, in a manner that destroys creation. When human activity leads to this second form of un-cultivation, where humanity's use of its technological power has rendered a portion of creation unfruitful, humanity takes something that had been ordered and fruitful and turns it into a barren waste.

If O'Connell was looking to Francis for a magisterial sequel to Al Gore's *An Inconvenient Truth*, he got instead an introduction to Guardini's *The End of the Modern World*, with its theologically rich social commentary, characterized by a sobering apocalyptic portrait of our present epoch. Following the rationale of Guardini, Francis characterizes human society today by way of diagnosing its inhumane posture toward nature. Guardini perceives the ingenuity of humanity in unlocking the mystery of the atom, to use an example to which Francis makes an appeal. Given the manner in which humanity put that discovery to use, we were faced with the atomic wasteland of Hiroshima and Nagasaki at the end of World War II. Having learned to employ our ingenuity to restructure reality, we can do so for the good of creation and society, or to destructive ends, leading ultimately to our own destruction.

Critiquing the Technocratic Paradigm: The Dissonance of Destruction (The Wounds of a Technocratic Apocalypse and an Integral Postmodern *Resourcement*)

"Nature is rising up in that very form which subdued the wilderness—in the form of power itself,"[90] Guardini recounts. We have lorded our power over the untamed wilderness, with our destructive "cultivation," and now, a chaos of wilderness (what Francis calls the bad kind of cultivation,[91] un-cultivation) arises from within human "culture" as a monstrous power before which we shrink in fear. What Francis perceives is that the narrative of anthropogenic climate change—according to which average

90. Guardini, *End of the Modern World*, 111.
91. Francis, "CM," para. 5.

temperatures across the globe are shifting and a growing proportion of the flooding, fires, significant damage to the natural habitat of the world's creatures and a myriad of natural disasters are the result of human activity—corresponds closely to the deeply-rooted rationale of Guardini's narrative of cultivation and un-cultivation. Humanity "stands again before chaos" Guardini recounts, "a chaos more dreadful than the first because most men go their own complacent ways without seeing, because scientifically-educated gentlemen everywhere deliver their speeches as always, because the machines are running on schedule and because the authorities function as usual."[92] Business as usual is a repulsive thing when we perceive—as the prophetic Guardini did and as Francis does—that chaos is "rising out of the very works of man," when chaos and destruction are arising directly from a complacent maintenance of business as usual in the machine of wealth creation and oppression.[93] The chaos that results from environmental degradation in the narrative told by environmentalists on the left today corresponds with Guardini's reading of modern technocracy.

In making reference to Guardini's notion of cultivation and un-cultivation (or non-cultivation), Francis points to what humanity did—particularly, what the US military did by order of Truman—to Hiroshima and Nagasaki in destroying them with an atomic bomb. This is a particularly stark example of that second form of what Francis, following Guardini, calls "un-cultivation." In contrast to the first form of "un-cultivation" (pre-cultivated nature), this second form of "un-cultivation" or "non-cultivation" refers to *post*-cultivated nature, after humanity has destroyed what *had* been ordered. Non-cultivation refers to society in its post-cultivated or *post-cultured* state. A bombed out city is an image of the polis within the cosmos *after* we've had our way with the cosmos and the polis, having raped mother earth, killed her, and left her dead, and left society, or a segment of society, in the same state. It's an image of human hearts distorted by a contraceptive and pornographic outlook. This image—that of the decimated and radiation-imbued city of Hiroshima—stands in stark contrast to the image of creation as it is handed to us by God, marked with the splendor of its meaning as gift, a meaning which we must honor in our cultivation of nature, in our collaboration with nature in a manner that honors the truth of her being. Leaving a

---

92. Guardini, *End of the Modern World*, 111–12.
93. Guardini, *End of the Modern World*, 112.

city bombed out and radiation imbued, leaving human hearts bombed out by pornography, and leaving wombs assaulted by the machinery of the state-funded corporate abortion industry are all aspects of household "management" that fall far short of our vocation and destiny as stewards of the common household of the earthly city.

What we do to creation in our abuse of the earth is inseparable from what we do to humanity, according to Francis's rationale. A crime against that which is outside of me is a crime against my own heart. Wounding that which is outside of me inflicts a wound upon my own heart. In assaulting another, I assault my own psyche. To objectify another by way of pornography, contraception, abortion, or any form of mere use and violence, is to objectify, misuse, and abuse my own heart. A wound on humanity's part inflicted upon that which is external to the human family is likewise a wound upon the heart of the human family. The destruction of Hiroshima is a singular crime against humanity, a crime against mother nature, a crime against the people of Japan and against the people of the US, a crime against President Truman's own heart, a crime against the heart of the bomber ordered to drop that bomb. In addition to contradicting an ethos of peace or even an ethos of justice (contrary as this action was to the ethic of just war), it is contrary to an integral human ecology, according to which we are called to responsibility for our common household. It is a singular destruction of the polis within the cosmic order. The wreckage we leave behind after having destroyed a city of civilians in war is both representative and is itself a manifestation of the very wreckage we leave behind by the economic systems at work within society and within the cities of the world even prior to a given act of destruction of any given city or town in war. It's an external image of the human heart distorted by contraception and pornography.

Opposition to mother nature is opposition to humanity, and vice versa. Such opposition to creation and to humanity manifests itself in the inextricably bound logic of modern warfare and the logic of the market as we know it, leaving more and more barren wastelands in its wake, destroying nature, destroying ancient culture, destroying new developments, destroying communities of human hearts.

Francis's Apocalypse in the Verano Cemetery

On the Feast of All Saints, 2014, in the Cemetery of Verano in Rome, Pope Francis celebrated Mass and, in his homily, meditated upon the reading from the book of Revelation in which was heard the "voice of the Angel crying a loud [*sic*] to the four Angels who were given power to damage the earth and the sea, 'Do not harm earth or sea or the trees.'"[94] At this point in his homily, the pontiff enters into the prophetic scene, Ignatian in manner, and responds directly to the crying angel, saying, "men are far more capable of doing this better than you."[95] Turning back to the faithful gathered in the Verano Cemetery, the pope as prophet exclaimed to them, confessing with them, "we are capable of destroying the earth far better than the Angels. And this is exactly what we are doing, this is what we do: destroy creation, destroy lives, destroy cultures, destroy values, destroy hope. How greatly we need the Lord's strength to seal us with his love and his power to stop this mad race of destruction!"[96] Our own power of destruction is what we need to be delivered from by the Lord, according to Pope Francis. What we need is "the Lord's strength" to prevent us from "destroying what He has given us," and to put a stop to the mad race of destroying "the most beautiful things that He has done for us."[97] We need to be sealed with his love and power in order to "nurture" the gifts of God so that they may "bear fruit,"[98] as the Lord intended for them in creating them, in giving his gifts to humanity, in performing his wonders for us. We need to be sealed, as the twelve thousand members of each of the twelve tribes of Israel were sealed "with the seal of the living God."[99]

The pope proceeded to share with his listeners that prior to the Mass he "looked at the pictures in the sacristy from 71 years ago [of the bombing of the Verano on 19 July 1943]."[100] He thought, "This was so grave, so painful," and yet, this gravity and pain of what he beheld in the bombed-out Verano, is, Francis reflected, "nothing in comparison to what is happening today."[101] For indeed, "man takes control of everything,

94. Francis, "Solemnity," para. 1; Rev 7:3.

95. Francis, "Solemnity," para. 1.

96. Francis, "Solemnity," para. 1.

97. Francis, "Solemnity," para. 1.

98. Francis, "Solemnity," para. 1.

99. Rev 7:2–8 RSV.

100. Francis, "Solemnity," para. 1 (brackets original).

101. Francis, "Solemnity," para. 1.

he believes he is God, he believes he is king. And wars, the wars that continue, they do not exactly help to sow the seed of life but to destroy. It is an industry of destruction."[102] It is from this "industry of destruction" that we must be delivered. Modern warfare is a prime example of how technocracy teaches us to deal with problems today: "When things cannot be fixed they are discarded: we discard children, we discard the old, we discard unemployed youth."[103] Whether by way of bombs, abortion, euthanasia, contraception, or careless and ruthless economic practices, the logic is the same—a logic of technocratically empowered irreverence, use, mere consumption, disposability, utilitarianism, all fueled by the perennial rationale of lust, which is to say, irreverence and disordered love—a failure in love, a failure to love, a failure to care and give a damn for the welfare of humanity and the meaning of the gifts of God. The devastation of war, and the devastation proper to our propensity to discard "has created the culture of waste. We discard people."[104]

Continuing with his meditation upon John's vision in Revelation 7, Francis beholds with John "a great multitude which no man could number, from every nation, from all tribes and peoples and tongues."[105] When Francis sees, through John's eyes, "the nations, the tribes," Francis perceives that "now it's starting to get cold."[106] In their plight, "those poor people" in the vision, who, in Francis's hermeneutical appropriation of the text, "have to flee for their lives, from their homes, from their people, from their villages, in the desert . . . they live in tents, they feel the cold, without medicine, hungry."[107] Their misery is the result of the destruction wrought by humanity in sin, a human society which could carry out the task of destruction far more effectively than any angel could do on its own. The nations and tribes have fled, Francis recounts, "because the 'man-god' has taken control of Creation, of all that good that God has done for us."[108] An unholy feast has been set forth by the man-god, by technocratic man. "But," Francis asks, "who pays for this feast? They do! The young, the poor,

---

102. Francis, "Solemnity," para. 1.

103. Francis, "Solemnity," para. 1.

104. Francis, "Solemnity," para. 1.

105. Francis, "Solemnity," para. 2; Rev 7:9.

106. Francis, "Solemnity," para. 2.

107. Francis, "Solemnity," para. 2.

108. Francis, "Solemnity," para. 2.

those people who are discarded."[109] This costly feast, Francis insists, "is not ancient history: it is happening today."[110] Some may regard such cataclysmic occurrences as "far away." Francis insists, on the contrary, that "it is here too, everywhere."[111] As Francis continues to reflect upon the apocalyptic scene, as though he were on the isle of Patmos on the Lord's Day with John the revelator, Francis observes that "it seems that these people, these children who are hungry, sick, do not seem to count, it's as if they were of a different species, as if they were not even human."[112] This is, for Francis, at one and the same time both a scriptural meditation and a social commentary on present realities. "This multitude" that Francis beholds as a multitude in the pages of the Apocalypse of John is likewise the multitude of the discarded populations of our own day, upon whom Francis, from the Chair of Peter and from his pulpit in the cemetery on All Saints' Day, has set his gaze. "This multitude is before God and asks, 'Salvation, please! Peace, please! Bread, please! Work, please! Children and grandparents, please! Young people with the dignity of being able to work, please!'"[113] The multitude is in a singular crisis of violence, hunger, unemployment, and family breakdown, all standing in need of salvation, all standing in need of having their dignity honored and their basic needs met.

Francis proceeds to recount that among the multitude crying out for salvation, for peace, for bread, for dignity, for family, for work, "are also those who are persecuted for their faith."[114] As Francis recounts, quoting from the scriptural text, "then one of the elders addressed me, saying, 'who are these, clothed in white, and when have they come?' . . . 'These are they who have come out of great tribulation; they have washed their robes and made them white in the blood of the Lamb' (7:13–14)."[115] Francis invokes these, whom he refers to as today's "unknown saints," who, "sinners like us, worse off than us," have been "destroyed."[116] Indeed, there is a "multitude of people who are in great distress," for "most of the world is in tribulation."[117]

109. Francis, "Solemnity," para. 2.
110. Francis, "Solemnity," para. 2.
111. Francis, "Solemnity," para. 2.
112. Francis, "Solemnity," para. 2.
113. Francis, "Solemnity," para. 2.
114. Francis, "Solemnity," para. 2.
115. Francis, "Solemnity," para. 2.
116. Francis, "Solemnity," para. 2.
117. Francis, "Solemnity," para. 2.

In the face of the devastation that the technocratic, lustful man-god brings upon the world, in the face of those whom our society discards, Francis calls us to hope, and calls us to the God in whom we can hope. Drawing from the second reading from that Mass, Francis quoted, "beloved, we are God's children now; it does not yet appear what shall be."[118] That unseen reality which *shall be* is that for which we hope, Francis suggests. We "hope that" God "will have mercy on His people," that he'll have "pity on those who are in great tribulation and compassion for the destroyers so that they will convert."[119] What we can count on, what we can hope in, is that "the holiness of the Church goes on" and "with these people" who cry out to God—the persecuted—we can live in the hope "that we will see God as He is."[120] As a "part of this multitude journeying to the Father, in this world of devastation, in this world of war, in this world of tribulation," we must assume as our own—"as we heard in the Gospel"—"the attitude of the Beatitudes."[121] Indeed the path of the Beatitudes "alone will lead us to the encounter with God. That path alone will save us from destruction, from destroying the earth, Creation, morality, history, family, everything. That path alone. But it too will bring us through bad things! It will bring us problems, persecution. But that path alone will take us forward."[122] What "these people who are suffering so much today" results from is "the selfishness of destroyers, of our brothers destroyers,"[123] and so the multitudes being chastened in the fires of our age "struggle onwards with the Beatitudes, with the hope of finding God, of coming face-to-face with the Lord in the hope of becoming saints, at the moment of our final encounter with Him."[124]

For Francis and the two previous popes, sin is what lies at the root of the singular crisis in liturgy, ecology, and solidarity. Human sin is what tears apart the harmony proper to humanity's origins, a harmony

118. Francis, "Solemnity," para. 3; 1 John 3:2.

119. Francis, "Solemnity," para. 3.

120. Francis, "Solemnity," para. 3.

121. In case someone might hold it against Francis for rhyming here, the original Italian does not rhyme: "*l'atteggiamento delle Beatitudini.*" Francis, "Solemnity," para. 3.

122. Francis, "Solemnity," para. 3.

123. Or "of our brothers who devastate," "our devastating brothers," "*dei nostri fratelli devastori.*" Francis recognizes the fraternity inherent to the humanity even of those of us who are destroyers—a fraternity that may be denied by our engagement in destruction but cannot be annihilated. Francis, "Solemnity," para. 3.

124. Francis, "Solemnity," para. 3.

for which it is destined, in relation to the entirety of the cosmos and in relation to the God by whom all creation is called and whom all creation is destined to worship.

5

. . . . .

The Truth about Work and the Worker

JP2 and Benedict against Economic Injustice

IN THE CRISIS OF COMMUNAL commitment as identified by Pope Francis, any and every notion of commitment is under threat. We've been seeing that a prominent aspect of the crisis of communal commitment is an ecological and economic crisis of endemic injustice, as a part of a global crisis of household mismanagement. For the papal trio, the overall crisis of truth, and specifically, moral truth, includes the crisis of ecological and economic injustice. In this chapter, JP2 and Benedict will take the lead in directing our attention to how moral truth, the truth of human dignity, and the truth about work are at stake in the logic of capitalism as we know it, in modern warfare, and in the havoc wrought upon the earth's ecosystems today.

Injustice in "the Barren Lands of the Earth"

In his catechesis on "a future more worthy of the human person," JP2 takes his listeners by the hand, as it were, and leads them to observe with him our shared societal surroundings. JP2 draws particular attention to the extreme extent of destructive violence in our own day, a violence in society perceived so vividly by St. John in the book of Revelation.[1] JP2 observes that today, "it seems, as in the vision of chapter 6 of Revelation, that horsemen are riding through the barren lands of the earth, bearing

1. "FMW," sec. 1.

now the crown of victorious power, now the sword of violence, now the scales of poverty and famine, now death's sharp sickle."[2] For JP2, not all is well in the world: "Unlike Moses, who beheld the promised land from the top of Mount Nebo, we look out over a troubled world in which the kingdom of God struggles to make headway."[3] Such is our existential location in the desert of moral relativism, secularization, a desert of injustice and violence that characterizes such a troubled dry and barren land. Speaking on behalf of his listeners, JP2 likens their just grievances to the grievances of the prophet Jeremiah, placing them alongside the prophet, placing his words into their own mouths. According to his account, alongside Jeremiah, JP2's contemporary audience cries out: "Righteous are you, O Lord, when I complain to you; yet I would plead my case before you. Why does the way of the wicked prosper? Why do all who are treacherous thrive?"[4] By dint of the treachery and injustice rampant in society, humanity falls short of the justice of God, and falls short of meeting the deepest longings of the human heart.

Talking Social Justice with a Cosmic Backdrop

At the outset of VS, JP2 roots his notion of truth in his vision of the cosmos. The demands of justice are accessible to the human heart because the splendor of truth shines forth universally.[5] Justice and its demands are transcribed into the very order of creation, and our hearts are built to perceive that order. JP2, citing St. Augustine, proposes that "every just law is transcribed and transferred to the heart of the man who works justice, not by wandering but by being, as it were, impressed upon it, just as the image from the ring passes over to the wax, and yet does not leave the ring."[6] Humanity can indeed stand in relation to the rest of the created order and look upon it and discern a manner of moving within it according to the demands of justice inherent to the cosmos. In JP2's Augustinian anthropology, the human person can indeed be shaped to know the demands of justice by way of practicing works of justice. The content of what justice demands isn't a matter of an unattainable and

2. "FMW," sec. 1.

3. "FMW," sec. 1.

4. "FMW," sec. 1.

5. VS, sec. 51, as discussed in chapter 1 of this book.

6. VS, sec. 51, citing Augustine, De Trinitate, XIV, 15, 21.

unsolvable puzzle, as though it were inaccessible to humanity. We practice works of justice, and in so practicing, our hearts are imprinted with the stamp of justice. In being "stamped" in this manner, the human person grows in knowledge of the demands of justice proper to the created order. The human heart, as it practices works of justice, learns to discern more clearly the difference between justice and injustice. This is because the human heart stands in integral relation to the cosmos of which it is a part, according to an "organic" order, which is an order of goodness, an order of justice perceptible to the human heart in the light of truth.

This vision of the human heart's place within an ordered cosmos renders relativism's vision of subjectivity antithetical to a Catholic notion of justice. JP2 insists that "the morality of human acts is not deduced only from one's intention" or "orientation."[7] My perspective as a subject is called to conform to the realities of my cosmic context, my creaturely nature within a created order. My perspective is liable to be warped by falsehood, and, in order to grow in my capacity to act justly, I must conform my actions to the truth of the universe in which I reside and of which I am an integral part. My "good intentions," if they do not truly take into account the realities of the created order, cannot render my unjust actions just.[8] For JP2, there is no such thing as an "intention devoid of a clearly determined binding content."[9] I am never let off the hook in my responsibility to conform my actions to the demands of justice inherent to the created order. While degrees of culpability can vary, this variance of culpability never turns that which is unjust into justice, and never dismisses me from my responsibility as a moral agent with a responsibility to strive to conform my actions to the truth of the goodness that fills the cosmos, with all the demands that the truth about the good makes upon my heart. I must be intent upon learning what is just, and strive to be just. This aim is proper to the human vocation as such.

Every intention underlying human action as well as every human moral act has binding content with respect to the demands of justice inherent to the nature of those people and things in relation to which I act, as a creaturely subject among other creatures in relation to which I stand within a created order. For JP2, an injustice carried out with a misdirected "good intention" does not render the unjust action just.

7. *VS*, sec. 67.

8. *VS*, sec. 92. See also *VS*, sec. 50.

9. *VS*, sec. 67.

An intention is not the only factor that comes into play with respect to determining the morality of an action. Rather, the morality of human acts always pertains to "the different obligations of the moral life."[10] The very nature of my own being and the nature of the people and things that surround me call forth from me a "corresponding positive effort to fulfill the different obligations of the moral life."[11]

All of this applies as much to economic life as to any sphere of life. The market is not a realm that receives from the pope a dispensation from honoring the demands of justice and charity. For JP2, that my efforts must be directed toward the shaping of my intentions according to the nature of the people and things in relation to which I act within the cosmic order means that my efforts within the market need to be directed toward shaping my intentions according to the demands of justice. Justice demands that I render the good I owe to whom I owe it in a manner true to "the dignity and integral vocation of the human person."[12] For the human person to arrive at wholeness and integration, JP2, citing Aquinas, insists that "the person must do good and avoid evil, be concerned for the transmission and preservation of life, refine and develop the riches of the material world, cultivate social life, seek truth, practise good and contemplate beauty."[13] The way of social justice—with the light of truth shedding light upon the integral meaning of the human person, of society, and of creation at large in relation to the Creator—is JP2's way of cosmic chastity.

JP2 proposes that the posture of *temperance* is a posture of reverence for human dignity in a particular way. It is the virtue called forth by the seventh commandment, which, as JP2 puts it, prohibits those "actions or enterprises which for any reason—selfish or ideological, commercial or totalitarian—lead to the enslavement of human beings, disregard for their personal dignity, buying or selling or exchanging them like merchandise."[14] As the late pontiff put it, "reducing persons by violence to use-value or a source of profit is a sin against their dignity as persons and their fundamental rights."[15]

10. *VS*, sec. 67.
11. *VS*, sec. 67.
12. *VS*, sec. 67.
13. *VS*, sec. 51.
14. *VS*, sec. 100.
15. *VS*, sec. 100.

An Anti-Capitalist and Anti-Socialist Call for the Transformation of the Economic Order: JP2's Distinctively Catholic Vision of Economic Justice

A key aspect of the JP2 legacy is his call for a transformation of the economic order. It is on the basis of his vision of temperance that he advocated and proposed "a struggle against an economic system"[16] if the economic system

> is understood as a method of upholding the absolute predomi-
> nance of capital, the possession of the means of production
> and of the land, in contrast to the free and personal nature of
> human work. In the struggle against such a system, what is be-
> ing proposed as an alternative is not the socialist system, which
> in fact turns out to be state capitalism, but rather *a society of
> free work of enterprise and of participation*. Such a society is not
> directed against the market, but demands that the market be ap-
> propriately controlled by the forces of society and by the State,
> so as to guarantee that the basic needs of the whole of society
> are satisfied.[17]

Replacing a socialistic state monopoly over the means of production with a system that hands over ownership of the means of production
to corporations doesn't cut it, for JP2. The kind of "capitalism" that JP2
endorses is something that JP2 is reluctant to even call by the name "capitalism," as he prefers the terms "business economy," "market economy,"
or "free economy,"[18] for the term "capitalism" contains within itself a
suggestion of the prioritization of capital over the person, over human
community, and over the meaning of creation—a prioritization that JP2
rejects. The kind of capitalism that JP2 rejects as inherently immoral is
that "system in which freedom in the economic sector is not circum-
scribed within a strong juridical framework which places it at the service
of human freedom in its totality and sees it as a particular aspect of that
freedom, the core of which is ethical and religious."[19]

We see then that that which is most appropriately termed "capitalism," from JP2's perspective, is something which JP2 rejects, and the sort
of economic system which JP2 endorses and which some might refer to

---

16. *CA*, sec. 35.

17. *CA*, sec. 35. See Boland, "Chesterton and JP2," para. 5.

18. *CA*, sec. 42.

19. *CA*, sec. 42.

as "capitalism" would, from his perspective, be more accurately referred to by another term. In endorsing a struggle against capitalism (i.e., the unjust system which JP2 thinks most accurately corresponds to the word "capitalism,") JP2 makes it clear that he is not endorsing what he refers to as "the socialistic system," which he refers to as "State capitalism,"[20] in which the state functions as the biggest corporation in the capitalist game, claiming a total monopoly on the means of production.[21] The "society of free work of enterprise and of participation" that JP2 endorses "is not directed against the market, but demands that the market be appropriately controlled by the forces of society and by the State, so as to guarantee that the basic needs of the whole of society are satisfied."[22] What capitalism as it developed in its early stages occasioned, in JP2's account, was "the conflict between capital and labour" that JP2 character-izes as "a conflict which sets man against man, almost as if they were 'wolves,' a conflict between the extremes of mere physical survival on the one side and opulence on the other."[23] In this conflict, JP2 recounts, Leo XIII "did not hesitate to intervene by virtue of his 'apostolic office.'"[24] Such a disparity between rich and poor, characteristic of that system which JP2 says is most accurately termed "capitalism," is unacceptable in JP2's vision of economic justice.

Against a popular impulse in sectors of North American society to identify a deregulated free market as essential for a society that honors basic human freedom, JP2 warns that "economic freedom is only one element of human freedom. When it becomes autonomous, when man is seen more as a producer or consumer of goods than as a subject who produces and consumes in order to live, then economic freedom loses its necessary relationship to the human person and ends up alienating and oppressing him."[25] For JP2, the state has a responsibility to place a significant check on corporate power, and to safeguard the good of the human person and of human community as the goal of market activity,

20. *CA*, sec. 35.

21. Here by "socialism" or "State capitalism," JP2 means a system in which the state has a monopoly on the means of production, which is to be distinguished from democratic socialism, which does not advocate for a state monopoly of the means of production.

22. *CA*, sec. 35. See Boland, "Chesterton and JP2," para. 5.

23. *CA*, sec. 5.

24. *CA*, sec. 5. Boland, "Chesterton and JP2," para. 6.

25. *CA*, sec. 39.

the goal of labor, the goal of consumption, the goal of production. No injustice is acceptable as a means to the end of wealth creation. Indeed, "it is the task of the State to provide for the defence and preservation of common goods such as the natural and human environments, which cannot be safeguarded simply by market forces. Just as in the time of primitive capitalism the State had the duty of defending the basic rights of workers, so now, with the new capitalism."[26] The state today, in JP2's call to temper corporate power, has the responsibility to guard both human dignity and the "common goods" of our common home. "The State and all of society" is tasked to carry out the "duty of *defending those collective goods* which, among others, constitute the essential framework for the legitimate pursuit of personal goals on the part of each individual."[27] What JP2 provides, in his social teaching, is an all-encompassing social critique of the intertangled web of economic injustices that spurn human dignity and spurn the grandeur of creation at large.

A Distinctively Catholic Vision of Labor: JP2 on Justice and the Truth about Work

The notion of justice, for JP2, is a notion that especially concerns itself with justice for the worker. In the midst of economic development and change in the process of production, JP2 insists that, far from trusting the mechanisms of the market with its prioritization of maximizing profit to take the lead in determining the course of events in social development, it must "be seen whether certain ethically and socially dangerous irregularities creep in, and to what extent."[28] We must be vigilantly on the lookout for any ethical and social danger in social development, and this vigilance in a special way includes a vigilant defense of the dignity of the worker. We must guard against both market mechanisms and state power that may pose a threat to human dignity at large. Any discussion about social justice true to the inheritance of JP2 and Benedict must include an analysis of the market, and an appraisal of how justice is or is not being arrived at in the market, which is to say, how charity's minimum measure of justice is or is not being met, and how that minimum measure can be both met and exceeded in economic life.

26. *CA*, sec. 40.
27. *CA*, sec. 40.
28. *LE*, sec. 8.

A Catholic Vision of the Truth about the Gospel of Human Work

As we began to see in chapter 1, the notion of social justice for JP2 is contingent upon a robust notion of truth. In exploring JP2's vision of social justice, we need to explore a Catholic vision of human work, which JP2 regards as the key to what Catholic social teaching calls "the social question."[29] Catholic social teaching's fundamental affirmations about work emerge precisely "from the wealth of Christian truth—especially from the very message of" what JP2 calls "the 'Gospel of work.'"[30] As JP2 recounts, "in the modern period, from the beginning of the industrial age, the Christian truth about work had to oppose the various trends of materialistic and economistic thought."[31] It is precisely by way of truth—and in particular the truth about work—that Catholic social teaching has in the modern era raised its voice against all that militates against this truth. It is precisely by way of proclaiming the truth of the gospel of work that Catholic social teaching has raised its voice against any force that systemically enables injustice in the domain of labor. In the industrial revolution in a particular way, the truth about work and the truth about the dignity of the worker was violated by social injustices in the domain of human work, especially by way of the mistaken idea that "work was understood and treated as a sort of 'merchandise' that the worker—especially the industrial worker—sells to the employer, who at the same time is the possessor of the capital, that is to say, of all the working tools and means that make production possible."[32] While since the nineteenth century, explicit verbal "expressions of this sort have almost disappeared, and have given way to more human ways of thinking about work and evaluating it," "the danger of treating work as a special kind of 'merchandise,' or as an impersonal 'force' needed for production . . . always exists, especially when the whole way of looking at the question of economics is marked by the premises of" what JP2 calls "materialistic economism" (which he likewise criticizes as "capitalism").[33] JP2 parenthetically observes that "the expression 'workforce' is in fact in common

29. *LE*, secs. 2, 3, and 14.
30. *LE*, sec. 7.
31. *LE*, sec. 7.
32. *LE*, sec. 7.
33. *LE*, sec. 7.

use," which he perceives as an expression of a depersonalizing vision of workers as constituting an impersonal "force" (i.e., a mere resource to be tapped into and used) in the process of production.[34]

The most appropriate term for the systemic denial of the truth about work, according to JP2, is "capitalism," which he also refers to as "materialistic economism," as we've been seeing.[35] In the humanism that JP2 advocates, the human person is the center and focus and end of all human activity, including economic activity. "Capitalism" or "materialistic economism," in contrast, is for JP2 the ideological and practical denial of the truth about work and the ideological and practical denial of the truth about justice for the worker. As such, humanism's antithesis is found in capitalism (materialistic economism), which puts capital rather than humanity at the center. Or, to use Francis's imagery to which we appealed in chapter 3, capitalism prioritizes bricks over people, while JP2's (and Francis's) humanism prioritizes people over bricks. "Capitalism" in the anti-humanist sense assigns to work and the worker a shallow, utilitarian meaning. Capitalism thus conceived regards the worker as a mere contributor to the system directed toward the end of amassing capital; the worker's meaning is thus shallowly rooted exclusively in a mechanistic system of wealth creation.

While recognizing positive historical developments that had taken place since the dawn of capitalism (thanks to society's widespread realization that much of what characterized the system of early industrial capitalism was inherently inhumane), JP2 warns that "the error of early capitalism"[36]—the error of treating man as a mere means of production—"can be repeated wherever man is in a way treated on the same level as the whole complex of the material means of production, as an instrument and not in accordance with the true dignity of his work—that is to say, where he is not treated as subject and maker, and for this very reason as the true purpose of the whole process of production."[37] For JP2, as a society we're not in a position to ease our consciences with the illusion that the days of capitalism's abuses are behind us.[38] Now, as in the days

34. *LE*, sec. 7.

35. *LE*, sec. 7.

36. *LE*, sec. 7.

37. *LE*, sec. 7.

38. Here JP2 uses the term "capitalism" in reference to that system which is not inherently anti-human, but has its own vulnerabilities to inhumanity, as was the case at the dawn of the Industrial Revolution. In the previously cited use of the word

of early capitalism and in the days of the initial development of industrialism, the outcry against economic abuse is justifiable, and indeed, is demanded by justice and charity. As JP2 insists, claiming continuity with the rationale of Leo, "the reaction against the system of injustice and harm that cried to heaven for vengeance and that weighed heavily upon workers in that period of rapid industrialization"[39]—an outcry led largely by secularists—"was justified from the point of view of social morality."[40] It is precisely from the "point of view of social morality"[41] that JP2 offers a distinctively Catholic critical voice for the economic circumstances of his day.

The song of justice as it is sung by Leo and taken up by JP2 decries all that offends justice, particularly in economics, in a context in which the humanity of the worker is systemically overlooked, and the worker's centrality as the subject of work is displaced by capitalism's false prioritization of capital, and its demotion of the worker as a means to the end of amassing capital. The injustice endured by the worker in the context of rapid industrialization was enabled "by the liberal socio-political system, which, in accordance with its 'economistic' premises, strengthened and safeguarded economic initiative by the possessors of capital alone."[42] This liberal system, JP2 relates, "did not pay sufficient attention to the rights of the workers, on the grounds that human work is solely an instrument of production, and that capital is the basis, efficient factor and purpose of production."[43] The truth about justice, which includes the truth about humanity and the truth about work and the worker, is thereby offended. This injustice continues well past the era of early industrialism. According to JP2's 1981 analysis, "various ideological or power systems, and new relationships which have arisen at various levels of society, have allowed flagrant injustices to persist or have created new ones."[44] While "on the

---

capitalism, JP2 identifies the term "capitalism" as the most accurate term for the inherently anti-human economic *modus operandi* that renders humanity a mere means of production geared toward the end of amassing capital for those nonworkers who own and control the means of production. "Capitalism," JP2 says, is the most fitting title for this false anthropology, in contrast to Catholic humanism.

39. *LE*, sec. 8.
40. *LE*, sec. 8.
41. *LE*, sec. 8.
42. *LE*, sec. 8.
43. *LE*, sec. 8.
44. *LE*, sec. 8.

world level the development of civilization and of communications has made possible a more complete diagnosis of the living and working conditions of man globally," the truth about work nonetheless continues to be denied.[45] Our perception of conditions globally has revealed new and various "forms of injustice, much more extensive than those which in the last century stimulated unity between workers for particular solidarity in the working world"—extensive forms of injustice that deny the truth about work in a manner that is more extensive than the denials of this truth proper to late-nineteenth-century industrial capitalism.[46] The denial of the truth about work and the worker has enabled a disturbing divergence between economic realities today on the one hand and the truth about the meaning of work and the worker on the other. As JP2 observes, both "in countries which have completed a certain process of industrial revolution" and "in countries where the main working milieu continues to be agriculture or other similar occupations,"[47] injustices more extensive than that of the era of rapid industrialization continue to offend the truth of human dignity and deny the good due to workers.

For JP2, "Every human being sharing in the production process . . . is the real efficient subject in this production process, while the whole collection of instruments, no matter how perfect they may be in themselves, are only a mere instrument subordinate to human labour."[48] JP2 identifies this truth as "part of the abiding heritage of the Church's teaching" that "must always be emphasized with reference to the question of the labour system and with regard to the whole socioeconomic system."[49] This truth about work is key to the truth about humanity, for, as JP2 stresses, "we must emphasize and give prominence to the primacy of man in the production process, the primacy of man over things,"[50] or, as Francis puts it, we must insist upon the priority of people over bricks.[51] Capital is for people; people do not exist for capital. Indeed, "everything contained in the concept of capital in the strict sense is only a collection of things,"

45. *LE*, sec. 8.
46. *LE*, sec. 8.
47. *LE*, sec. 8.
48. *LE*, sec. 12.
49. *LE*, sec. 12.
50. *LE*, sec. 12.
51. *LUD*, 117.

whereas "man, as the subject of work, and independently of the work that he does—man alone is a person."[52]

"The structure of the present-day situation," JP2 reflected, giving a not-so-rosy picture of 1980s capitalism, "is deeply marked by many conflicts caused by man, and the technological means produced by human work play a primary role in it."[53] JP2 emphasizes the import of recalling "a principle that has always been taught by the Church: the principle of the priority of labour over capital."[54] As the worker is the end, not the means, the work itself, likewise, has a dignity above that of capital. Capital is at the service of work, and work is at the service of the human person. As JP2 explains, "this principle directly concerns the process of production: in this process labour is always a primary efficient cause, while capital, the whole collection of means of production, remains a mere instrument or instrumental cause."[55] The worker is not mere capital, as a part of the means of production, nor is the worker a mere means to gain financial capital. "This principle" of the priority of the worker as distinct from the means of production "is an evident truth that emerges from the whole of man's historical experience."[56]

Catholic social teaching has from its beginning allied itself with the "just social reaction" against economic injustice and the "great burst of solidarity between workers, first and foremost industrial workers"[57] who were resisting the injustices proper to the logic of the market in the late nineteenth century and since. The days of injustice for the worker by dint of the market's own mechanisms and the days of a need to resist the logic of the market as we know it are not over: "various ideological or power systems, and new relationships which have arisen at various levels of society, have allowed flagrant injustices to persist or have created new ones."[58] For JP2, "In order to achieve social justice in the various parts of the world, in the various countries, and in the relationships between

52. *LE*, sec. 12.

53. *LE*, sec. 12.

54. *LE*, sec. 12.

55. *LE*, sec. 12.

56. *LE*, sec. 12.

57. *LE*, sec. 12.

58. *LE*, sec. 8.

them, there is a need for ever new movements of solidarity of the workers and with the workers."[59]

That period "marked and in a sense symbolized by the publication of the Encyclical *Rerum novarum* . . . is by no means yet over," JP2 recounts.[60] As he explains, "the issue of work has of course been posed on the basis of the great conflict that in the age of, and together with, industrial development emerged between 'capital' and 'labour.'"[61] According to JP2 in 1981, the era of *RN* is not over. The conflict between capital and labour that arose at the dawn of industrial capitalism was "between the small but highly influential group of entrepreneurs, owners or holders of the means of production, and the broader multitude of people who lacked these means and who shared in the process of production solely by their labour."[62] In JP2's account, "the conflict originated in the fact that the workers put their powers at the disposal of the entrepreneurs, and these, following the principle of maximum profit, tried to establish the lowest possible wages for the work done by the employees."[63] This logic must be resisted by advocates of economic justice, along with "other elements of exploitation, connected with the lack of safety at work and of safeguards regarding the health and living conditions of the workers and their families."[64]

JP2 critiques capitalism's utilization of the worker as a means to the end of production, as opposed to the utilization of production as a means to the flourishing of those who labor and the flourishing of the families among whom they live. JP2 thus critiques the exploitative system that "did not originate merely in the philosophy and economic theories of the eighteenth century" but "originated in the whole of the economic and social practice of that time, the time of the birth and rapid development of industrialization," a context "in which what was mainly seen was the possibility of vastly increasing material wealth"—which can be viewed rightly if it is strictly regarded as a *means* to the flourishing of humanity, but unfortunately began to be treated as the end of the economic system in place—while the true "end, that is to say, man, who should be served

59. *LE*, sec. 8.
60. *LE*, sec. 8.
61. *LE*, sec. 8.
62. *LE*, sec. 8.
63. *LE*, sec. 8.
64. *LE*, sec. 8.

by the means, was ignored."[65] This was a "practical error that *struck a blow* first and foremost against human labour, against *the working man* and caused the ethically just social reaction already spoken of above."[66]

Benedict and JP2 against the Logic of Capitalism

Benedict insists that "the moral aspect of authentic economic develop-ment is . . . of fundamental importance to the well-being and peaceful progress of a nation," and that it is in authentic economic development "that the demand for justice is satisfied."[67] For Benedict, "The right to meaningful work and an acceptable standard of living, the assurance of a fair distribution of goods and wealth, and the responsible use of natural resources all depend upon a concept of development" that highlights "the dignity of the human person—who is the proper subject of all progress—and thereby enhance the common good of all humanity."[68] Benedict's humanism insists on economic justice by calling for the upholding of human dignity in the sphere of economics, which, he said, demands "the support of the entire international community" as well as support "at the level of regional initiatives."[69] Society must thus abandon "excessive nationalism . . . so that the profound value of communal solidarity be permitted to find expression in local agreements conducive to regional economic and social cooperation."[70]

Benedict in *Africae munus*, quoting JP2's *Ecclesia in Africa*, laments that "despite the modern civilization of the 'global village,' in Africa as elsewhere in the world the spirit of dialogue, peace and reconciliation is far from dwelling in the hearts of everyone."[71] On the contrary, "wars, conflicts and racist and xenophobic attitudes still play too large a role in the world of human relations."[72] Today, "concern for our neighbor transcends the confines of national communities and has increasingly

65. *LE*, sec. 8.
66. *LE*, sec. 8.
67. Benedict, "St. Lucia," para. 5, citing *SRS*, sec. 10.
68. Benedict, "St. Lucia," para. 5.
69. Benedict, "St. Lucia," para. 5.
70. Benedict, "St. Lucia," para. 5.
71. Benedict, *Africae munus*, sec. 12.
72. Benedict, *Africae munus*, sec. 12.

broadened its horizon to the whole world.'"[73] This means "the intrinsic relationship between charity and justice needs to be more clearly understood and emphasized."[74] Benedict thus draws attention to "three specific challenges facing our world, challenges which I believe can only be met through a firm commitment to that greater justice which is inspired by charity."[75] Of these challenges, "the first concerns the environment and sustainable development."[76] As Benedict recounts, "the international community recognizes that the world's resources are limited."[77] This means that "it is the duty of all peoples to implement policies to protect the environment in order to prevent the destruction of that natural capital whose fruits are necessary for the well-being of humanity."[78] This calls for "a capacity to assess and forecast, to monitor the dynamics of environmental change and sustainable growth, and to draw up and apply solutions at an international level."[79] Ecological and economic realities, in Benedict's "interdisciplinary approach"[80] requires that "particular attention . . . be paid to the fact that the poorest countries are likely to pay the heaviest price for ecological deterioration."[81] In his critique of the commercial logic, Benedict cries out that "the violent hoarding of the earth's resources . . . are the consequences of an inhumane concept of development."[82] Benedict continues: "if development were limited to the technical-economic aspect, obscuring the moral-religious dimension, it would not be an integral human development, but a one-sided distortion which would end up by unleashing man's destructive capacities."[83] Hence Benedict calls for moral reform: "In meeting the challenges of environmental protection and sustainable development, we are called to promote and 'safeguard the moral conditions for an authentic "human ecology,"'"[84] which "in turn calls for a responsible relationship not only with creation

73. Benedict, "Glendon," para. 5, quoting Benedict, *Deus caritas est*, sec. 30.

74. Benedict, "Glendon," para. 5.

75. Benedict, "Glendon," para. 5.

76. Benedict, "Glendon," para. 6.

77. Benedict, "Glendon," para. 6.

78. Benedict, "Glendon," para. 6.

79. Benedict, "Glendon," para. 6.

80. Benedict, "Glendon," para. 6.

81. Benedict, "Glendon," para. 6.

82. Benedict, "Glendon," para. 6, citing Benedict, "Day of Peace," sec. 9.

83. Benedict, "Glendon," para. 6, citing Benedict, "Day of Peace," sec. 9.

84. Benedict, "Glendon," para. 6, citing *CA*, sec. 38.

but also with our neighbours, near and far, in space and time, and with the Creator,"[85] according to God's plan of harmony.

A second challenge Benedict identifies "involves our conception of the human person and consequently our relationships with one other [*sic*]"[86] within the triad of harmony. "Despite the recognition of the rights of the person in international declarations and legal instruments, much progress needs to be made in bringing this recognition to bear upon such global problems as the growing gap between rich and poor countries."[87] For Benedict, "the unequal distribution and allocation of natural resources and of the wealth produced by human activity" and "the tragedy of hunger, thirst and poverty on a planet where there is an abundance of food, water and prosperity; the human suffering of refugees and displaced people; the continuing hostilities in many parts of the world; the lack of sufficient legal protection for the unborn; the exploitation of children; the international traffic in human beings," international traffic in "arms and drugs; and numerous other grave injustices"[88] are interrelated manifestations of injustice arising from disorder in the human heart.

Catholic social teaching's concern with work, the worker, and economics is rooted in its concern for this challenge identified by Benedict, which we are called to face in view of achieving harmony within the human family, on micro and macro levels. Catholic social teaching's interest in work is rooted in the reality that "work bears a particular mark of man and of humanity, the mark of a person operating within a community of persons," as JP2 said.[89]

JP2 assigns work and the worker a central place in his anthropology, recounting that "work, as a human issue, is at the very centre of the 'social question' to which, for almost a hundred years, since the publication of" *RN*, the "Church's teaching and the many undertakings connected with her apostolic mission have been especially directed."[90] JP2 observed: "the ninetieth anniversary of the Encyclical *RN*" in 1981 came "on the eve of new developments in technological, economic and political conditions which, according to many experts, will influence the world of work and

85. Benedict, "Glendon," para. 6, citing *CA*, sec. 38.
86. Benedict, "Glendon," para. 7.
87. Benedict, "Glendon," para. 7.
88. Benedict, "Glendon," para. 7.
89. *LE*, prefatory blessing.
90. *LE*, sec. 2.

production no less than the industrial revolution of the last century."[91] Among the many facets of this development proper to our epoch, JP2 identifies "the widespread introduction of automation into many spheres of production, the increase in the cost of energy and raw materials, the growing realization that the heritage of nature is limited and that it is being intolerably polluted."[92] JP2 identifies as an inherent part of the circumstances of our day "the emergence on the political scene of peoples who, after centuries of subjection, are demanding their rightful place among the nations and in international decision-making."[93]

The injustices in the era of rapid industrialization occasioned a popular call for an alternative, more humane logic of solidarity. "The call to solidarity and common action addressed to" nineteenth-century workers, "especially to those engaged in narrowly specialized, monotonous and depersonalized work in industrial plants, when the machine tends to dominate man—was important and eloquent from the point of view of social ethics."[94] Workers' solidarity across the globe is perceived by JP2 as integral to the promotion of social ethics. This solidarity of workers "was the reaction *against the degradation of man as the subject of work*, and against the unheard-of accompanying exploitation in the field of wages, working conditions and social security for the worker. This reaction united the working world in a community marked by great solidarity."[95] In light of these circumstances, Leo XIII birthed Catholic social teaching properly speaking.

In our epoch, according to JP2, "there must be continued study of the subject of work and of the subject's living conditions," for "in order to achieve social justice in the various parts of the world, in the various countries, and in the relationships between them, there is a need for ever new movements of solidarity of the workers and with the workers."[96] For JP2, there is a need for a solidarity of workers today that pushes back against the logic of the market insofar as it is characterized by a prioritization of capital and a false relegation of workers to the category of an impersonal work force, as a part of the means of production whose meaning is

91. *LE*, sec. 1.

92. *LE*, sec. 1.

93. *LE*, sec. 1.

94. *LE*, sec. 8.

95. *LE*, sec. 8.

96. *LE*, sec. 8.

shallowly taken to be exclusively a means to the end of amassing financial capital. To the extent that human beings are objectified and used in this manner, the solidarity of workers "must be present."[97] Solidarity must be present, for JP2, "whenever it is called for by the social degrading of the subject of work, by exploitation of the workers, and by the growing areas of poverty and even hunger."[98] Today, "the 'poor' appear under various forms; they appear in various places and at various times; in many cases they appear as a result of the violation of the dignity of human work."[99] They are made poor today "either because the opportunities for human work are limited as a result of the scourge of unemployment, or because a low value is put on work and the rights that flow from it, especially the right to a just wage and to the personal security of the worker and his or her family."[100] For JP2, "the Church is firmly committed to this cause" of solidarity, "for she considers it her mission, her service, a proof of her fidelity to Christ, so that she can truly be the 'Church of the poor.'"[101]

Benedict's Call for a Complete Reexamination of Development

Following JP2, Benedict recognized that "many areas of the globe today have evolved considerably, albeit in problematical and disparate ways, thereby taking their place among the great powers destined to play important roles in the future."[102] What "should be stressed" is "that *progress* of a *merely economic and technological kind is insufficient*"[103]— a point that Francis would later stress, as we've seen. For Benedict, "development needs above all to be true and integral."[104] Indeed, "the mere fact of emerging from economic backwardness, though positive in itself, does not resolve the complex issues of human advancement, neither for the countries that are spearheading such progress, nor for those that are already economically developed, nor even for those that

97. *LE*, sec. 8.
98. *LE*, sec. 8.
99. *LE*, sec. 8.
100. *LE*, sec. 8.
101. *LE*, sec. 8.
102. *CV*, sec. 23.
103. *CV*, sec. 23.
104. *CV*, sec. 23.

are still poor, which can suffer" both "through old forms of exploitation" as well as "from the negative consequences of a growth that is marked by irregularities and imbalances."[105] Economic injustice is not relegated to a socialism of the past, Benedict insists. Following the very rationale of JP2 in *SRS* and *CA*, Benedict said that "after the collapse of the economic and political systems of the Communist countries of Eastern Europe and the end of the so-called opposing blocs, a complete re-examination of development was needed."[106]

In the upcoming chapter we will see Francis lead us in this reexamination of development for which Benedict called—at the most fundamental level of the human spirit, offering a paradigm of chastity against the technocratic paradigm. Francis transmits his paradigm of chastity by presenting themes that serve as central images at the core of his social message and most characteristic of his papacy: the figure of St. Francis as an icon of solidarity and reverence for the gifts of creation, the figure of St. Joseph as an icon of chastity in every sphere of life, and the literary-theological contrast between the rich young man on the one hand and Zacchaeus on the other. It is to these key images of Francis's teaching that we now turn, as we explore the ontology of creation-as-gift as it manifests itself in JP2's and Francis's shared earnest call to vocational commitment, which is foundational for a reexamination of development on a personal, communal, and societal level. Central to the upcoming chapters is cosmic chastity's understanding of the place of humanity within creation, in contrast to technocratic lust's empty anthropology and cosmology. It is this empty anthropology and cosmology that governs so much of so-called "development" today, which is why it stands in need of reexamination, as the Redeemer appeals to our hearts in calling us to give ourselves in a life of self-giving love.

105. *CV*, sec. 23.
106. *CV*, sec. 23.

6

· · · · ·

JP2 and Francis on the Call of Christ

*A Fight for Love-Fueled Responsibility
and Vocational Commitment*

DURING THEIR RESPECTIVE VISITS to the US, JP2 and Francis each placed before the nation's youth a choice to respond to the divine call to freedom, or to turn their backs upon it. In examining JP2's and Francis's placement of the rich young man on the American landscape, we'll see here how Christ calls us from possessiveness to dispossession. Responsibility and solidarity in the rationale of JP2 and Francis are integral aspects of dispossession and of the chastity to which Christ calls us in seeking to set us free from lust's grasp.

JP2 and the Rich Young Man on Boston Common

At the start of his first visit as pope to the US in October 1979, JP2 celebrated Mass on Boston Common. There, he addressed his homily to the young people of the United States. JP2 placed the youth of America in the shoes of the rich young man whom Christ encountered on his way to Jerusalem. "Tonight, I want to repeat what I keep telling youth,"[1] JP2 said. "Tonight, in a very special way, I hold out my hands to the youth of America."[2] JP2 proceeded to present the rich young man as one upon

---

1. JP2, "Homily," sec. 4.
2. JP2, "Homily," sec. 3.

whom Christ looked with love, whom Christ called, and who didn't respond to the call.

"The Gospels preserves for us a striking account of a conversation Jesus had with a young man. We read there that the young man put to Christ one of the fundamental questions that youth everywhere ask: 'What must I do . . . ?' (Mk 10:17), and he received a precise and penetrating answer."[3] JP2 proceeded to observe that "this deeply penetrating event, in its concise eloquence, expresses a great lesson in a few words."[4] This narrative event "touches upon substantial problems and basic questions that have in no way lost their relevance."[5] In society, JP2 observed, "everywhere young people are asking important questions—questions on the meaning of life, on the right way to live, on the true scale of values,"[6] such that the words of the rich young man are the words on the lips of the youth of the United States: "'What must I do . . . ?' 'What must I do to share in everlasting life?'"[7] In this question, JP2 discerns a testimony to "*your* thoughts, *your* consciences, *your* hearts and wills"[8]—so the pope said to his youthful audience. "This questioning tells the world that you, young people, carry within yourselves a special openness with regard to what is good and what is true. This openness," JP2 proposed, "is in a sense, a 'revelation' of the human spirit."[9] The young man's inquiry addressed to Christ the teacher is the inquiry that the pope's own audience addresses to Christ. It's a question that reveals a fundamental aspect of humanity: "in this openness to truth, to goodness and to beauty, each one of you can find yourself; indeed, in this openness you can all experience in some measure what the young man in the Gospel experienced: 'Jesus looked at him with love.'"[10] This inquiry into the truth of existence is what disposes humanity, and in particular, youth, to perceive the truth of their own meaning and the truth of Christ's love for them. Quoting from the version of the story found in Mark, JP2 recounted the answer that came from Christ in response to the young man's initial question: "Then, Jesus

3. JP2, "Homily," sec. 4.

4. JP2, "Homily," sec. 4.

5. JP2, "Homily," sec. 4.

6. JP2, "Homily," sec. 4.

7. JP2, "Homily," sec. 4.

8. JP2, "Homily," sec. 4.

9. JP2, "Homily," sec. 4.

10. JP2, "Homily," sec. 4.

looked at him with love and told him . . . Come and follow me."[11] JP2 then beckoned his listeners to "see what happens" next in the narrative: "the young man, who had shown such interest in the fundamental question, went away sad, for he had many possessions."[12] Indeed, "he went away, and—as can be deduced from the context—he refused to accept the call of Christ."[13]

Zacchaeus and the Rich Young Man with Francis in Philly

During the 2015 World Meeting of Families, Francis placed before the eyes of his episcopal audience at St. Charles Borromeo Seminary and before the eyes of those listening in on the Ben Franklin Parkway two contrasting literary figures whom Christ encountered on his way to Jerusalem in the narrative of Luke's Gospel: that of the rich young ruler, and that of Zacchaeus the tax collector. Francis's description of the young ruler's turn away from Christ serves as an archetypical portrait, against which Francis's portrait of Zacchaeus stands in striking contrast. We see in these figures two portraits of the yearning of the human heart. That morning, Francis proposed that "for every rich young man who with sadness feels that he has to calmly keep considering the matter" of whether to make a complete gift of self in following Christ by way of the sacrament of matrimony, "an older publican will come down from the tree and give fourfold to the poor, to whom, before that moment, he had never even given a thought."[14] The first responds—or fails to—by continuing to clutch on to what he possesses; the other—though perhaps late in life—at long last rushes down from the tree in response to Christ's call, receives Christ into his home, gives his possessions to those in need, and becomes a testimony to the Son of Man's coming to seek and to save the lost, among whom Zacchaeus had been numbered.

The young man is an image, in Francis's discussion with his fellow bishops in Philadelphia, of the reluctance of young adults in society today to marry, while Zacchaeus symbolizes the desperado who at long last responds to the call with an unhindered willingness to give all in

11. JP2, "Homily," sec. 4.
12. JP2, "Homily," sec. 4.
13. JP2, "Homily," sec. 4.
14. "WMF," para. 22.

following Christ in the sacrament of holy matrimony. In Francis's presentation of Zacchaeus as a template for finally responding to Christ's call to dispossession and self-gift, we see parallels with Francis's presentation of the figure of Joseph—who responds, though perhaps earlier in life than Zacchaeus—just as decisively to the call when it's heard. Francis painted a portrait of Joseph at the vespers service the previous evening on the Parkway, and would paint a parallel portrait of Joseph five years later at the start of the Year of St. Joseph in *PC*.[15] The responses of both figures—Zacchaeus and Joseph—in their respective dramatic literary contexts, stand in marked contrast to the final decision of the rich young man, who turned from Christ, his heart clutching to his possessions. Zacchaeus approximates St. Joseph's responsiveness, which Francis describes as the response of chaste love.

St. Joseph as Icon of Cosmic Chastity

Throughout his papacy, Francis has clearly presented the chastity of Joseph as the exemplary response to the divine call and the answer to today's social ills. As John Paul was "convinced that by reflection upon the way that Mary's spouse shared in the divine mystery, the Church—on the road towards the future with all of humanity—will be enabled to discover ever anew her own identity within" the Lord's "redemptive plan, which is founded on the mystery of the Incarnation,"[16] so Francis had the same conviction. Central to Francis's portrait of Joseph as fundamental for the Church's self-understanding is *Joseph's chastity*, which Francis describes as "freedom from possessiveness in every sphere of one's life."[17] This is the "punch line,"[18] if you will, of Francis's *Patris corde* and of the social teaching of Francis and the two previous popes. It is the meaning of cosmic chastity.

The willingness to give oneself away in marriage and raising children and to remain steadfast in this life of givenness requires the all-encompassing freedom-from-possessiveness that Francis attributes to

15. *PC*, secs. 1, 3, and 7.

16. John Paul II, *Redemptoris custos*, sec. 1.

17. *PC*, sec. 7.

18. Michael Gorman commends this question that J. Christiaan Beker "asked of every text and in every class" at Princeton Theological Seminary: "What is the punch line?" Gorman, *Biblical Exegesis*, 115.

Joseph. Joseph is a figure who stands out prominently as fundamentally *responsive* to the divine call to make a gift of self, and therefore functions as a template for such a response on our part. Joseph found the freedom that the rich young man *did not find*, the freedom away from which the rich young man turned. The rich young man was *not* free in the very way that Joseph most chaste *was* free. Joseph exemplifies the freedom of chaste love, a freedom reflected in the conversion of Zacchaeus, whose newfound freedom was manifest in his unimpeded response of love to Christ's call, giving to the poor that wealth to which he had previously clung so tightly, which he had obtained so unjustly, so uncharitably, so lustfully in his striving. It's precisely this freedom that is found in following Christ en route to Jerusalem, in embracing the sacrament of matrimony, by which those thus bound participate in Christ's self-gift.

The Existential Landscape of the Evangelical Call

Even if the rich young man whom Christ called on his way to Jerusalem and the youth gathered in Boston in 1979 are separated by a few thousand years and by the vast space of sea, air, and land between the green New England common and that dusty stretch of highway between Mount Tabor and Jericho, the existential space in which the young man traveled, set as he was upon penetrating the deepest truths of life as he approached the Teacher with his probing question—is the very existential space where the youth of the twentieth and twenty-first centuries journey, which JP2 entered through his preaching that evening in Boston. Even if the rich young man and the not-so-rich young man—Joseph of Nazareth—are separated from the youth gathered in Philadelphia in 2015 by the same ocean and a vast expanse of time, for Francis, the rich young man and Joseph most chaste inhabit the same existential space as the youth gathered for the World Meeting of Families—an existential space Francis penetrated that weekend in Philly.

Love and Responsibility

Francis took up with the bishops gathered in Philly a prevalent concern of pastors the world over, as we saw in chapter 2. So many young adults today are not equipped to take the bold risk of assuming the responsibilities of marrying and having children. A core aspect of Joseph's chastity in Francis's portrayal is the way Joseph exercises precisely this kind of *responsibility*. Joseph's exercise of responsibility is a key expression of his chaste love.

Far from refusing responsibility, love entails an immense amount of responsibility. Love enlivens in the human heart the capacity to begin to exercise the responsibility proper to any vocation. It involves a responsibility to *not merely use others*, but to authentically *will the good of others*, in accordance with an outlook of justice and charity. Authentic responsibility is quite different from the possessiveness of the unchaste, mis-exercised fatherhood critiqued by Francis. The cultivation of authentic human solidarity requires what Wojtyla referred to as "a sense of love and its essential 'flavor.'"[19] According to young Wojtyla, "this 'flavor' of love is bound with the sense of responsibility for the person."[20] The call to develop a taste for the flavor of love is as essential to responsibility in Wojtyla's thinking as is the call to develop an ear for the cry of the poor, the infirm, and nature in Francis's thinking. Indeed, it's one and the same call. This kind of responsibility—characterized by a taste for the flavor of love and by an ear for the cry of the poor—is key to an integral vision of *solidarity*, which is inherent to the human call to love and responsibility.

The truth about chaste love is that it's not possessive. This does not mean that chaste love is marked by *indifference*, apathy, or complacency with regard to the well-being of others. Far from it, chaste love drives a sense of investment proper to solidarity in contrast to the self-indulgent, self-serving investment of possessive lust, which is disinterested in the good of others, interested only in the satisfaction of my own disordered desires. The chaste love proper to solidarity is characterized by a driven interest in the other's good as my own good. The sense of the flavor of love of which Wojtyla writes and an ear for the cry of the poor[21]—of which Francis writes in *FT*[22]—"implies concern for the true good of the person," which is "the quintessence of all altruism and at the same time an infallible sign of some expansion of one's 'I,' of one's existence" to iden-tify itself with another "I."[23] It's a sense of my own investment in another's good as my own good. Love's concern for others and its sense of

19. *LR1*, 112.

20. *LR1*, 112.

21. Francis bids us to develop sensitivity to the sound of the cry of the earth. See *LS*, secs. 33, 84–88, 97, 117, 221.

22. *FT*, secs. 11, 34, and 48.

23. *LR1*, 112.

responsibility for others results from the expansion of the "I" to include others within its own field of concern, such that the "I" is expanded to include *another's* existence.[24] By way of this expansion of the "I," "what comes to light in it is not a constriction or impoverishment of man, but precisely his enrichment and expansion."[25] The truth of my relationship to others is perceived authentically by way of chaste love, whereas the possessiveness that Francis warns against fails to safeguard the good of others. By way of what Wojtyla calls *a sense of the flavor of love*, we're concerned for the true good of others. To turn away from love, by contrast, is to turn away from the authentic growth of the self. "Love separated from the sense of responsibility" is love's "denial of itself," which is to say a false love, which is what JP2 calls "egoism."[26] St. Joseph's "I," in contrast—Francis shows us—was expanded to include within its purview Mary and Christ, such that he could perceive that, given his relation to them, their good was his very own. He thus assumed the responsibility proper to chaste spousal and paternal love, and was invested in their welfare as his own.

The Chaste Freedom of Joseph in an Age of Lust's Bondage

Francis identifies the chastity of Joseph as emblematic of *the* alternative to authoritarianism, servility, oppression, a welfare mentality, and destruction.[27] The title "most chaste father" attributed to Joseph "is not simply a sign of affection" but is rather "the summation of an attitude that is the opposite of possessiveness."[28] Self-gift is the posture of chastity called for today as an alternative to the ways that lust's possessiveness manifests itself in society. While society doesn't recognize its longing as something that can be fulfilled by the chastity proper to authentic spousal and paternal love, it is precisely this that society is hankering

24. *LR1*, 112. The logic of cosmic chastity sees our identity as rooted in the cosmic order, not only in the human family. The rest of the cosmos, in a sense, is included within the purview of the human creature's "I" standing in integral relation to other creatures and creation as a whole as a singular order. I do not exist apart from other creatures or the cosmic whole.

25. *LR1*, 113.

26. *LR1*, 113.

27. *PC*, sec. 7.

28. *PC*, sec. 7.

for, deep down, according to Francis's portrayal of Joseph in the context of contemporary social circumstances: "Joseph found happiness not in mere self-sacrifice but in self-gift."[29] The Christian logic of sacrifice means nothing apart from the inherently connected notion of self-gift. As Francis puts it,

> Every true vocation is born of the gift of oneself, which is the fruit of mature sacrifice. The priesthood and consecrated life . . . require this kind of maturity. Whatever our vocation, whether to marriage, celibacy or virginity, our gift of self will not come to fulfilment if it stops at sacrifice; were that the case, instead of becoming a sign of the beauty and joy of love, the gift of self would risk being an expression of unhappiness, sadness and frustration.[30]

What meets our longings, according to Francis, is giving ourselves away, as St. Joseph did in exercising his fatherhood and as Mary's spousal collaborator. Our longings are not met by the indulgence of our appetites. Francis's reflections on Joseph universalize the notion of chastity—in the very manner of JP2 in his proposal for a positive alternative to the three forms of lust. Such chastity includes within itself the notion of sexual chastity without narrowly focusing upon sexuality *apart from the context of the social-cosmic whole.* Francis's explication of Joseph's chastity likewise presents chastity as key to authentic freedom and authentic love in all spheres of life. Here, Joseph's fatherhood is an icon of chastity as a posture of love and freedom. "Only when love is chaste, is it truly love," Francis says.[31] "A possessive love ultimately becomes dangerous: it imprisons, constricts and makes for misery. God himself loved humanity with a chaste love . . . The logic of love is always the logic of freedom, and Joseph knew how to love with extraordinary freedom."[32] Indeed, "he never made himself the centre of things. He did not think of himself, but focused instead on the lives of Mary and Jesus."[33] Authentic love is by definition other-centered and free.

29. *PC*, sec. 7.

30. *PC*, sec. 7.

31. *PC*, sec. 7.

32. *PC*, sec. 7.

33. *PC*, sec. 7. Thanks to Ana Sofia Corona Gaxiola for pointing out that the Spanish version of this text makes it explicit that Joseph "decentered himself." In the pope's mother tongue, the text reads: "*Supo cómo descentrarse, paraponer a María y a Jesús en el centro de suvida.*" The Latin text: "*Novit se de medio removere, in medium locum vitae*

Francis proposes that in the Joseph story, we can perceive that "the 'good news' of the Gospel consists in showing that, for all the arrogance and violence of worldly powers, God always finds a way to carry out his saving plan."[34] Joseph's chastity played a key role in the divine plan. As Francis observes,

> Our lives may at times seem to be at the mercy of the powerful, but the Gospel shows us what counts . . . Arriving in Bethlehem and finding no lodging where Mary could give birth, Joseph took a stable and, as best he could, turned it into a welcoming home for the Son of God come into the world (cf. Lk 2:6–7). Faced with imminent danger from Herod, who wanted to kill the child, Joseph was warned once again in a dream to protect the child.[35]

In response, Joseph "rose in the middle of the night to prepare the flight into Egypt."[36] By way of chaste love, we stand in defiance against the possessiveness of the "Herods" of society today, and we protect human dignity and all creation from lust's possessive, consumeristic grasp, so characteristic of our technocratic age.

The Three Forms of Lust and the Masters of Suspicion

The appetites of today's "Herods" are found in our hearts—not only in the state or in big corporations. Herod isn't found exclusively in the government or on Wall Street. Herod's appetites are found within the "governments" of our hearts, in the "Wall Street" of our self-serving minds and souls. The lust found on Wall Street and in state power springs from no place other than the human heart with its distorted appetites. The lusts of corporate power and of the military state spring forth from the heart. Marx, Freud, and Nietzsche, whom JP2 refers to as the "masters of suspicion,"[37] have at the foundations of their respective anthropologies "suspicions about the illusions of consciousness" informing their

---

suae Mariam et Iesum collocare" (he knows how to remove himself from the middle). The Italian likewise makes clear that Joseph knew how to decenter himself.

34. *PC*, sec. 5.

35. *PC*, sec. 5.

36. *PC*, sec. 5.

37. JP2 adopts this phrase from Paul Ricoeur.

interpretation of the meaning of "the *humanum* itself."[38] Are we at the most basic level nothing but a bunch of lusting, grasping, despotic Herods? What fundamentally drives the human person and society? This is the underlying question for the masters of suspicion. In their answers, JP2 perceives "a significant convergence with, and . . . a fundamental *divergence from*, the hermeneutics that has its source in the Bible."[39]

If Benedict and Neusner found themselves present at Christ's Sermon on the Mount, JP2 found himself at the same mount, listening to the same sermon, alongside Marx, Freud, and Nietzsche, among the crowds in first-century Palestine, as Christ turned toward Jerusalem. The Polish pope takes each of these brilliant masters of suspicion on as conversation partners at that very mount, and draws them into a conversation with the carpenter-rabbi from Nazareth. These influential "rabbis" of the twentieth century—Marx, Freud, and Nietzsche—stand alongside Jesus as fellow "teachers." In a manner parallel to that of Rabbi Jesus, these famed rabbis of secularism accuse the human heart, as Christ accuses our lustful hearts. Marx, Freud, and Nietzsche accuse the human heart of fundamental illusions of consciousness driving humanity. In Christ's analysis of the human heart in the Sermon on the Mount, we find a diagnosis of the heart in its sickness. But accompanying this diagnosis is a *call* upon the heart, "a call that springs precisely from the affirmation of the personal dignity of the body and of sexuality," a call which confirms the affirmation of personal dignity and the dignity of the body and sexuality—a dignity from which the call springs.[40] "One must interpret Christ's words . . . in the light of" the "complex truth about man."[41] For JP2, "even if" Christ's words "contain a certain 'accusation' of the human heart, all the more do they turn to it with an appeal. The accusation of the moral evil that the 'desire' born from carnal intemperate concupiscence contains within itself is at the same time a call to overcome this evil."[42] What Marx, Freud, and Nietzsche accuse the human heart of, Christ likewise accuses it of. But Christ's accusation points beyond itself to a higher call upon the heart to rise above its own lusts. It's a call to chaste love. Christ's identification of lust/concupiscence as characteristic of the

38. *MW*, 46:1.
39. *MW*, 46:1.
40. *MW*, 46:1.
41. *MW*, 45:4.
42. *MW*, 45:4.

human heart is an identification at the service of calling the human heart to transcend that lust/concupiscence. Christ's identification of lust in the heart is not an explanation of what humanity fundamentally is or what humanity is condemned to be; it's an identification of how humanity has fallen short of its fundamental meaning. Identifying the problem of the human heart as *lust*, Christ calls humanity to the *more* human orientation of chaste love.

JP2 observes that the masters of suspicion "seem to judge and accuse the human heart" for what Johannine language "calls concupiscence, the threefold concupiscence,"[43]—the three forms of lust. Nietzsche charges the human heart with "what biblical language calls 'pride of life'";[44] Marx charges the heart with the "lust of the eyes," while Freud accuses the human heart of "lust of the flesh."[45] The option before us as we engage in a hermeneutics of humanity is whether to limit "ourselves to putting this heart in a state of continual suspicion," like the rabbis Marx, Freud, and Nietzsche, or to follow Scripture, which, according to its own hermeneutics of humanity, perceives the terrible power of lust in its three forms in the human individual, society, and throughout history, but "does not allow us to stop here."[46] In Scripture's hermeneutics of humanity, we are shown (particularly in the Sermon on the Mount) "the whole reality of desire and concupiscence"[47] (i.e., propensity toward lust). Scripture doesn't "allow us to turn such concupiscence into the absolute principle of anthropology . . . or into the very nucleus of the hermeneutics of man."[48] The three forms of lust "is without doubt an important coefficient for understanding man, his actions," JP2 says.[49] But such lust doesn't supply *the* interpretive key to understanding humanity and humanity's actions. "The three forms of lust do not correspond to the fullness of" humanity, but rather correspond "precisely to the loss, the deficiencies, the limitations that appeared with sin."[50] For JP2, "lust is explained as a lack."[51] Lust is a shallowness

43. *MW*, 46:1.
44. *MW*, 46:2.
45. *TOB*, 8.22.80.
46. *MW*, 46:2.
47. *MW*, 46:2.
48. *MW*, 46:2.
49. *MW*, 46:2.
50. *TOB*, 5.14.80.
51. *TOB*, 5.14.80.

of the human spirit, a deficiency, the heart settling for the superficial, in contrast to the depths and profundity more fundamentally true to the longings of the heart, more proper to the depth of the meaning of its longings, according to the heart's fundamental design and destiny. When we characterize the human heart as driven exclusively by lust in any of its forms, we indeed describe a prominent aspect of human existence, but we fail to plumb its depths. Lust is humanity's failure to draw from the depths of its own meaning.

While for each of the masters of suspicion, one of the three forms of lust is the fundamental driving force of human life, for JP2, humanity is built to be driven by *chaste love*. By divine design, chaste love is meant to be humanity's fundamental driving force—in economics (in corollary relation to Marx's insights regarding avarice), in sexuality (correlating with Freud's insights on sexual lust), and in the practice of authority and the taking on of responsibility (in corollary relation to Nietzsche's insights on the will to power).

If the three forms of lust explain humanity at its most shallow level, what are we to say of the depths to which Christ calls humanity? Christ directs us toward an alternative outlook, which JP2 refers to as the *ethos of redemption*. Christ's accusation of humanity points to his "call to what is true, good, and beautiful" that—"in the ethos of redemption"—involves "the necessity of overcoming what derives from the threefold concupiscence" or lust.[52] In the anthropology of the Sermon on the Mount, we see that Christ's appeal to the human heart means there is an emphatically implied possibility and necessity "of transforming what has been weighed down by the concupiscence [lust] of the flesh."[53]

In his theology of the body, JP2 focuses on the redemption of humanity as it pertains to humanity's brokenness *sexually*. Scripture—so we're beginning to see—contains a call *to* (and the implied possibility *for*) an alternative to the lust of the flesh, the lust of the eyes, and the pride of life. According to a biblical anthropology, humanity is defined by the call to love. At humanity's core as history's fundamental driving force is an impetus to love chastely, in a manner that transforms the lust of the flesh, the lust of the eyes, and the pride of life into an all-encompassing chaste love.

52. *MW*, 47:5.
53. *MW*, 47:5.

Rehabilitating the Cosmos

The replacement of the threefold lust with the threefold chastity according to Scripture's ethos of redemption requires a rehabilitation of virtue, and in particular, a rehabilitation of the virtue of chastity in every sphere of life. This requires—so we shall explore here—a rehabilitation of the cosmos. Let me explain.

Wojtyla sounded a call for what he called a *rehabilitation of chastity*. Wojtyla picked up this idea of the rehabilitation of chastity from Max Scheler's call for a rehabilitation of virtue at large. As Wojtyla recounts, "When we speak of rehabilitation, we think of somebody (or something) that has lost his (or its) good name and the right to be esteemed among people. Rehabilitation restores his good name and the right to be esteemed."[54] Among the virtues, "chastity above all has been deprived by resentment of many rights in the human soul, in the will and the heart of man."[55] Chastity is, for Wojtyla, an entity that itself pertains to justice, which has its own rights, and to which we owe honor. Chastity has the right to citizenship in our hearts and our communities.[56] Likewise, a posture of reverence, by which we render the honor due toward all things according to what I'm calling cosmic chastity, took a serious blow in modernity.

Wojtyla asks, "Has virtue lost its good name? Has the virtue of chastity lost its good name? Is it that people do not regard chastity as a virtue?"[57] Yes, virtue—and the virtue of chastity in particular—has lost its good name. But the problem goes deeper. "Not only a good name is at stake here," Wojtyla says.[58] "The mere name of the virtue and a nominal esteem do not solve the problem, for the point is the right of citizenship in the human soul, in the human will."[59] Virtue and the virtue of chastity in particular are to have a prominent place within the human soul. Chastity's name needs to be restored in the hearts of men and women so that it may have an honored place there. What's due to virtue, and to chastity in particular, is "citizenship in the human soul, in the human will."[60] What

---

54. *LR1*, 125.
55. *LR1*, 126.
56. *LR1*, 125–26.
57. *LR1*, 125.
58. *LR1*, 125.
59. *LR1*, 125.
60. *LR1*, 125.

this means is that chastity needs to be rehabilitated not merely to a place of esteem, for "Mere esteem for the words 'virtue' and 'chastity,'" in JP2's account, "would . . . lack" the significance required for the rehabilitation of chastity.[61] "Scheler saw a need for the rehabilitation of virtue because he perceived in contemporary man a characteristic spiritual attitude unfavorable to a genuine esteem for virtue."[62] The antithesis of this esteem for virtue, for Scheler, is "resentment."[63]

Resentment, Wojtyla explains, "consists in an erroneous, distorted relation to value."[64] Resentment "is a lack of objectivity in assessment and valuation . . . a lack whose sources lie in the weakness of the will."[65] To render something the honor that is its due (which is precisely what justice demands), to render the reverence due where it is due, calls for the *opposite* of resentment. A person beset by resentment is beset by a weakness of will, and, in his weakness of will, excuses himself for not rendering the honor due to a person or thing according to its objective value, and treats that person or thing in a manner that falls short of the honor due. In order to excuse ourselves from valuing something according to its objective value, to excuse ourselves from honoring something in proportion to what is its due (which we have a tendency to fall short of, as is to be expected, given our state of concupiscence, such that rendering such honor "demands a greater effort of the will"),[66] we must tell ourselves a false story about the actual value of a thing or person, as though that thing or person doesn't have the value that we actually know it to have.

According to a posture of resentment, which easily accompanies a posture of lust, we diminish the meaning of the object of lust, though it objectively "obliges us to acknowledge the good."[67] The meaning of an entity—the goodness proper to it—is written within the being of that thing as a part of the cosmic order. Resentment "possesses typical characteristics of the cardinal vice of sloth."[68] Acedia, according to Thomas's definition, which JP2 appropriates as his own, is "sorrow proceeding

61. *LR1*, 125.
62. *LR1*, 125.
63. *LR1*, 125.
64. *LR1*, 125.
65. *LR1*, 125.
66. *LR1*, 125.
67. *LR1*, 125.
68. *LR1*, 125.

from the fact that the good is difficult."[69] This is the very sorrow of the rich young man who turned away sad from the Teacher whom he had just identified as good. Whereas this sorrow in itself "does not falsify the good,"[70] and in actuality "even indirectly sustains in the soul an esteem for its value,"[71] resentment "goes further: not only does it falsify the image of the good, but [it] also depreciates what should merit the esteem, so that man does not have to take pains to measure up to the true good, but can 'safely' acknowledge as the good only what suits him, what is convenient for him."[72]

Here, we can begin to see the way in which *cosmic* resentment is one of the underlying foundations of modernity, in modernity's emptying the cosmos of its inherent value, in view of convenience and utility. According to modernity's cosmic resentment, the raw materials of creation do not contain in themselves an inherent meaning as gift, but are at my disposal according to what suits *me*. Guardini warned against precisely this aspect of modernity. This is what's at stake in the battle between the dictatorship of relativism on the one hand and the liberating truth of cosmic chastity on the other. The dictatorship of relativism, fundamentally, is a dictatorship of resentment, in that "resentment is contained in the subjectivistic mentality"[73] such that (by way of the lust of the flesh) "pleasure replaces a superior value,"[74] as does the will to power (the pride of life) and avarice (for profit—the lust of the eyes). The idol of capital gain is pursued to sustain the feeding of my unhindered appetite for pleasure or to achieve (or sustain) the possession of power.

In the papal trio's proposal for what we can call *a rehabilitation of the cosmos* according to Wojtyla's call for the rehabilitation of chastity and Francis's call for chastity in every sphere of our lives, what is proposed is a posture of reverence that renders the honor due to created things—the cosmos at large, in our dealings with our fellow creatures, as members of the earthly city within God's creation, and, as a part of that earthly city, as human persons in relation to one another as citizens of the earthly city. We are called to honor one another according to our true value, and not

69. *LR1*, 125.
70. *LR1*, 125–26.
71. *LR1*, 126.
72. *LR1*, 126.
73. *LR1*, 126.
74. *LR1*, 126.

to diminish one another according to a false narrative that we easily tell ourselves when we are looking for an excuse to take the easier way, which is the way of sloth, resentment, and lust, by which we fail in justice, failing to render the honor due to whom and to what it is due according to its inherent value and meaning. A rehabilitation of chastity then, involves moving beyond modernity, to the other side of modernity, by way of a rehabilitation of the cosmos in the hearts of men and women, a rehabilitation in the human heart of a sense of the cosmic order and its inherent meaning, a rehabilitation of the right of the cosmos to be esteemed as a citizen of the human heart.

The Technocratic Pursuit of Pleasure and Loss of Joy

The problem, in the widespread state of what Wojtyla, following Scheler, calls resentment, as resentment's disregard for the good is shored up and empowered by technology according to a technocratic paradigm (in which technological prowess and resentment form an unholy anti-human, anti-creation alliance), is that, in Francis's words, "we have come to see ourselves as" sister earth's "lords and masters, entitled to plunder her at will."[75] We easily base action exclusively on what suits us according to our desires, and we employ technology for this purpose.[76] By way of technology, we rule over nature, and meanwhile easily reject any notion of truth or justice. The only meaning of a person or a thing is its suitability to feed my appetites. This, Francis recounts, is an external manifestation of "the violence present in our hearts, wounded by sin,"[77] a violence which is today "reflected in the symptoms of sickness evident in the soil, in the water, in the air and in all forms of life. This is why the earth herself, burdened and laid waste, is among the most abandoned and maltreated of our poor; she 'groans in travail' (Rom 8:22)."[78] What we "have forgotten," according to Francis, is that "we ourselves are dust of the earth (cf. Gen 2:7); our very bodies are made up of her elements, we breathe her air and we receive life and refreshment from her waters."[79] A certain form of creaturely solidarity, then, is called for, on the part of humans, as we

75. *LS*, sec. 2.
76. *LR1*, 126.
77. *LS*, sec. 2.
78. *LS*, sec. 2.
79. *LS*, sec. 1.

stand within creation as a part of creation, subject to the laws of nature, bound, by justice, to honor the meaning of creation, to honor the Creator as the gift-giver who has generously provided for us. We must not spurn these gifts he has given to us.

Francis of Assisi, who models for Pope Francis "an integral ecology lived out joyfully and authentically,"[80] likewise is a model for Pope Francis of what it means to be a proclaimer of the gospel, who, precisely by way of his posture of reverence and delight in the Creator and his creation, cuts through the most prominent barriers that prevent us from assuming a posture of attentiveness to God's will in the practical household management of our ecosystem, by way of an integral ecology and economics. The world today, in Pope Francis's assessment, is pervaded by consumerism, and as such stands in great danger of "the desolation and anguish born of a complacent yet covetous heart."[81] This is sloth, and sloth's worsened form as resentment, in the lexicon of Wojtyla. In today's world pervaded by consumerism, we are faced with the danger of that "feverish pursuit of frivolous pleasures" as well as "a blunted conscience,"[82] as Pope Francis puts it, both of which are inherent to consumerism, and are characteristic of what we are calling technocratic lust. Whereas St. Joseph, in Pope Francis's characterization, "did not think of himself, but focused instead on the lives of Mary and Jesus,"[83] the pervasion of consumerism in today's world has exacerbated the vulnerability of "our interior life" to become "caught up in its own interests and concerns," such that there is "no longer room for others, no place for the poor,"[84] such that "God's voice is no longer heard, the quiet joy of his love is no longer felt, and the desire to do good fades."[85] In such a context, lust, sloth, and resentment begin to increasingly shape our hearts, fed as they are by a technocratically empowered mentality of consumption.

Believers and unbelievers alike are vulnerable to find themselves without a sense of love, without a desire to do good, without a sense of room for others, without a place in their hearts for the poor, in a word, deprived of a sense of solidarity. Indeed, "this is a very real danger for

80. *LS*, sec. 10.

81. *EG*, sec. 2.

82. *EG*, sec. 2.

83. *PC*, sec. 7.

84. *EG*, sec. 2.

85. *EG*, sec. 2.

believers,"[86] Francis warns. "Many fall prey to it, and end up resentful, angry and listless."[87] What Christ calls us to—as he called the rich young man, as he called Zacchaeus, as he called St. Joseph, and St. Francis—is a radical alternative to this resentment, lust, and sloth. Believers the world over fall prey to these effects of consumerism. "This is no way to live a dignified and fulfilled life," Pope Francis insists, adding that "it is not God's will for us, nor is it the life in the Spirit which has its source in the heart of the risen Christ."[88] It is precisely in this context that Pope Francis calls us to an encounter with Christ—to an encounter like that of the rich young man, upon whom Christ looked with love, or like that of Zacchaeus, who responded to Christ's desire to share a meal with him in his home. It is in this context that Pope Francis invites "all Christians, everywhere . . . to a renewed personal encounter with Jesus Christ."[89] In the midst of our vulnerability to sloth, lust, and resentment, a vulnerability facilitated especially today by way of the technocratic paradigm according to a consumeristic mindset, "we are tempted to find excuses" for our lack of joy in the love of the Lord, "and complain, acting as if we could only be happy if a thousand conditions were met."[90]

Francis attributes this listless striving, in part, to what Paul VI referred to as our "technological society"[91] that, according to Paul VI's assessment appropriated by Pope Francis, "has succeeded in multiplying occasions of pleasure, yet has found it very difficult to engender joy."[92] Joy, according to Francis, is not contingent upon the availability of pleasures to indulge in; it is not contingent upon the endless conditions set by a consumeristic society ruled by the dictatorship of relativism, which hands us over to an enslavement to our own egos. Instead, joy is found in the encounter with Jesus Christ, an encounter that "blossoms into an enriching friendship"[93] with him. Joy is ultimately found only in this encounter, an encounter by which "we are liberated from our narrowness

86. *EG*, sec. 2.

87. *EG*, sec. 2.

88. *EG*, sec. 2.

89. *EG*, sec. 3.

90. *EG*, sec. 7.

91. *EG*, sec. 7.

92. *EG*, sec. 7.

93. *EG*, sec. 8.

and self-absorption."[94] Our hearts, in this liberation, are expanded in the manner of the authentic altruism characteristic of St. Joseph, that expansiveness of heart proper to St. Francis as he stood before all creation and before his neighbor in particular with awe and delight, in love as he was with the beauty of God's creation.

This is the joy of St. Benedict, who was purified by way of his encounter with God and in the expansion of his "I" to cosmic proportions. As much as St. Francis provides for Pope Francis an alternative to resentment, to technocracy, to acedia and lust, so St. Benedict provides the chaste and loving paradigm for Pope Benedict, which is at the same time, for him, a paradigm for evangelization and the restoration of culture. The alternative to *acedia* and lust is born primarily by way of an encounter with Jesus Christ, the papal trio helps us to see. "Only through men who have been touched by God can God come near to men,"[95] Ratzinger proposed in Subiaco.[96] "We need men like Benedict of Nursia," Ratzinger said—eighteen days before he would make the name Benedict his own. The answer for us today, living as we are "in a time of great dangers and great opportunities for man and the world,"[97] is found in men like St. Benedict who, in a time not unlike our own—"a time of dissipation and decadence"—have been "plunged into the most profound solitude," and who, "succeeding, after all the purifications he had to suffer, in ascending again to the light, and" who "returning" proceeded to build communities of love like "Monte-Casino, the city on a mountain that, with so many ruins, gathered together the forces from which a new world was formed."[98] In our own day, with the historical backdrop of "the past century" during which "man's possibilities and his dominion over matter grew by truly unthinkable measures,"[99] what we need are people animated by a zeal "that removes one from vices and leads to God and to eternal life."[100] This is the zeal that leads to a chaste love cosmic in scope. As St. Benedict reflected, in a paragraph with which Ratzinger closed his address at Subiaco on the threshold of his papacy, "just as there is a bitter

---

94. *EG*, sec. 8.

95. Ratzinger, "Europe's Crisis of Culture," 335.

96. Ratzinger, "Europe's Crisis of Culture," 325.

97. Ratzinger, "Europe's Crisis of Culture," 325.

98. Ratzinger, "Europe's Crisis of Culture," 335.

99. Ratzinger, "Europe's Crisis of Culture," 325.

100. Ratzinger, "Europe's Crisis of Culture," 335.

zeal that removes one from God and leads to hell, so there is a good zeal that removes one from vices and leads to God and to eternal life. It is in this zeal that monks must exercise themselves with most ardent love."[101]

Quoting from Pope Benedict's encyclical *Deus caritas est*—a quote which Pope Francis says he never tires of repeating, Francis reiterates that "being a Christian is not the result of an ethical choice or a lofty idea, but the encounter with an event, a person, which gives life a new horizon and a decisive direction."[102] This is the christological and evangelical core of cosmic chastity. It is the constant enlivening wellspring for Christian vocation, the constant inspiration to make of our existence a gift. This fundamentally is what shaped the hearts of St. Francis, St. Benedict, and St. Joseph.

Cosmic Solidarity: Universal Brotherhood and the Church's Task in the Public Square

Following Pope Benedict's refusal of an individualistic spirituality that relegates religion to the private sphere,[103] Pope Francis insists that "no one can demand that religion should be relegated to the inner sanctum of personal life, without influence on societal and national life, without concern for the soundness of civil institutions, without a right to offer an opinion on events affecting society."[104] Faith, Francis insists, is "never comfortable," never satisfied with conditions as we know them within society suffering the effects of war, poverty, and the all-encompassing brokenness characteristic of the human family globally. By way of faith "we love this magnificent planet on which God has put us, and we love the human family which dwells here,"[105] according to a singular chaste love that is at the same time both cosmic and political. Faith doesn't pose a threat to the common good. Faith, in truth, is what fuels a concern for the common good.

"The earth is our common home and all of us are brothers and sisters," says Francis in *EG*, summarizing, in a single sentence, the message of cosmic love at the heart of his later encyclical *LS* and the message of

---

101. Ratzinger, "Europe's Crisis of Culture," 335.

102. *EG*, sec. 7, citing *Deus caritas est*, sec. 1.

103. See Pope Benedict's *SS*, as discussed in chapter 4 of this book.

104. *EG*, sec. 183.

105. *EG*, sec. 183.

political love at the heart of *FT*'s call for solidarity. Francis proceeds to insist, quoting Pope Benedict, that "if indeed 'the just ordering of society and of the state is a central responsibility of politics,' the Church 'cannot and must not remain on the sidelines in the fight for justice.'"[106] The Church must exercise a chaste paternal and maternal love in exercising influence in the public square. The chaste love to which the Church is called demands of us an effort to exercise influence in such a manner.

A Not-So-Rich Young Man and a Not-So-Rich Young Woman in Philadelphia: Joseph Most Chaste and Mary of Nazareth

The evening before his discussion about the rich young man and the reluctance of many youth today to take the risk of starting a family, Pope Francis appealed in Philadelphia to the figure of another young man—St. Joseph—whom he presented as a young man "full of dreams . . ."[107] As Francis recounts, "along comes this surprise which he doesn't understand"—namely, the surprise of Mary's pregnancy.[108] "He accepts, he obeys. And in the loving obedience of this woman, Mary, and this man, Joseph, we have a family into which God comes. God always knocks on the doors of our hearts."[109] Responding to God's call—responding to God's knock at the door of our hearts and all that this knock will demand of our hearts after that knock is initially heard—means for Francis *a response of dispossession* on our part, which is inherent to Francis's notion of *chastity pertaining to all things in every sphere of our lives*, and is inherent to Francis's theology of marriage and family. The dispossessiveness modeled by that young couple's receptivity to God's sudden knock at the door of their hearts, involved for Joseph, a dispossession of his previous dreams and a "yes" to what God was now asking of him.

In his December 2020 Apostolic Letter on St. Joseph, Pope Francis describes Joseph as the shadow of God the Father and zeroes in upon Joseph's chaste love, which, in Francis's account, is revealed in the exercise of his fatherhood. For Francis, St. Joseph shadows God the Father precisely by shadowing the chaste love of God the Father. In order to

106. *EG*, sec. 183, quoting *Deus caritas est*, sec. 28.
107. Francis, "Prayer Vigil," para. 5.
108. Francis, "Prayer Vigil," para. 5.
109. Francis, "Prayer Vigil," para. 5.

make this point, Pope Francis engages the tradition's portrait of Joseph, and, in that portrait which the tradition has handed down to us, Francis discerns a quintessential emblem of the kind of all-encompassing chastity to which Francis calls society and its members.

Francis's presentation of the figure of Joseph is part of a story that Francis and the two previous popes have been telling for decades. It's a story whose characters include the forces of secularization and technocracy—the antagonists in the narrative plot in which we find ourselves as members of society today. It's the story of any young couple's call to strive to cultivate new life in an age of contraception, consumption, pornography, self-service, and disposability. It's the very story that Wojtyla was recounting for Paul VI and the papal household in the Lenten retreat of 1976—the story of the Catholic youth of Poland finding the splendor of God in the beauty of creation in the midst of a hostile secularist regime. The story Francis tells about St. Joseph, picking up where the two previous popes left off, is a story whose setting is the turn of the millennium— the closing decades of the twentieth century and the opening decades of the twenty-first. The portrait of Joseph as presented by Pope Francis functions as an emblematic critique of the very utilitarian mentality[110] that JP2 critiqued.

Joseph, for Francis, is a prophetic emblem of chastity in an age of utilitarian lust—a lust that is deeply seated in the history of humanity, and which manifests itself in particularly powerful ways today. The figure of Joseph as presented by Francis is as much a prophetic figure crying out against contemporary technocratic manifestations of lust as he is a prophetic figure crying out—by way of his chaste silence—against the manifestations of lust perennially characteristic of fallen humankind's acts of abuse and domination and against the deafening noise through human history since Adam and Eve's first grasp of the fruit from the tree of the knowledge of good and evil in the garden.

Pope Francis on St. Joseph's and St. Francis's Listening Hearts: From Narcissism to Authentic Altruism

Pope Francis's presentation of the meaning of chastity as the opposite of possessiveness—as modeled by the figure of St. Joseph—is a hallmark

---

110. For JP2, the utilitarian mentality was the "characteristic property of contemporary man's mentality and his attitude toward life" (*LR1*, 19).

of Francis's ongoing rhetorical project of calling for a conversion from narcissism to authentic altruism. Francis calls for a conversion from a narcissism that allies itself with technocratic power, a narcissism that seizes on to technological power for the feeding of our own self-indulgent impulses at the expense of our dignity, at the expense of our neighbors' dignity, at the expense of the dignity of the human community, at the expense of the dignity of God's creatures, and at the expense of the honor due to God the Creator. "Today's world is largely a deaf world," Francis laments.[111] It's a world deaf to St. Joseph's prophetically silent outcry. "At times, the frantic pace of the modern world"—a pace set by technocracy and the pace of the accompanying logic of the market, that governing arm of the dictatorship of practical relativism—"prevents us from listening attentively . . . We must not lose our ability to listen."[112]

St. Francis, like St. Joseph, is someone who found narcissism's chaste alternative by way of cultivating a *listening* heart. His heart grew into a heart that is able to listen. St. Francis, in Pope Francis's account, "heard the voice of God, he heard the voice of the poor, he heard the voice of the infirm and he heard the voice of nature."[113] Such hearing, arising from *listening* to God, to the poor, to the infirm, and to nature became for St. Francis in his chastity "a way of life."[114] It is by such *listening*—deep listening—proper to chaste love, that we honor people and things for who and what they are. The listening of St. Francis's heart was a cosmically chaste listening to other creatures as they are and according to their meaning. The chaste heart is a heart that "hears" the social meaning, as it were, of each person and each creature, listening as the chaste heart does for the meaning of creatures according to the law inscribed into their very being as creatures within a cosmos ordered by love. This kind of listening is proper to the chaste heart because it listens not to the self-indulgent impulses of one's own heart disordered by lust, but listens for that which is lovely, for that which demands our respect and love, for the dignity of the creature, to safeguard that dignity. The silence of St. Joseph stands in prophetic contrast to the noise of our lustful desires.

111. *FT*, sec. 48.
112. *FT*, sec. 48.
113. *FT*, sec. 48.
114. *FT*, sec. 48.

Receiving the Fisherman's Ring and the Responsibility of St. Joseph

At the Mass marking the beginning of his Petrine ministry in 2013, the newly installed Pope Francis pointed to the figure of St. Joseph as a model of human responsibility, according to a theology of Christian vocation. In this context, Francis proposed that in Joseph "we learn how to respond to God's call, readily and willingly."[115] On this score, Francis pointed to Joseph as a model for his own Petrine ministry as universal shepherd, which, he said, "involves a certain power"—as the taking on of responsibility proper to any vocation "involves a certain power."[116] The Pope asked, concerning the power conferred upon Peter by Jesus, "what sort of power was it?"[117] The power conferred upon Peter by Christ, Francis suggests, is the power associated with the commands Jesus gave to Peter: "feed my lambs, feed my sheep."[118] In these commands, we are reminded of something that, Francis says, we must "never forget," namely, "that authentic power is service, and that the Pope too, when exercising power, must enter ever more fully into that service which has its radiant culmination on the Cross."[119]

In the vocational theology of Pope Francis, the service rendered by St. Joseph is a service whose culmination is found on the cross. This power that is put at the service of self-gift upon the cross of Christ is the meaning of every humane exercise of power and responsibility in Francis's theology of vocation. The amphitheater of Catholic social teaching contains within itself this very vision of human responsibility—the responsibility proper to any given state of life and office. The song of cosmic chastity resounds precisely within the context of this theology of vocation. The *true power* of service is revealed on the cross, where we see the heart of the meaning of the power and authority proper to the task of feeding lambs and sheep—which serves as an image for the vocation of the pope, the vocation of a bishop, the vocation of a parish priest, the vocation of married couples and parents, the vocation of those in

---

115. Francis, "Mass, Imposition of the Pallium," para. 5.

116. Francis, "Mass, Imposition of the Pallium," para. 10.

117. Francis, "Mass, Imposition of the Pallium," para. 10.

118. Francis, "Mass, Imposition of the Pallium," para. 10.

119. Francis, "Mass, Imposition of the Pallium," para. 10.

consecrated life—in ways proper to the divinely bestowed responsibilities found within each and every vocation.

The power of service in every vocation reaches its culmination on the cross, Francis shows us. It is a power that stands in stark contrast to the anti-human power of possessiveness, which is the anti-human power of lust, which is the power that fills the void of truth in the dictatorship of relativism governed by the motive of self-indulgence in a liberal market armed and outfitted by all the technological resources at our disposal. Following the alternative rationale that perceives *authentic power as service*, the newly enthroned Pope Francis said that the pope "must be inspired by the lowly, concrete and faithful service which marked Saint Joseph and, like him,"[120] the pope "must open his arms to protect all of God's people and embrace with tender affection the whole of humanity, especially the poorest, the weakest, the least important, those whom Matthew lists in the final judgment on love."[121] This is what the chaste and loving service in exercising the power of a protector looks like, according to the template of St. Joseph, as presented by Pope Francis's vocational theology. "Only those who serve with love are able to protect!"[122] Francis insists. The love proper to an authentic exercise of authority is a dispossessive love, not a possessive love. The ordered love proper to an authentic exercise of authority sustains the power of *service* and *protection*—of guardianship and stewardship—over and against possessiveness, exploitation, and lust.

In Francis's and JP2's respective presentations of the figure of the rich young man, the rich young man has the very vulnerabilities which manifest themselves in the youth of the US in the twentieth and twenty-first centuries. In contrasting the figure of the rich young man with that of Zacchaeus, Francis shows that where Zacchaeus becomes liberated from possessiveness by way of responding to Christ's call, the rich young man remains bound by his own possessiveness—a bondage that manifests itself in his turn away from Christ's call to freedom, as he turns his back upon Christ's gaze of love. The figures of Zacchaeus and St. Joseph model for Francis the posture of this freedom from possessiveness, this posture of chastity. It is this posture that Francis commends to the disciples of Christ today.

120. Francis, "Mass, Imposition of the Pallium," para. 10.
121. Francis, "Mass, Imposition of the Pallium," para. 10.
122. Francis, "Mass, Imposition of the Pallium," para. 10.

The Harmony of Moral Truth against the Cacophony of Relativism

7

. . . . .

Francis and the Tradition
of Cosmic Chastity against
the Dictatorship of Relativism

PART III OF THIS BOOK zeroes in on how the papal trio's song of truth stands in direct opposition to relativism, beginning with this chapter's exploration of Francis's direct attack upon relativism's dictatorship. After this chapter, we continue in chapter 8 with an examination of JP2's and Francis's ardent commitment to the harmony of moral truth, and end with chapter 9's survey of Francis's vision of marriage and family as a part of an integral ecology foundational for all three papacies.

A Franciscan Opposition to the Poverty of Relativism

The choice before humanity in the midst of what Benedict's biographer Peter Seewald refers to as modern "uncivilizing developments" is the choice articulated by one of Benedict's favorite novelists, Herman Hesse.[1] As Seewald draws from the lips of Hesse's character Steppenwolf, "humans have the capability to devote themselves" to "the quest to approach the divine, the ideal of the holy" or "on the other hand . . . also have the capability to surrender wholly to instinct, their sensual desires, and direct all their efforts toward momentary pleasure. One way leads to becoming holy, a martyr . . . giving yourself up to God. The other

1. Seewald, *Benedict XVI*, 1:190.

167

way leads to becoming a libertine, a martyr to instincts, giving yourself up to corruption."[2] Seewald goes on to recount that "even in old age, Ratzinger remembered what had particularly captivated him in Hesse's book" as a young student.[3] In Ratzinger's own words, there is in the novel *Der Steppenwolf* "a ruthless analysis of degraded humanity in it. It is a manifestation of what is happening to humanity today"[4]—i.e., society's "uncivilizing developments." This is what Francis, following Guardini, refers to as the "uncultivation" that takes place, we can say, in the wake of relativism's destruction, as we saw in chapter 4. Relativism is the culprit for many of the economic and ecological injustices in the world today, is responsible for the destruction of marriage and family, and itself constitutes one of the most fundamental poverties of society that Francis seeks to address.

According to Francis in *LS*, "when human beings place themselves at the centre, they give absolute priority to immediate convenience and all else becomes relative."[5] Such anthropocentrism leads to what Pope Francis refers to as "practical relativism."[6] In Francis's view, "we should not be surprised to find, in conjunction with the omnipresent technocratic paradigm and the cult of unlimited human power, the rise of a relativism which sees everything as irrelevant unless it serves one's own immediate interests."[7] We stand in opposition to relativism on the immediate practical level by way of making definitive commitments, which is to say, by way of making a definitive gift-of-self. We likewise stand in opposition to relativism by way of *authentic* dialogue. As Francis observed in his address to the bishops visiting Rome from the Czech Republic in February of 2014, "Although the Church in your country was oppressed for a long time by regimes founded on ideologies contrary to human dignity and freedom, today you are faced with other pitfalls, such as secularism and relativism."[8] For Francis, here as elsewhere, the work of authentic dialogue is precisely an antidote to relativism, as opposed to a capitulation to it. Given the pitfalls of secularism and relativism that threaten

2. Seewald, *Benedict XVI*, 1:190–91.
3. Seewald, *Benedict XVI*, 1:191.
4. Seewald, *Benedict XVI*, 1:191.
5. *LS*, sec. 122.
6. *EG*, sec. 80.
7. *LS*, sec. 122.
8. "CR," para. 1.

the Church today, "It is necessary to dialogue constructively with all people, even those who are far away from every religious sympathy, while proclaiming the values of the Gospel tirelessly."[9] Francis insists upon the need for *proclamation* as well as *dialogue,* and he insists that a pursuit of dialogue apart from proclamation on the part of the Church's shepherds would be a failure in fidelity to the Church's mission.

At the very beginning of his pontificate, Francis linked his own ministry with Benedict's bold opposition to relativism. In articulating his own choice of the name "Francis," Pope Francis identified St. Francis's *"love for the poor"* as "one of the first reasons" for the choice of his new name. "How many poor people there still are in the world!"[10] Identifying the poor as "the sick, orphans, the homeless and all the marginalized," Pope Francis identified "another form of poverty" to which many today fall prey: "It is the spiritual poverty of our time, which afflicts the so-called richer countries particularly seriously. It is what my much-loved predecessor, Benedict XVI, called the 'tyranny of relativism.'"[11] Thus, Pope Francis's all-encompassing concern for the poor is, for him, an explicit link to Pope Benedict's battle cry against relativism's dictatorship, which is a fundamental culprit for both material and spiritual poverty. Injustices and failures in charity leave many of the sick without healthcare, leave many children unparented, many of society's members without housing, and relegate a myriad of our brothers and sisters to society's margins. Relativism is a root ideological cause of poverty in our day.

The spiritual poverty of relativism's tyranny "makes everyone his own criterion and endangers the coexistence of peoples,"[12] Francis warns, explaining that his name Francis is itself a nod to St. Francis's care for the poor, including those lacking a robust sense of truth due to the tyranny of relativism. Far from advocating a vision of the kind of neutered "coexistence" proper to relativism, Francis warns that relativism is a threat to the *authentic* coexistence of peoples.[13] "And that brings me to a second reason for my name,"[14] Francis says. "Francis of Assisi tells us we should work to build peace. But there is no true peace without truth! There cannot be

---

9. "CR," para. 1.

10. Francis, "Diplomatic Corps," para. 3.

11. Francis, "Diplomatic Corps," para. 4.

12. Francis, "Diplomatic Corps," para. 4.

13. Francis, "Diplomatic Corps," para. 4.

14. Francis, "Diplomatic Corps," para. 4.

true peace if everyone is his own criterion, if everyone can always claim exclusively his own rights, without at the same time caring for the good of others, of everyone."[15] The name "Francis," for Pope Francis, stands in direct opposition to moral relativism by way of standing *for* the poor over and against the spiritual poverty caused by relativism, over and against the spiritual poverty that is likewise the cause of relativism, and over and against the violence inherent to a world of autonomous individuals unmoored and drifting according to the dictates of moral relativism, which are the dictates of passing whims and fads proper to the lust-filled heart. The name "Francis" signifies authentic justice and charity for the poor, and signifies authentic peace in a world of violence—a peace rooted in truth, a peace that cannot exist without truth. Pope Francis's cry, his song of protest today, in concert with Pope Benedict, is *No truth, no peace! No justice, no peace!*[16] *No truth, no justice!* Concern for social justice, which is to say, "caring for the good others," is founded "on the basis of the nature that unites every human being on this earth."[17]

The Need for Authentic Dialogue

Francis's alternative to the spiritual poverty of relativism's tyranny is the precise context in which, at the beginning of his papacy, he proposes authentic dialogue. "One of the titles of the Bishop of Rome is Pontiff, that is, a builder of bridges with God and between people."[18] The enmity between peoples and between individuals places a chasm between them, as humanity's broken relationship with God likewise places a chasm between humanity and God. What is needed, in Francis's vision, is bridge-building.[19] "My wish is that the dialogue between us should help to build bridges connecting all people, in such a way that everyone can

---

15. Francis, "Diplomatic Corps," para. 4.

16. A defining slogan of the movement protesting racial injustice in the summer of 2020, following the police killing of George Floyd, and with roots going back to the protests in reaction to the 1986 killing of Michael Griffith. See *Wikipedia*, s.v. "No Justice, No Peace," paras. 1–2, https://en.wikipedia.org/wiki/No_justice,_no_peace.

17. Francis, "Diplomatic Corps," para. 4.

18. Francis, "Diplomatic Corps," para. 5.

19. See Reno, "Building Bridges," paras. 3–4. As opposed to Reno, Francis is convinced we do have isolated, wall-ringed ideological enclaves, on both sides of the culture wars, precisely in "an era that puts transgendered people on the covers of magazines," to reappropriate Reno's phrase (Reno, "Building Bridges," para. 4).

see in the other not an enemy, not a rival, but a brother or sister to be welcomed and embraced!"[20] Authentic dialogue, we can see, is integral to Francis's vision of solidarity.

Francis reflects in this context upon his "own origins," which, he says, impels him "to work for the building of bridges," given his own Italian background in Argentina.[21] "This dialogue between places and cultures a great distance apart matters greatly to me, this dialogue between one end of the world and the other, which today are growing ever closer, more interdependent, more in need of opportunities to meet and to create real spaces of authentic fraternity."[22] Such spaces for authentic fraternity—which is what is pursued in any authentic pursuit of dialogue between religions and between Churches and ecclesial communities—must steer clear of illusory forms of dialogue in which the parties involved lose sight of what it is upon which their own respective identities are based, by which each party loses its identity in a substanceless, purposeless, "peace."

In his meeting with leaders of various religions and Christian denominations in Albania in 2014, Francis warned against this form of pseudo-dialogue, founded upon the sands of relativism, which, Francis warns, "is always an illusion."[23] Against the temptation to suppose that "everything is relative," Francis proposed that the "important and beautiful" task before leaders of various religions and ecclesial communities "is to walk together without betraying our own identity, without disguising it, without hypocrisy."[24] This pseudo-dialogue is a temptation of what Francis calls *the carnival of worldly curiosity*. Whereas in much of society today, a dichotomy is easily placed between acceptance, reconciliation, peace, and "cultural encounter" on the one hand and an authentic reverence for truth and orthodoxy on the other, no such dichotomy exists in the thinking of Francis. Indeed, Francis instructs the bishops of the Czech Republic that "in order to foster in the faithful a correct understanding of Jesus Christ and personal encounter with Him, you are called first and foremost to multiply appropriate pastoral initiatives aimed at a solid preparation for the Sacraments and an active participation in the

---

20. Francis, "Diplomatic Corps," para. 5.
21. Francis, "Diplomatic Corps," para. 4.
22. Francis, "Diplomatic Corps," para. 5.
23. Francis, "Meeting with Leaders," para. 10.
24. Francis, "Meeting with Leaders," para. 10.

liturgy."[25] Francis commends to the bishops of the Czech Republic the sacraments, catechesis, and liturgy as constituting a radical alternative to the regime of relativism. In this context, "Commitment to religious education and a qualified presence in the world of education and culture" on the part of Catholics "is necessary."[26]

Francis went on to insist to the Czech bishops that

> every person in their own role is called to make a generous contribution so that the Good News may be proclaimed in every environment, even the most hostile or distant from the Church; so that the proclamation reaches the outskirts, the various categories of people especially the weakest and those without hope.[27]

Reaching out to the outskirts is Francis's battle plan in his war on relativism. On the *ideological* peripheries, much work is needed on the part of the faithful, for precisely in these locations do we see the most severe alienation from the Church. Likewise, on the *socio-economic* peripheries, it is precisely relativism that is the culprit for injustice. The relegation of certain categories of people to the socio-economic peripheries is deeply connected, for Francis, with family breakdown and ideological and practical relativism. By way of relativism's antagonism toward ethics, our ethics-deprived society leaves many struggling in inhumanely "precarious conditions" that are "threatening various levels of society, especially families, the elderly and the sick."[28] It is in this context that we must face "the moral and spiritual fragility of so many people, above all among the youth."[29]

St. Dominic and the Apostle Paul against Relativism: Urgent in Season and Out

In his homily at St. John Lateran on the occasion of the eight-hundredth anniversary of the confirmation of the Order of Preachers in 2017, Francis presented to the Dominicans gathered for the Mass he celebrated on that occasion "two opposing human scenarios: on the one hand the

25. "CR," para. 1.
26. "CR," para. 1.
27. "CR," para. 1.
28. "CR," para. 2.
29. "CR," para. 2.

'carnival' of worldly curiosity, and on the other the glorification of [God] the Father through good works."[30] As is characteristic of exhortations of Pope Francis, he places before his audience a clear choice, in a manner true to the Ignatian spirit. The choice between a human collaboration to glorify God the Father on the one hand and falling for the temptation of the carnival of worldly curiosity on the other is the very choice placed before those to whom "Saint Dominic with his first brothers" preached eight hundred years ago. "Our life always moves between these two scenarios."[31] This is the choice before us at every moment, in "every age, as shown by the words Saint Paul addressed to Timothy,"[32] in which Paul tasked Timothy to "preach the word," to "be urgent in season and out of season," to "convince, rebuke, and exhort," to "be unfailing in patience and in teaching."[33] Paul exhorted Timothy to assume this task precisely in view of the fact that "the time is coming when people will not endure sound teaching, but having itching ears they will accumulate for them-selves teachers to suit their own likings, and will turn away from listening to the truth and wander into myths."[34]

To preach the word, to be urgent in season and out of season, to convince, rebuke, and exhort, to be unfailing in patience and in teaching, in the context of the perennial temptation to "wander into myths,"[35] is to work for "the glorification of God the Father," as Francis puts it, over and against falling into the debauchery of "the 'carnival' of worldly curiosity."[36] According to Francis's gloss of St. Paul, "Paul advises Timothy that he will have to proclaim the Gospel in a context where the people always seek new 'teachers,' 'myths,' different doctrines, ideologies . . . 'Having itching ears.'"[37] This "is the 'carnival' of worldly curiosity, of seduction" and it is "for this reason" that "the Apostle instructs his disciple also by using powerful verbs . . . 'be urgent,' 'convince,' 'rebuke,' 'exhort,' and then 'be steady,' 'endure suffering.'"[38]

30. Francis, "Closing," para. 2.

31. Francis, "Closing," para. 1.

32. Francis, "Closing," para. 1.

33. 2 Tim 4:2 RSV. See Francis, "Closing," para. 2.

34. 2 Tim 4:3–4. See Francis, "Closing," para. 2.

35. 2 Tim 4:4b.

36. Francis, "Closing," para. 1.

37. Francis, "Closing," para. 2, citing 2 Tim 4:3.

38. Francis, "Closing," para. 2, citing 2 Tim 4:2, 5.

Francis observed that "already then, 2,000 years ago, the Apostles of the Gospel faced this scenario, that up to our days it has really evolved and globalized due to the seduction of subjective relativism."[39] What at the time of the initial proclamation of the gospel confronted the apostles as an expression of the perennial "tendency of human beings to seek their own newness" by way of a superficial, fabricated novelty manifests itself in particularly powerful and seductive ways today, as this tendency "finds the ideal environment in the society of appearances, in consumption, in which old things are often recycled, but the important thing is to make them seem new, attractive, captivating."[40] Relativism's recycling culture then proves to be part and parcel with a throwaway culture, for it is precisely in this recycling culture in which "even the truth is disguised"[41]— such that our irreverence for materiality, our mass consumption, is disguised beneath by the shiny, the new. The same lust for novelty runs rampant in our recycling as the opposite side of the same coin of our landfill culture—but more deceptively so, as "we move" today "within the so-called 'liquid society,' without fixed points . . . lacking sound and steady references; in the ephemeral culture of the disposable."[42] We refuse maintenance, stewardship, and care, all the while easily falling into the habit of patting ourselves on the back for recycling rather than dumping.

It is "in the face of this worldly 'carnival'" in which "the opposite scenario clearly stands out,"[43] the scenario to which Dominic called his brother Dominicans, and to which Pope Francis calls his listeners. We find this contrasting scenario between the carnival of worldly curiosity on the one hand and glorifying God the Father on the other hand "in the words of Jesus": "give glory to your Father who is in heaven."[44] The call to glorify God the Father as the source of all that exists is the call to pass "from pseudo-celebratory superficiality to glorification, which is true celebration."[45] It's a call to take on "the good works," "becoming disciples of Jesus," who, in following him, become "'salt' and 'light.'" Christ's exhortation to the disciples to "let your light so shine before men" is a

---

39. Francis, "Closing," para. 3.

40. Francis, "Closing," para. 3.

41. Francis, "Closing," para. 3.

42. Francis, "Closing," para. 3.

43. Francis, "Closing," para. 4.

44. Francis, "Closing," para. 4. Matt 5:16.

45. Francis, "Closing," para. 4.

call—Francis says—to let the light of Christ shine precisely "in the midst of the 'carnival' of yesterday and today."[46] Christ called his disciples to let this light shine in the "carnival" of worldly curiosities in the day of the first generation of gospel proclamation, in the day of St. Dominic eight hundred years ago, and in our own day, as that carnival grows ever more insane. We are called to let the light of the gospel of Christ shine so that those who seek truth "'may see your good works and give glory to your Father who is in heaven,'" Francis suggests.[47]

To let the light shine—as Christ called his disciples to do—"is the response of Jesus and of the Church."[48] Over and against relativism, the Church offers "sound support in the midst of the 'liquid' environment: the good works that we are able to do thanks to Christ and to his Holy Spirit, and which make grow in our heart thanksgiving to God the Father."[49] What Francis calls "the restlessness of the world" will respond to this sure "testimony of the Gospel" with thanksgiving, with a thanksgiving that grows in otherwise restless hearts.[50] If the restless heart stops short of such thanksgiving, the restless hearts of this restless world will at the very least "wonder and the question: 'why?'"[51] will grow in their restless hearts. The gospel as it is proclaimed by word or deed is what has the capacity to inspire restless hearts to ask what the shining light of Christ is all about. The proclamation of the gospel in this context is, in Francis's characterization of its effect, a "shaking up" that can only take place if the salt, i.e., Jesus' disciples, does "not lose its taste."[52] "Jesus says it very clearly: if salt loses its taste it is no longer good for anything. Woe to salt that loses its taste! Woe to a Church that loses its taste! Woe to a priest, a consecrated person, a congregation that loses its taste!"[53]

Salt and light are the antidote to relativism, Francis suggests, as the salt and light that characterized St. Dominic served as the antidote to the temptations to falsehood in his time. "Today we give glory to the Father for the work that Saint Dominic, full of the light and salt of Christ,

46. Francis, "Closing," para. 5.
47. Francis, "Closing," para. 4. Matt 5:16.
48. Francis, "Closing," para. 5.
49. Francis, "Closing," para. 5.
50. Francis, "Closing," para. 5.
51. Francis, "Closing," para. 5.
52. Francis, "Closing," para. 6.
53. Francis, "Closing," para. 6.

carried out 800 years ago: a work in service to the Gospel, preached with his words and with his life."[54] Dominic's work of preaching was

> a work that, with the grace of the Holy Spirit, allowed many men and women to be helped so as not to be lost in the midst of the "carnival" of worldly curiosity, but rather to have tasted the flavour of healthy doctrine, the taste of the Gospel, and to have become, in their turn, light and salt, artisans of good works.[55]

Paul VI as Proclaimer of the Gospel against Relativism

Pope Francis helps us to see that the salt and light that characterized St. Dominic's work of gospel proclamation in his day, as an alternative testimony to the carnival of worldly curiosity, likewise characterized Paul VI's work of gospel proclamation. An aspect of the salt and light characterizing Pope Paul's sense of mission was his "sincere desire for encounter and dialogue" on the part of the Church "with humanity as a whole," such that the Church might "be able to present herself to" the world as it was "rapidly changing," Francis recounts.[56] The Church must present herself and her message to the world in a manner true "to her deepest and most authentic identity," Francis insists, summarizing the vision Paul VI had for dialogue between the Church and society.[57] As much as Dominic believed the Church had good news to offer the world, so Paul VI believed the same. For Pope Paul, and for Francis after him, for such evangelization to take place, "the Church must enter into dialogue with the world in which it lives."[58] In Pope Paul's own words, quoted by Francis, the Church "has something to say, a message to give, a communication to make," something beautiful to transmit, which can only take place in the context of an authentic encounter, an authentic dialogue, an authentic mutual exchange of thoughts, words, ideas, concerns.[59] For

54. Francis, "Closing," para. 7.

55. Francis, "Closing," para. 7.

56. Francis, "Interreligious Dialogue," para. 3.

57. Francis, "Interreligious Dialogue," para. 3.

58. Francis, "Interreligious Dialogue," para. 3, citing Paul VI, *Ecclesium suam*, sec. 65.

59. Francis, "Interreligious Dialogue," para. 3, citing Paul VI, *Ecclesium suam*, sec. 65.

Francis, entering into dialogue is key to having the opportunity to share the truth of the gospel that we have to offer.

We must enter into dialogue precisely because we firmly believe that the gospel contains within itself the definitive revelation of truth in a manner that calls for the allegiance of all human hearts. By way of such a commitment to truth, we must seek to build a society of justice and charity. Building a society of justice and charity in a pluralistic context requires authentic dialogue. Such dialogue, Francis insists in his summary of Pope Paul's vision for dialogue, is "not meant to relativize the Christian faith" and is not meant "to set aside the longing that resides in the heart of every disciple, to proclaim to all the joy of encounter with Christ and his universal call."[60] For indeed, according to Francis, "dialogue is possible only by beginning with" safeguarding the integrity of "one's own identity."[61] Here Francis appeals to the figure of JP2 as a model of one engaged in both proclamation and dialogue in a manner according to which dialogue and proclamation are complementary, not contradictory: "As the Holy Father Saint John Paul II would show frequently through words and gestures, dialogue and proclamation do not exclude one another, but are intimately connected."[62] A perception of the authentic connection between proclamation and dialogue includes within itself a perception of "their distinction," which "must be maintained" such that "the two should never be confused or instrumentalized or judged equivalent or interchangeable," Francis insists, citing JP2.[63] Proclamation is one thing, and dialogue is quite another. But that does not make them mutually exclusive and incompatible. Disciples of Christ must be bold proclaimers of the truth while also maintaining a posture of dialogue with other traditions that posit truth claims, some of which are compatible with the Catholic faith and some of which are incompatible. JP2 demonstrated precisely this tension. Indeed, according to Francis's appropriation of Paul VI's and JP2's vision for dialogue, a Christian engagement in authentic dialogue presupposes the very type of conviction that is required for the task of gospel proclamation.

In exhorting his flock to engage in authentic dialogue, Francis displays a great deal of confidence in the guidance of the Spirit in both

60. Francis, "Interreligious Dialogue," para. 4.

61. Francis, "Interreligious Dialogue," para. 4.

62. Francis, "Interreligious Dialogue," para. 4.

63. Francis, "Interreligious Dialogue," para. 4; JP2, *Redemptoris missio*, sec. 55.

dialogue and in gospel proclamation. Quoting JP2, Francis insists that "in truth, 'it is always the Spirit who is at work, both when he gives life to the Church and impels her to proclaim Christ, and when he implants and develops his gifts in all individuals and peoples, guiding the Church to discover these gifts, to foster them and to receive them through dialogue.'"[64]

Francis's optimism regarding the compatibility of authentic dialogue and authentic gospel proclamation does not render Francis naïve. Francis's eyes are wide open to the ways in which dialogue can become diabolically falsified. In a morning meditation in the chapel of the *Domus Sanctae Marthae* on an October morning in 2015, Francis narrated the way in which an individual can end up being "destroyed by the well-mannered method the devil uses, by the way the devil convinces him to do things."[65] What is the name of this "well-mannered" technique of the devil, according to Francis? Relativism.[66] Again, there is no mincing of words here for Francis. According to Francis's account, the devil, with his good manners, assures the one he tempts with sentences that begin with the phrase "But it is not . . . ," or "But it is not much . . . ," or "No, relax, be calm . . ."[67] These are the good mannered phrases of the devil as he employs relativism to seduce us in the face of temptation.

It is by way of succumbing to these tactics of the devil that the conscience is numbed, and we compromise our moral convictions. Though we may be tempted to compromise our conviction for the sake of an alleged peace, we must assume a posture of discernment and vigilance "in order to avoid the risk of 'anaesthetizing one's conscience,'"[68] as Francis put it. For indeed, the evil spirit, according to Francis, "always tries to deceive, to lead us and make us choose the wrong path."[69] In the face of this, "vigilance is necessary, because the enemy may come."[70] Often, "the evil one is hidden" and "he comes with his very polite friends, knocks on the door, asks permission, enters and lives with that man, in his daily

---

64. Francis, "Interreligious Dialogue," para. 4; JP2, *Redemptoris missio*, sec. 29.

65. Francis, "Well-Mannered Evil One," para. 7.

66. Francis, "Well-Mannered Evil One," para. 7. For the characteristics of polite relativistic devils, see Francis, "Midday Prayer," paras. 8–11, 13.

67. Francis, "Well-Mannered Evil One," para. 7.

68. Francis, "Well-Mannered Evil One," para. 1.

69. Francis, "Well-Mannered Evil One," para. 4.

70. Francis, "Well-Mannered Evil One," para. 6.

life, and little by little gives him instructions."[71] This is when the devil convinces us "to do things" by the seduction of relativism, as Francis warned.[72] For Francis, we must look to the Lord for deliverance from the diabolical forces of relativism.[73]

The Cry of the Poor against Relativism

Among the demands of chastity is what Francis calls "the duty of hearing the cry of the poor"[74] (which, Francis shows, is integrally connected with the cry of the earth itself).[75] The theology of the Bible testifies to the truth of the call of justice and charity in response to the plight of the poor, a truth that, Francis says, "greatly influenced the thinking of the Fathers of the Church and helped create a prophetic, counter-cultural resistance to the self-centred hedonism of paganism."[76] In Francis's own presentation, this scriptural theology calls for an equally prophetic, countercultural resistance to the self-centered manifestations of pagan hedonism—largely in the form of practical relativism—so prevalent today. The truth of the call to charity—for one another, and particularly, for those deprived of the basic necessities of life—(a truth to which Scripture and the Fathers testify)—is a truth that, Francis insists, we mustn't relativize.[77] Francis locates his social ethic within its integral homeland—the homeland of doctrine and moral truth proper to the church fathers.

Among the "various means of masking reality" that Francis says we must reject is "the dictatorship of relativism."[78] This "relativistic subjectivism" is greatly responsible for the breakdown of the faith in cultures globally.[79] The temptation "to relativize or conceal their Christian identity and convictions" likewise all too often prevents the Church's pastors from embracing their task as missionaries, prevents them from boldly proclaiming the gospel, affected as they are by "our media culture and

71. Francis, "Well-Mannered Evil One," para. 7.

72. Francis, "Well-Mannered Evil One," para. 7.

73. See Francis, "Well-Mannered Evil One," para. 7.

74. *EG*, sec. 193.

75. See *LS*, secs. 49, 53, 117.

76. *EG*, sec. 193.

77. *EG*, sec. 194.

78. *EG*, sec. 231.

79. *EG*, sec. 70.

some intellectual circles" that "convey a marked scepticism with regard to the Church's message, along with a certain cynicism."[80] Thus, in Francis's diagnosis of the societal sickness of relativism today, the Church's pastors can "fall into a relativism which, whatever their particular style of spirituality or way of thinking, proves even more dangerous than doctrinal relativism" in that "it has to do with the deepest and inmost decisions that shape their way of life" and deforms their hearts in relation to the world around them according to an utterly falsified and lustful manner.[81] Even if it is *believed* by the "practical relativist" that God exists, such pastoral workers, Francis warns, can easily fall into the trap of living, in many ways, "as if God did not exist, making decisions as if the poor did not exist, setting goals as if others did not exist, working as if people who have not received the Gospel did not exist."[82] All this, Francis observes, comes at the expense of "missionary enthusiasm,"[83] which is suffocated by relativism's choke hold. "It is striking that even some who clearly have solid doctrinal and spiritual convictions frequently fall into a lifestyle which leads to an attachment to financial security or to a desire for power or human glory at all cost, rather than giving their lives to others in mission."[84] What the truth of the gospel demands of its adherents is a missional drive to share that truth.

Francis on Beauty and Authentic Dialogue

Relativism is as antithetical to the notion of beauty as much as it is to the notion of truth and goodness, as beauty, truth, and goodness are inseparably intertwined. For this reason, Pope Francis is concerned with aesthetic relativism as much as he challenges moral relativism and practical relativism. Whereas the counter-Christian task of "fostering an aesthetic relativism," which, according to Francis, downplays "the inseparable bond between truth, goodness and beauty," Francis proposes "a renewed esteem for beauty as a means of touching the human heart and enabling the truth and goodness of the Risen Christ to radiate within it."[85] This is

80. *EG*, sec. 80.
81. *EG*, sec. 80.
82. *EG*, sec. 80.
83. *EG*, sec. 80.
84. *EG*, sec. 80.
85. *EG*, sec. 167.

what Francis proposes as an authentic, integral catechesis that attends "to the 'way of beauty' (*via pulchritudinis*)" in the tradition of Pope Benedict.[86] According to Francis, "Proclaiming Christ means showing that to believe in and to follow him is not only something right and true, but also something beautiful, capable of filling life with new splendour and profound joy, even in the midst of difficulties. Every expression of true beauty can thus be acknowledged as a path leading to an encounter with the Lord Jesus."[87]

An encounter with the Lord Jesus by way of the path of beauty is key to a robust catechetical and evangelistic response to the forces of relativism on the prowl across the globe today. In his meeting with the bishops of Asia in 2014, Francis warned against "the deceptive light of relativism" that "obscures the splendor of truth and, shaking the earth beneath our feet, pulls us toward the shifting sands of confusion and despair."[88] This relativism "is a temptation which nowadays also affects Christian communities, causing people to forget that in a world of rapid and disorienting change, 'there is much that is unchanging, much that has its ultimate foundation in Christ, who is the same yesterday, and today, and forever'" explained Francis, quoting *Gaudium et spes*.[89] Francis goes on to explain, as is characteristic of his war against relativism, that the threat of relativism today manifests itself not "merely as a system of thought" but as "that everyday practical relativism which almost imperceptibly saps our sense of identity," again insisting that authentic dialogue can only take place when both parties in dialogue are secure in where they stand.[90] While the Church on the "vast continent" of Asia "is called to be versatile and creative in her witness to the Gospel through dialogue and openness to all," "we cannot engage in real dialogue unless we are conscious of our own identity."[91] Indeed, "we can't dialogue, we can't start dialoguing from nothing, from zero, from a foggy sense of who we are. Nor can there be authentic dialogue unless we are capable of opening our minds and hearts, in empathy and sincere receptivity, to those with whom we

86. *EG*, sec. 167.

87. *EG*, sec. 167.

88. Francis, "Bishops of Asia," para. 3.

89. Francis, "Bishops of Asia," para. 3.

90. Here Reno's image of a bridge requiring firm foundations on either side is a fitting illustration for what Francis is insisting upon as a criteria for authentic dialogue. Reno, "Building Bridges," paras. 2–3.

91. Francis, "Bishops of Asia," para. 2.

speak."[92] This is the tension Francis consistently holds, in speaking of dialogue. Authentic dialogue requires "a clear sense of one's own identity *and* a capacity for empathy."[93] But commitment to the truth of the God that has made his claim upon us, for Francis, is "the point of departure for all dialogue."[94] As Francis puts it, "If we are to speak freely, openly and fruitfully with others, we must be clear about who we are, what God has done for us, and what it is that he asks of us."[95] For Francis, a firm foundation upon which we stand never negates a capacity for an openness of heart and mind, and an openness of heart and mind never means that one doesn't stand firmly upon the foundations of belief. Such conviction is a prerequisite for dialogue. At the same time, "If our communication is not to be a monologue, there has to be openness of heart and mind to accepting individuals and cultures."[96] Such dialogue is engaged in boldly and "fearlessly, for fear is the enemy of this kind of openness."[97]

Standing firmly on our side of the bridge—what Francis calls "the solidity of our Christian identity,"[98] "does not always prove easy, however, since—being sinners—we will always be tempted by the spirit of the world, which shows itself in a variety of ways."[99] "The world threatens the solidity of our Christian identity" by way of "superficiality," which Francis describes as "a tendency to toy with the latest fads, gadgets and distractions, rather than attending to the things that really matter."[100] We are, as Francis points out, in the midst of "a culture which glorifies the ephemeral, and offers so many avenues of avoidance and escape"[101] such that the temptation of superficiality "can present a serious pastoral problem"[102]—the very problem JP2 was addressing in speaking with his youthful audience in Boston in 1979.

According to Pope Francis's humanism, we become fully human "when we let God bring us beyond ourselves in order to attain the fullest

92. Francis, "Bishops of Asia," para. 2.
93. Francis, "Bishops of Asia," para. 2 (emphasis added).
94. Francis, "Bishops of Asia," para. 2.
95. Francis, "Bishops of Asia," para. 2.
96. Francis, "Bishops of Asia," para. 2.
97. Francis, "Bishops of Asia," para. 2.
98. Francis, "Bishops of Asia," para. 4.
99. Francis, "Bishops of Asia," para. 3.
100. Francis, "Bishops of Asia," para. 4, citing Phil 1:10.
101. Francis, "Bishops of Asia," para. 4.
102. Francis, "Bishops of Asia," para. 4.

truth of our being."[103] Cosmic chastity is a name for that posture of our hearts toward all around us that we can assume by way of that encounter with Christ, an encounter which brings us, as we have said, "beyond ourselves,"[104] becoming like St. Joseph in his relation to the Christ Child and Mary his spouse, a "self-gift."[105] It was only in that gift of self that St. Joseph found happiness, Francis says, and only in that gift of self that "we find the source of inspiration of all our efforts at evangelization."[106]

The Ethos of Redemption

What JP2 calls the ethos of redemption is, as he presents it, *the* alternative to lust. The ethos of the redemption of the body is an integral aspect of the ethos of redemption at large. The ethos of cosmic chastity is the name I'm giving to what JP2 speaks of as an ethos of redemption, an aspect of which is an ethos of the redemption of the body, which includes a restored outlook upon human sexuality in contrast to the lust of the flesh. We have seen that the lust of the flesh is what humanity is condemned to be driven by exclusively—so we'll believe if we are to subscribe to a Freudian anthropology proper to a Freudian hermeneutics of our psyches, translated into the language of the Church's theological tradition. But in JP2's scriptural anthropology, which is an anthropology of hope, we have seen, neither the lust of the flesh in particular nor lust in its three forms has the final say regarding the fundamental orientation of the human person. Marx and Adam Smith[107] would have it that the lust of the eyes is what drives humanity (avarice). Nietzsche would have it that the pride life (part and parcel with the lust for power/the will to power) drives the *humanum*. And as we've said, for Freud, it's the lust of the flesh that drives the *humanum* in all he does (sexual lust). But for JP2's scriptural anthropology, which acknowledges the incredible power of these three forms of lust, and which perceives how the three forms of lust poison all of human activity and indeed have played and continue to play an enormous role in driving our psyches, driving our action, driving society, and driving history, there is contained within the blueprint

103. *EG*, sec. 8, 24.

104. Francis, *EG*, sec. 8, 24.

105. *PC*, sec. 7.

106. Francis, *EG*, sec. 8.

107. See Schindler, *Ordering Love*, 2–3.

of humanity (individually and collectively) and of history a plan for the restoration of humanity's sexual desire, humanity's relationship to material creation, and humanity's handling of power and authority—a plan of restoration that is already in the process of being implemented. This plan of redemption, which is in active motion within history and within humanity, specifically contains within itself a redemption of our sexual desire and of our sexuality at large. The redemption of our sexual outlook is part of an all-encompassing redemption that is cosmic in scope, in that it restores our ethos as it pertains to the whole of creation. The blueprint of chaste love will ultimately override the blueprint's distortion by way of lust.

JP2 follows St. Paul's eschatology at length, recounting that in the Letter to the Romans, Paul "contrasts the 'slavery of corruption'; (8:21) and the submission 'to transitoriness' (8:20) . . . to the desire for the 'redemption of our bodies' (8:23)."[108] As JP2 explains, "The whole creation has come to share" in humanity's subjection to transitoriness "because of sin."[109] The desire for redemption is fundamental to humanity's orientation in the history of a broken world, and this desire for redemption pertains to humanity with regard to human sexuality, but is not relegated to sexuality exclusively. Our relationship to the cosmos is broken, and the cosmos itself is participatory in humanity's brokenness. But the cosmos likewise stands in a participatory relationship with humanity's deep-seated longing for redemption. In the context of explicating humanity's slavery to corruption coupled with humanity's longing for redemption, "the Apostle speaks about the groans of 'the whole creation,' which cherishes the hope that it itself will be set free from the slavery of corruption to enter into the freedom of the glory of the children of God."[110] Humanity's slavery to corruption manifests itself in the three forms of lust, in JP2's biblical anthropology. And what is restored, as JP2 discusses it in his vision of an ethos of redemption, is humanity's capacity for chaste love in the realm of sexuality, which replaces the lust of the flesh with a chaste love in a restoration of our sexuality. This replacement of the lust of the flesh with chaste love in the ethos of redemption is part of the restoration of the human person at large, such that our relationship with the whole of creation is restored in a manner of cosmic chastity, such that the lust

108. *MW*, 49:2.
109. *MW*, 49:2.
110. *MW*, 49:2.

of the eyes (avarice, particularly in economic life, as commented upon by Marx, though in atheological language) and the pride of life (the will to power, as commented upon by Nietzsche) are transformed into a chastity of the eyes and a humility of life proper to creaturely existence.

Solomon's Apostasy and Christ's Call: From a Regime of Lust to the Option of Love

In recounting the call that Christ was making upon the rich young man and Christ's call to American youth gathered on Boston Common in 1979, JP2 warned his audience of the temptation to seek an escape from the responsibility inherent to the love to which Christ calls us. Our tendency to seek an escape from the responsibility to which Christ calls us manifests itself in an "escape in selfishness, escape in sexual pleasure, escape in drugs, escape in violence, escape in indifference and cynical attitudes,"[111] JP2 warned. "But today, I propose to you the option of love, which is the opposite of escape."[112]

In the ethos of cosmic chastity characteristic of the teaching of JP2, what is proposed is "the option of love"—authentic love—over and against an escape from reality and its demands of justice and love.[113] What is proposed is the option of love over and against the escape from the meaning of the universe, an escape from the truth of the meaning of the human person, the truth of the meaning of the human family, the truth of the meaning of fraternity and paternity, the truth of the meaning of sorority and maternity, the truth of the meaning of materiality, the truth of the meaning of existence. Such striving escapism from the truth of reality is inherent to lust, and is inherent to technocracy's regime of feeding the lust of the human heart according to its myriad disordered desires by way of technological power. By way of lust, we clutch on to our many possessions and turn away from the Calvary-bound Christ who calls us to follow him. By Christ, we are called out of such escapism.

This was JP2's first call to cosmic chastity on American soil, as well as his first word of defiance on American soil against the regime of technocratic lust. In being called by Christ, we are called to take responsibility by way of christological generosity. "If you really accept that love from

111. JP2, "Homily," sec. 5.
112. JP2, "Homily," sec. 5.
113. JP2, "Homily," sec. 5.

Christ"—that supremely chaste love with which Christ looked upon the rich young man and with which he looked upon the youth in Boston in 1979—"it will lead you to God."[114] Accepting that gaze of love from Christ will lead youth in their vocational path: "Perhaps in the priesthood or religious life; perhaps in some special service to your brothers and sisters: especially to the needy, the poor, the lonely, the abandoned, those whose rights have been trampled upon, or those whose basic needs have not been provided for."[115] Regardless of the form our respective responses take, "whatever you make of your life," JP2 says, we are to "let it be something that reflects the love of Christ."[116] The Church depends upon it, as "the whole People of God will be all the richer because of the diversity of your commitments. In whatever you do, remember that Christ is calling you, in one way or another, to the service of love: the love of God and of your neighbor."[117] Christ is calling us out of ourselves, to give of ourselves, to let go of what we grasp onto so tightly with lust's deadly choke hold, and to make a gift of ourselves in following Christ in response to his call and his gaze of love, participating in his self-gift.

In this context, toward the end of his homily that night, JP2 again directs the attention of the youth gathered in Boston to the rich young man's tragic turn from love and responsibility: "Coming back to the story of the young man in the Gospels, we see that he heard the call—'Follow me'—but that he 'went away sad, for he had many possessions.'"[118] JP2 observes that "we could be tempted to think that many possessions, many of the goods of this world, can bring happiness."[119] When we are clutching, clinging, possessing, grasping to gain life, it is intuitive for us to think that such power of possession is what brings happiness. But, as JP2 recounts, "We see instead in the case of the young man in the Gospel that his many possessions had become an obstacle to accepting the call of Jesus to follow him. He was not ready to say yes to Jesus, and no to self, to say yes to love and no to escape."[120]

114. JP2, "Homily," sec. 5.
115. JP2, "Homily," sec. 5.
116. JP2, "Homily," sec. 5.
117. JP2, "Homily," sec. 5.
118. JP2, "Homily," sec. 6.
119. JP2, "Homily," sec. 6.
120. JP2, "Homily," sec. 6.

JP2 gives a description of just what it is that we are called to by Christ, expounding upon the content of the invitation of Christ to us, who stands before us, responding to our questioning hearts, as he stood before the rich young man of the ancient near east some two thousand years ago: "Real love is demanding."[121]

This temptation to escape from the responsibilities laid upon us by reality, and to do so by way of superficiality, lures not only lay youth who haven't made a vocational commitment, but likewise lures "ministers of the Church" by way of "an enchantment with pastoral programs and theories, to the detriment of direct, fruitful encounter with our faithful, and others too, especially the young who need solid catechesis and sound spiritual guidance."[122] To seek an escape from fruitful encounters with the lay faithful and with those outside the fold is to seek an escape from reality, from responsibility, from the demands of the truth about justice and love. In this culture of fleeting commitment which glorifies the ephemeral, we are foundationless, and "without a grounding in Christ," Francis says, "the truths by which we live our lives can gradually recede, the practice of the virtues can become formalistic, and dialogue can be reduced to a form of negotiation or an agreement to disagree."[123] Francis rejects this option as a dangerous distortion of dialogue: "An agreement to disagree . . . so as not to make waves . . . This sort of superficiality does us great harm."[124]

Francis's attacks on relativism are frequently accompanied by attacks on relativism's evil twin, which he identifies as the temptation of fundamentalism. But this too is an escape from truth, from reality, from responsibility, if in a hidden way. Francis describes to the bishops of Asia the temptation to escape into fundamentalism as "the apparent security to be found in hiding behind easy answers, ready formulas, rules and regulations"[125]—the temptation of fundamentalism that is increasing with the rise and intensification of relativism's regime, as many desperately (and understandably) seek an alternative to relativism's shaky ground. Yet, as Francis points out, "Jesus clashed with people who would hide

121. JP2, "Homily," sec. 6.
122. Francis, "Bishops of Asia," para. 4.
123. Francis, "Bishops of Asia," para. 4.
124. Francis, "Bishops of Asia," para. 4.
125. Francis, "Bishops of Asia," para. 5.

behind laws, regulations and easy answers . . . He called them hypocrites."[126] Grasping for easy answer, ready formulas, rules, and regulations—which is a living temptation, particularly for young adults fed up with relativism and seeking a clear and definitive alternative to the void of meaning it leaves—will not satisfy our need for a sure foundation. It is not a viable alternative to relativism. And yet, tribalistic fundamentalisms abound in society today, in tandem with relativism, its evil twin.[127] "It is our living faith in Christ which is our deepest identity, our being rooted in the Lord. If we have this, everything else is secondary. It is from this deep identity— our being grounded in a living faith in Christ—it is from this profound reality that our dialogue begins, and this is what we are asked to share, sincerely, honestly and without pretence, in the dialogue of everyday life, in the dialogue of charity, and in those more formal opportunities which may present themselves.[128]

Just as it is in everyday life—in subtle interactions, in small conversations—that our commitment to the truth, our commitment to mission, our commitment to authentic dialogue—is to be most frequently lived out, as Pope Francis suggested to the bishops with whom he met in Asia in 2014, so it is in the small exchanges and interactions of everyday life that the temptation of relativism presents itself to us.

Back in Rome, during a weekday Mass at *Domus Sanctae Marthae* over five years later, Francis directed attention to Solomon's apostasy as a warning against "being led astray,"[129] against sliding into sin, as Solomon did. "This also occurs in our lives," Francis warned.[130] "Most of us do not commit great sins but the danger lies in 'letting ourselves slide slowly, because it is an anaesthetized fall.' Without realizing it, things become relativized and we lose our faithfulness to God. How 'often we forget the Lord and begin to deal with other gods such as money, vanity and pride!'"[131] The "slippery slide" of relativism, Pope Francis suggests, "is directed towards worldliness."[132] We are easily swayed by societal breezes, believing that

---

126. Francis, "Bishops of Asia," para. 6.

127. Thanks to Phillip Cary for helping me to identify fundamentalism as relativism's "evil twin."

128. Francis, "Bishops of Asia," para. 6.

129. Francis, "Beware of Sliding," para. 2.

130. Francis, "Beware of Sliding," para. 2.

131. Francis, "Beware of Sliding," para. 2.

132. Francis, "Beware of Sliding," para. 3.

such and such "is alright because 'everyone is doing it.'"[133] But, Francis warns, "as we justify ourselves in this way, we lose our faithfulness to God and embrace modern idols."[134] Francis identifies this fickleness of heart as the "sin of worldliness" by which we lose "the authenticity of the Gospel, the authenticity of the Word of God."[135] Francis identifies the crossroad at which Solomon stood prior to going the way of idolatry as the crossroad before which each of us stands throughout our lives every day, moment by moment: to go down the road of relativism, which is the way of worldliness, or to go the way of gospel truth.

Back in 2013, about a month after the famous Spadaro interview[136] came out, Pope Francis made reference to the shared Catholic and Jewish patrimony in the Decalogue as "our common witness to the truth,"[137] which functions, as Francis puts it (citing Benedict XVI), "as a solid foundation and source of life for our society, which is so disoriented by an extreme pluralism of choice and direction, and marked by a relativism which leads to no longer having sure and solid points of reference."[138] Indeed, for Francis, "ours are times of unbridled relativism which undermines the edifice of faith and strips away the meaning of the very idea of Christian fidelity."[139] We are "confronted by a superficial culture which reveres the possession of material goods and promises happiness through dangerous shortcuts," and we must "not fail to encourage young people to temper the spirit and to form a mature character, capable of strength but also of tenderness."[140] This is a key aspect of what Francis would in 2020 call our "moral pandemic."[141] And against this pandemic of moral relativism, Francis offers an evangelical antidote, which he calls "the greatest joy": "speaking to young people about Jesus, reading the Gospel with them, correlating it with life . . . This is the best path for building a solid future."[142] In today's context, there are many barriers to belief in the truth of the risen Christ—who is the standard of all moral truth and

133. Francis, "Beware of Sliding," para. 3.

134. Francis, "Beware of Sliding," para. 3.

135. Francis, "Beware of Sliding," para. 3.

136. Francis, "Big Heart Open."

137. Francis, "Jewish Community of Rome," para. 6.

138. Francis, "Jewish Community of Rome," para. 6.

139. Francis, "Oblates of Saint Joseph," para. 5.

140. Francis, "Oblates of Saint Joseph," para. 6.

141. Francis, "Day of Fraternity," para. 2.

142. Francis, "Oblates of Saint Joseph," para. 6.

the path of fullness of life. Today "it is easier to believe in a ghost than in the living Christ! It is easier to go to a magician who predicts the future, a fortune-teller than to have faith and hope in a victorious Christ, in a Christ who triumphed over death! It is easier to have an idea, an imagination, than docility to this Lord who rose from the dead than to go and learn what he has in store for" us![143]

Against the moral pandemic, Pope Francis offers an evangelical antidote as well as the antidote of authentic pluralism, which "entails an authentic and fruitful dialogue," a dialogue "which spurns relativism and takes the identity of each" party in the conversation "into account," for "what the various religious expressions have in common is . . . the good will to do good to one's neighbour, without denying or diminishing their respective identity."[144] Together, then, the plurality of religious traditions are antithetical to moral relativism. What we must do, Francis insists, in the face of moral relativism, is to face it head-on with authentic dialogue and gospel proclamation, two things which, as we have already seen, were lived out and modeled by JP2 in his commitment to moral truth.

Francis on the Sacramental Life of the Church against Relativism

The theological virtue of hope is the antidote to relativism, for Pope Francis. Among the chief "difficulties that religious life faces today," Francis identifies "the snares of relativism."[145] Precisely "in these circumstances we raise our hope to the Lord, the only One who can aid and save us."[146] In the face of relativism, along with its complex system of accompanying snares and consequences, Francis directs our attention to the promise uttered by God through the prophet Jeremiah: "I will give you a future full of hope."[147] What "the Church needs" is for "us to be prophets, that is, men and women of hope . . . We have to live with humble audacity."[148]

At the opening of his address to the annual youth meeting in Medjugorje in June of 2020, Francis celebrated the reality that what the

---

143. Francis, "Thanksgiving Mass," para. 1.

144. Francis, "General Audience," September 2014, para. 2.

145. Francis, "Spanish Conference of Religious," para. 4.

146. Here Francis cites "To All Consecrated Persons," sec. 3.

147. Francis, "Spanish Conference of Religious," para. 3.

148. Francis, "Spanish Conference of Religious," para. 6.

annual event in Medjugorje offers is "a time rich in prayer, catechesis and fraternity" and an "opportunity to encounter the living Jesus Christ, especially in the Eucharist where he is praised and adored, and in the Sacrament of Reconciliation."[149] In this very way, what is on offer by way of adoration, reconciliation, catechesis, prayer, and fraternity—is "another way of living," which stands in stark contrast with "the one offered by our ephemeral culture, according to which nothing can be definitive and the only thing that matters is enjoying the present moment"[150]—an observation that resonates with the comment of Hesse's character *Steppenwolf* with which we opened this chapter. The bold action of eucharistic adoration; the existential trust entailed in and implied by the Sacrament of Reconciliation; the exquisite and all-encompassing truth claims inherent to all authentically Catholic catechesis, the raw spiritual action of prayer, the encounter with Christ in a Christian experience of brotherhood and sisterhood, and the encounter with Christ posited by each of these thoroughly Catholic ways of being, if you will, presents within the very heart of a relativistic world in a relativistic age a very different outlook from that of relativism, with all the serious truth claims and the underlying claims upon the human heart made by every aspect of such a gathering as the 2020 youth gathering held in Medjugorje. This is the very sort of alternative formation and deeper feeding of our heart's desires that we saw Benedict putting forward as the chaste alternative to being fattened for the slaughter of technocracy's technocratic regime in chapter 3. The option of "uncivilizing developments" is the choice articulated by one of Benedict's favorite novelists, Herman Hesse. As Seewald draws from the lips of Hesse's character in *Steppenwolf,* we have a capacity to "surrender wholly to instinct" and "direct all . . . efforts towards momentary pleasure" and a capacity for martyrdom, a capacity to devote ourselves to "the quest to approach the divine, the ideal of the holy."[151] In light of this contrast between the prevailing culture and the outlook on life cultivated by the annual conference in Medjugorje, Francis remarked that in today's "climate of relativism, in which it is difficult to find true and certain answers, the guiding words of the Festival, 'Come and see' (Jn 1:39), addressed by Jesus to the disciples, are a blessing."[152] Francis proposes to his youthful

149. Francis, "Medjugorje Annual Meeting," para. 1.

150. Francis, "Medjugorje Annual Meeting," para. 1.

151. Seewald, *Benedict XVI*, 1:190–191.

152. Francis, "Medjugorje Annual Meeting," para. 1.

audience that in the context of the pilgrim festivities and devotional practices at Medjugorje, "Jesus directs his gaze" "to you too" "and invites you to go and be with him"[153]—a possibility that explodes the closed box of relativism, which forbids the claim upon all human hearts made by the Master from Galilee, and the claim made upon hearts by his mother, from the banquet hall of Cana to the hilltops of Bosnia. Every aspect of every assertion made by the Medjugorje gathering bursts through every confine of relativism's regime.

Seven years earlier, as World Youth Day 2013 came to an end in Rio de Janeiro, Francis, in addressing young volunteers at the event, reminded them (as he would say in a similar manner two years later in Philadelphia, as we've seen, and to many other audiences of young adults across the globe), "God calls you to make definitive choices . . . God calls each of us to be holy, to live his life . . ."[154] Ever seeking to safeguard the import of the vocation to holy matrimony, Francis explained that while "some are called to holiness through family life in the sacrament of Marriage," we are confronted with the challenge of the fact that "today, there are those who say that marriage is out of fashion."[155]

The regime of relativism is defied on the practical level by way of making definitive commitments. Pope Francis's call to youth to not fear the sacrament of holy matrimony is one of Pope Francis's key strategies in his war on relativism. Relativism's regime forbids the commitments entailed by this sacramental vocation, and it is precisely to these commitments that Francis calls youth the world over. The global Socrates, Francis, "corrupting" the youth of a relativistic global Athens, seeking to lure them to a way of life whose rationale refuses to offer incense, as it were, to our own egos, as the regime of relativism bids us, asks, "Is it" (that is, marriage) "out of fashion?"[156] Francis calls into question the taken-for-granted irrelevance of definitive commitment in marriage, commenting that "in a culture of relativism and the ephemeral, many preach the importance of 'enjoying' the moment. They say that it is not worth making a life-long commitment, making a definitive decision, 'for ever,' because we do not know what tomorrow will bring."[157] Over and against

153. Francis, "Medjugorje Annual Meeting," para. 1.
154. Francis, "Meeting with Volunteers," para. 3.
155. Francis, "Meeting with Volunteers," para. 3.
156. Francis, "Meeting with Volunteers," para. 3.
157. Francis, "Meeting with Volunteers," para. 3.

this caution—which is the careful, calculating caution of the rich man to which Francis alluded a few years later in Philadelphia—Francis exhorted the young volunteers gathered in Rio to "instead . . . be revolutionaries."[158] Francis went on: "I ask you to swim against the tide; yes, I am asking you to rebel against this culture that sees everything as temporary and that ultimately believes you are incapable of responsibility, that believes you are incapable of true love."[159] Pope Francis calls the world's youth to defy the demands of the throwaway culture. Over and against the consensus that young adults are incapable of the kind of love to which the Church calls us, the Pope exhorted the youth in Rio to "have the courage 'to swim against the tide.'"[160]

The social-theological rhetorical achievement of Francis's frequent attacks on relativism is found in the fact that these attacks are accompanied by his singular call to the sons and daughters of the Church to go boldly to the ideological peripheries—that is, to go boldly into those spheres of ideological influence most thoroughly alienated from the Church's faith. The widespread alienation from the Church's life in the context of relativism's regime is for Pope Francis the fundamental poverty of our time—a poverty that this new Francis seeks to address with the spirit of peace and charity that animated the poverello of Assisi. Pope Francis's call is a singular call to an integral ethos of love, responsibility, proclamation, authentic dialogue, and vital catechesis rooted in the sacramental life of the Church. It's a call to an existential confidence in the power of the sacrament of reconciliation, and an allegiance to the most blessed sacrament of the Eucharist, as well as the bold definitive embrace of husband and wife in the sacrament of holy matrimony, the bold definitive commitment required by consecrated life and the life of the ministerial priesthood, as forms of life that enable and require a definitive gift of self. Francis presents each of these as positive alternatives to relativism, and as sure ways of overcoming relativism's stranglehold on our hearts, its stranglehold in our age of technocracy's regime of expendability. They are what make up a culture of life rooted in truth. The war on relativism with which Pope Benedict began his pontificate is the very war that the culture warrior Pope Francis has boldly made his own, in his fight for cosmic chastity over and against the relativistic rationale of technocratic lust.

158. Francis, "Meeting with Volunteers," para. 3.
159. Francis, "Meeting with Volunteers," para. 3.
160. Francis, "Meeting with Volunteers," para. 3.

8

·····

An Ode to Truth

*JP2's and Francis's Shared Insistence on Moral Truth
in the Crucible of Family Life Today*

IN POPE FRANCIS'S ACCOUNT, as the Soviet regime fell, another regime—
the more subtle regime of relativism—rose to power, as we saw in Francis's
address to bishops of a former Soviet country in the previous chapter.
Both communism and relativism oppose an integral notion of truth. For
those of us who live after the fall of Soviet communism, Francis sounds
an earnest warning that the struggle on behalf of truth is not over, for the
power of relativism is subtle and strong. What Francis has to offer is the
song of another regime, whose power arises from the beauty of truth. As
we shall see, JP2 and Francis's shared insistence upon moral truth is an
integral part of their rejection of a throwaway culture, a rejection proper
to the human ecology they both advocate.

Francis on the Task of Pastors and the Lay Faithful in the Public Square

An understandable common response of "the Christian community as a
whole . . . beginning with pastors, and markedly with the Bishop" to the
widespread societal opposition to the Church and her moral teachings
is to feel "questioned," Francis says.[1] As the faith and its representatives
are challenged, accused, and called into question by moral relativism, the

1. "CR," para. 2.

194

bishop, Francis suggests, is called by God "to offer . . . the response of Christ, by dedicating himself wholeheartedly to the service of the Gospel, by sanctifying, teaching and guiding the People of God."[2] In Francis's understanding of the task of the bishop, the shepherd is called to be no pushover when it comes to offering resistance to the dictatorship of relativism, but a bold apostle and evangelist.

As is characteristic of Francis when he diagnoses the social ills of our day, what stands out for him is how moral relativism cripples youth in their *capacity to give themselves to God and neighbor in the form of a definitive vocational commitment.* Robust vocational commitment is forbidden by relativism. When vocational commitment and family life are under threat, "the fabric of the ecclesial community and of civil society itself"[3] indeed stands in need of renewal.

The response that's called for is "to persevere in prayer, to be generous in serving . . . full of zeal in proclaiming the Word."[4] In addition, the bishops are called, Francis says to the Czech bishops, "to foster, especially in the young, the quest for meaning and gift of self to God and neighbour."[5] They are likewise called to "let your attention also focus on the pastoral care of families."[6] For indeed, as Francis reminds his fellow pastors, "the family is a load-bearing element of the life of society and only by working to promote the family can you renew the fabric of the ecclesial community and of civil society itself."[7]

Cultivating vocations of definitive commitment and safeguarding the welfare of the family is key to the development of a culture of moral truth in the midst of relativism's regime. Determined prayer, unstinting service, and faithful evangelism are the things that cultivate the sort of gusto needed to stand in opposition to relativism's denial of moral truth. Given this context, Francis rhetorically asks the bishops, "how can we fail to see, then, the importance of the presence of Catholics in public life, as well as in the sector of communications?"[8] A big part of what Catholics

2. "CR," para. 2.
3. "CR," para. 3.
4. "CR," para. 3.
5. "CR," para. 3.
6. "CR," para. 3.
7. "CR," para. 3.
8. "CR," para. 3.

can bring to the public square by way of involvement in the political arena and communications is *the Church's commitment to moral truth.*

The task of lay Catholics in government and in communications is intimately linked with the task of the bishops "to ensure that one can always hear the voice of truth in the problems of the moment and one can perceive the Church as an ally of men and women, at the service of their dignity."[9] Advocacy for truth is advocacy for humanity. In addressing the Latvian and Estonian bishops, Francis directed attention to the fact that they minister in a context in which the Soviet regime that had explicitly opposed the foundations of human freedom and dignity has been replaced by the shrewder regime of relativism, which tears away at the very same foundations of human freedom and dignity.

"The Lord has chosen you," Francis said to his brother bishops of Latvia and Estonia, "to work in a society that, after being long oppressed by regimes founded on ideologies contrary to human dignity and freedom, is called today to measure itself against other dangerous hidden perils, such as secularism and relativism."[10] These "may render your pastoral action more difficult" Francis said.[11] "I exhort you to continue tirelessly," precisely in this context, "without ever losing confidence in proclaiming the Gospel of Christ, [the] word of salvation for men of all times and all cultures."[12]

As lay Catholics involved in the public square are key collaborators for bishops in the context of widespread relativism in the Czech Republic, so in Latvia and Estonia, "the involvement of the laity is . . . indispensable to the mission of evangelization," Francis recounts, underscoring for them that "your closeness and solicitude" with the lay faithful "will help them to carry forward those responsibilities" of evangelization in society.[13] Francis reminds the bishops that "entrusted to you is the task of watching over and motivating" the faithful "so that . . . they can shape their conscience and deepen their sense of the Church, in particular the knowledge of her Social Doctrine," for it is precisely the lay faithful who are "the living means between what we Pastors preach and the different social environments."[14]

9. "CR," para. 3.

10. "L&E," para. 3.

11. "L&E," para. 3.

12. "L&E," para. 3.

13. "L&E," para. 7.

14. "L&E," para. 7.

Far from encouraging a relativizing form of dialogue, what Francis advocates to the bishops of Estonia and Latvia is a sustained dialogue on the part of the bishops and the lay faithful on the one hand, and with society at large on the other, a dialogue which is at the service of "social peace," a peace which seems far-fetched, given the conflicts surrounding "ethnic and linguistic difference" and the forms of enmity that have arisen between those separated by these distinctions.[15] Authentic dialogue can help to secure social peace in a context in which many are at enmity. This dialogue is to be undertaken, for Francis, with eyes wide open to relativism's hidden dangers and temptations. It's not a task that is to be undertaken in compliance with the regime of relativism—which works for a pseudo-peace by way of bulldozing and flattening the landscape with an imposed ideological homogeny in the name of an alleged toler-ance and an alleged affirmation of diversity.

In this context of proposing a vision of moral truth over and against relativism, Francis reiterates a theme that has run as a red thread through-out Francis's papacy, namely, relativism's efforts to *dismantle the family*.[16] "I . . . wish to share with you the firm will to promote the family, as a gift of God for the fulfillment of man and woman created in his image and as the 'fundamental cell of society,' a place 'where we learn to live with others,'" Francis said to the Estonian and Latvian bishops, drawing from the very themes of *Evangelii gaudium* that we began to explore in this book's second chapter.[17] Here, Francis warns against the widespread relativistic and technocratic distortion of the notion of marriage today, according to which marriage is regarded as "a form of affective gratifica-tion which can be constituted in any way and modified according to each one's sensibility."[18] Something that needs to be of primary concern to the pastors of the flocks of Estonia and Latvia, Francis says, is the unfortu-nate reality that this "reductive concept" of marriage as mere affective gratification constructed and modified according to my own particular

15. "L&E," para. 8.

16. Francis would again bring to the fore this prominent danger of relativism—precisely as a foremost danger of relativism—at the Philadelphia World Meeting of Families in September of the same year. He had already brought it to the fore in *EG* in the first autumn of his papacy (November 2013).

17. "L&E," para. 9.

18. "L&E," para. 9.

sensibilities "also influences the mentality of Christians, facilitating the recourse to divorce or *de facto* separation."[19]

Francis and JP2 against the Technocratic-Relativistic Distortion of Marriage and for an Integral Catechesis

As we discussed in chapter 2, in a context in which marriage is perceived as something merely at the service of the gratification of my desires and which can be constituted and modified according to my arbitrarily determined sensibilities and preferences—which is to say, in a cultural context in which marriage is viewed utterly according to the terms set by relativism and technocratically empowered consumerism—if my marriage or some other form of sexual partnership falls short of gratifying my expectations, I can toss it out. This is where we see the integral link between what Francis calls the throwaway culture on the one hand and relativism on the other. The marriage preparation for which pastors, families, and Church communities are responsible, then, has to bolster an authentically Christian vision of marriage over and against the technocratic and relativized distortion of it.

In the face of feeling questioned and thus threatened by the surrounding culture, Francis suggests that he and his fellow pastors should be *questioning themselves*: "We Pastors are called to question ourselves on the marriage preparation of engaged young people and also on how to assist all those who experience these situations, so that children do not become the first victims."[20] Catholic couples have fallen prey to the popular distortions of marriage by way of the alternative catechesis offered by relativism and technocracy, and Christian communities, with their pastors, need to prepare Catholic couples to embrace marriage according to the very different Christian vision of it. If we fail to meet the challenge of preparing Christian unions by way of a robustly countercultural catechesis in marriage, we are asking—in a manner of speaking—for uncatechized married Catholics to "feel excluded from God's mercy and the solicitude of the Church."[21] In falling short of living according to the Church's moral teaching on marriage without having been equipped

19. "L&E," para. 9.
20. "L&E," para. 9.
21. "L&E," para. 9.

to understand this teaching according to an integral Catholic outlook, many Catholic couples, Francis perceives, live according to a vision of relativism and technocracy that has formed them, even as they strive to live as Catholics. They're trying to simultaneously play two games with two mutually opposed sets of rules. They continue to gaze upon the world through the lens of relativism and technocracy, and so, when representatives of the Church voice a "no" to them (for example, by way of barring access to the Eucharist, due to the use of contraception, or due to the existence of a previous sacramental bond with a partner other than the current partner), it is, from their perspective, an incomprehensible "no." To gaze upon the Church, as a member of it, but with the lens of technocracy and relativism as opposed to the lens of an integral sexual outlook, is to gaze upon a Church that by all appearances makes arbitrary demands—what may seem to be archaic, unmerciful, inflexible, exclusionary demands, even misogynistic demands, what may seem to be demands that disempower women and that deny women's reproductive "rights," for example, or to stifle an alleged liberty that is in fact a false, consumeristic, throwaway mentality. To look upon the Church through the lenses of a technocratic and relativistic society is to look upon an incomprehensible universe. Catholic social teaching can only be comprehended by way of a catechesis as thorough as the cultural "catechesis" that the regime of relativism and technocracy offers to society's members today. That we have not been able to transmit on a wide-scale societal level a robust alternative is on *us*, Francis suggests to his fellow bishops, and through them, to their cooperators—priests, consecrated, and the committed core lay faithful at large. We need to offer an alternative catechesis—so that wayward pilgrims who otherwise have not found the resources of Catholic formation to know any better can be "helped in their journey of faith and" in "the Christian education of the children."[22]

JP2 offers a direct alternative to today's technocratic "catechesis." That is to say, JP2 offers an alternative to society's deformation of the human heart. For JP2, human agency is not meant to be handed over to the power of technological mechanisms.[23] JP2 seeks to foster the integrity of human agency, allowing it to remain intact, strengthening human hearts to govern over their own actions as responsible subjects, using technology in a humane manner, as intentional stewards of their own

22. "L&E," para. 9.

23. The ways in which the technology of contraception or pornography determines our behavior and our relationships is a prime example of this.

actions. JP2's alternative catechesis consists of responding to Christ's call upon every "man, male and female" to be a "responsible subject of his own action," to be "a subject who decides his own actions in the light of the integral truth about himself, inasmuch as it is the original or fundamental truth of authentically human experiences."[24] Christ leads us to seek this truth, JP2 suggests, in a gaze upon the "beginning."

As "various cultural tendencies" that are "based on . . . partial truths" in the context of our own day "insert themselves," by way of a falsifying catechesis, proposing to us today certain patterns of behavior and "ways of *relating to 'man*.'"[25] What happens, then, in Paul VI's and JP2's identification of what Francis later came to call technocracy, is that "man then becomes more an object of certain technologies than the responsible subject of his own action."[26] This is quintessential technocracy. It is the objectification of humanity under technology's rule, as opposed to humanity's responsible use of technology for the authentic benefit of humanity. What is needed in the face of technocracy's rule, which is part of the package of ideological and practical relativism alike, is a catechesis in an all-encompassing chastity, in an all-encompassing reverential love for what it is that God has handed to humanity at large and to every human person. What is needed is a formation in a reverential love for what God has placed before our gaze, and with which he seeks to gladden our hearts—the gift of life, the gift of our bodies, of our sexuality, of our neighbors, whole and entire.

Because Catholic communities of our era have major work to do in the area of forming the hearts of the Church's members, JP2 sets out in VS to treat "'more fully and more deeply the issues regarding the very foundations of moral theology,' foundations which are being undermined by certain present day tendencies."[27] JP2 insists that for the sake of humanity, the Church must maintain its commitment to moral truth, precisely at the service of humanity, for the sake of human flourishing, and not in opposition to humanity. It is a denial of humanity to deny moral truth—and the human heart testifies to the existence of such truth.

As we saw in chapter 1, for JP2, "in the depths of his heart"— that is, "man's" heart, i.e., in the depths of the heart of every man and

---

24. *TOB*, 4.2.80.

25. *TOB*, 4.2.80.

26. *TOB*, 4.2.80.

27. *VS*, sec. 5, citing JP2, *Spiritus Domini*.

woman—"there always remains a yearning for absolute truth and a thirst to attain full knowledge of it."[28] Just as "this is eloquently proved by man's tireless search for knowledge in all fields," it is likewise "proved even more by his search for the meaning of life"[29]—which is precisely where questions of moral truth begin to arise with great urgency—for all of humanity in every age, standing alongside the rich young man (where JP2 places us near the beginning of VS),[30] and standing alongside the Pharisees in their discussion with Jesus concerning the indissolubility of marriage (where JP2 places us in significant portions of his catechesis on a theology of the human body).

It is precisely here that Francis is greatly suspect by many—suspect for diverging radically from JP2's insistence on moral truth. For many, Francis seems to be calling into question, even directly denying, the indissolubility of marriage. Francis's advocacy for inculturation is widely interpreted in terms of the very dichotomy between faith on the one hand and morality on the other—a dichotomy that JP2 vehemently rejects. While JP2 refuses any dichotomization between faith on the one hand and morality on the other, and rejects any relegation of the latter to the subjective realm, Francis is accused of promoting such a dichotomy and such a subjectification of morality.[31]

The place where Francis is most thoroughly suspect for doing this is in *AL*, where, over and against JP2's insistence upon moral truth, Francis relegates the question of adultery to the subjective realm—or at least, so he has been charged. It is to this charge and to the most hotly debated sections of *AL* to which we must now direct our attention.

In *AL*, I propose, Francis clearly insists upon the moral truth concerning marriage, and expresses a deep-seated confidence in the mercy of God to work through the Church to call those who are in "forms of union" that "radically contradict"[32] the inherent meaning of Christian marriage to adhere to the call and demands of the gospel. Why, then, are some of the faithful concerned that Francis might be calling into question—or even directly opposing—moral truth as it pertains to marriage?

28. *VS*, sec. 1.

29. *VS*, sec. 1.

30. *VS*, sec. 6.

31. *AL*, para. 302, for instance, is taken by some to be such a challenge to moral truth. For the *dubia* themselves and an explanation of the concerns expressed by them, see Pentin, "Full Text," esp. *dubia* nos. 2–5.

32. *AL*, sec. 292.

The question of providing pastoral care to those who are in unions that fall short of the true meaning of marriage—that fall short of what Francis calls the gospel ideal of marriage—is where Francis gets people worried that he's buying into relativism and technocracy. This is where Matthew Schmitz of *Compact* (formerly of *First Things*) began charging Francis with rendering obeisance to the regime of technocracy, and allegiance to the throwaway culture.[33] But does he?

Readings and Misreadings of *AL*

According to the summary of *AL* offered by the Bishops of the Pastoral Region of Buenos Aires and published by Pope Francis as an official Act of the Apostolic See as the definitive magisterial interpretation of the exhortation, the exhortation at its heart "calls us, above all, to encourage the growth of love between spouses and to motivate young people to opt for marriage and a family."[34] In their letter to Francis, the Buenos Aires bishops spell out an explication of the meaning of some of the most hotly debated portions of *AL*.

What, then, is Francis up to in the hotly debated portions of *AL*? As JP2 recognizes in *FC*, "there are those who have entered into a second union for the sake of the children's upbringing, and who are sometimes subjectively certain in conscience that their previous and irreparably destroyed marriage had never been valid."[35] This recognition corresponds to Francis's recognition that "conscience can do more than recognize that a given situation does not correspond objectively to the overall demands of the Gospel," and corresponds to his recognition that conscience "can also recognize with sincerity and honesty what for now is the most generous response which can be given to God and come to see with a certain moral security that it is what God himself is asking amid the concrete complexity of one's limits, while yet not fully the objective ideal."[36] Francis here places side by side two different things of which the conscience

33. "A pope who speaks with singular eloquence of our need to resist the technocratic logic of the 'throwaway culture' seems bent on leading his Church to surrender to it. What is more typical of the throwaway culture than the easy accommodation of divorce and remarriage?" (Schmitz, "How I Changed My Mind," para. 12). Schmitz's relationship with Francis is worth tracking.

34. Bishops of Buenos Aires, "Directive," para. 1.

35. *FC*, sec. 84.

36. *AL*, sec. 303.

is capable. The first is the conscience's capacity to perceive when "a given situation does not correspond objectively to the overall demands of the Gospel."[37] This capacity of the conscience to perceive our situation in direct relation to the demands of the gospel is key to equipping us to respond to the demands of the gospel. What of the second task of the conscience to which Francis here makes reference—that of recognizing "with sincerity and honesty what for now is the most generous response which can be given to God" and the accompanying perception of "what God himself is asking" in the midst of a situation that falls short of "the objective ideal"?[38] What Francis refers to here in this context as "the objective ideal" is the "objective ideal" of marriage and child-rearing. This objective ideal consists of a couple raising children within the context of a sacramental union. But there are plenty of instances of someone raising children with a partner other than the partner with whom they had previously been married in the Church—at least, a previous sacramental union, valid or invalid, is on the books. As both JP2 and Francis recognize, someone can be certain in conscience that the previous marriage was not valid, though an annulment has as of yet not been granted. While not corresponding to the ideal of marriage and family life, when someone finds that their decisions have led them into this situation, they might have grounds upon which to make the discernment to live *as a sibling* with a new partner even prior to an annulment of the previous bond, for the sake of the upbringing of the children. Again, this falls short of what Francis refers to as the "objective ideal" of marriage, but it's not a sin. Indeed, in the rationale of both JP2 and Francis, this may be precisely what justice and charity demand in the given situation. The welfare of the children may well suggest a collaborative raising of the children with the new partner.

The objective ideal consists of two members bound in a legitimate marriage, consummated by sexual intercourse, together raising the children of their union, and remaining in their union until death. But what is to be done when clarity of conscience arises for someone in the midst of an irregular situation—the situation of already having children to raise, and of beginning to do so with someone with whom the said individual is not in a legitimate union, and with whom this individual cannot—at least as of yet—enter into a legitimate union, as the official process of

37. *AL*, sec. 303.
38. *AL*, sec. 303.

annulment has not yet been completed? Francis (with the bishops of Buenos Aires) suggests precisely JP2's proposed line of action: when the light of conscience makes it clear that the welfare of the children of the more recent partnership requires that the couple raise the children together in a singular household, the man and the woman of this partnership are to live together as brother and sister, that is to say, with the firm resolve to abstain from sexual intercourse.[39] As already established, this scenario falls short of the ideal.[40] But falling short of the ideal, *the circumstances can be faced with a newfound resolve, such that the demands of justice and charity in response to the circumstances can be fully pursued.* Falling short of the ideal here refers to the fact that the family household is marked in a particular way by the breaking of a previous bond. Previous sins on the part of at least one of the adults in the new partnership may have led to the breaking of the previous union, or perhaps the previous union's breakup was due more exclusively to the previous spouse. Regardless, as Francis recognizes, the light of conscience in such a context can indeed make it clear (with what Francis calls "a certain moral security")[41] that raising the children with a new partner with whom that parent lives as a sibling "is what God himself is asking amid the concrete complexity of one's limits, while yet not fully the objective ideal."[42] Something closer to the objective ideal can indeed be achieved if an annulment of the previous union is granted, and the couple can live as husband and wife in the bond of holy matrimony. Whether or not this is the appropriate course of action—that is, to pursue an annulment and to enter into a new union by way of holy matrimony—is to be determined in view of a whole array of variables. (It is precisely in view of enabling individuals in such circumstances to navigate their family situations according to the demands of moral truth, the demands of justice, the demands of charity, that this portion of *AL* is written.) Still, even if an annulment is granted, the new union, which would likely bear the fruit of more children, still falls short of the ideal of lifelong fidelity to a singular spouse.[43]

39. Bishops of Buenos Aires, "Directive," no. 5.

40. *AL*, sec. 298.

41. *AL*, sec. 303.

42. *AL*, sec. 303.

43. "The ideal of marriage" according to Francis is "marked by a commitment to exclusivity and stability" (*AL*, sec. 34). Already, in the above case, exclusivity and stability had been shattered, and social consequences of the previous shattering still have to be faced.

What concerns many of the core faithful about Francis's language of something *not corresponding to the objective ideal*, though being the *most generous response God is asking for now*, is that this has been popularly misread as meaning that in some cases, living in adultery may be the most generous response one can give for now, and that it is even what God is asking, and that if this is what God is asking, then such a couple can receive the blessed sacrament.[44] But nowhere does Francis permit such a course of action. Such a course of action contradicts the entire framework of Francis's moral message. Schmitz concludes that Francis has bought into technocracy and the throwaway culture in suggesting that you can abandon your spouse and children without abandoning the altar of Christ.[45] But such a reading ignores Francis's own insistence upon applying a hermeneutic of continuity with JP2's teaching.

With the interpretation of *AL* as interpreted by the Buenos Aires bishops, JP2's insistence that a lesser degree of culpability not be used to justify giving absolution and communion to those who have not resolved to live as brother and sister is still on the books. For JP2's insistence on this matter to remain on the books, as Francis insists it does, what the Argentine bishops identify as the place for admission to the sacraments of individuals in second unions is those situations of couples, "where one party is not a Christian or is not practicing the faith—where abstaining from conjugal relations is 'not feasible.'"[46] Commenting upon this, Raymond de Souza explains that

> The situation foreseen here is apparently that of one party desiring such abstinence, but the other refusing and threatening dire consequences in the absence of conjugal life. The first party then agrees to sexual relations against his or her will, for example, to preserve the welfare of the children.
>
> In such cases, the practicing Catholic party may not be guilty of serious sin and could therefore, in some cases, be admitted to the sacraments of reconciliation and the Eucharist. This case, it should be noted, could be treated in such a manner even before *Amoris Laetitia*, according to application of the standard principles of moral theology and confessional practice,

---

44. See Schindler, "Conscience, Moral Theology, Modernity," 334–85.

45. Schmitz, "How I Changed," para. 11.

46. De Souza, "What Argentina's Guidelines Mean," para. 15.

analogous to the determination of the moral culpability of contraception when the spouses do not agree.[47]

Point five of the magisterial Buenos Aires guidelines states that *AL*
"offers the possibility of having access to the Sacrament of Reconciliation
if the partners fail in this purpose" (their purpose of living as brother and
sister, in chaste celibacy), identifying *AL*'s "footnote 364, recalling the
teaching that Saint John Paul II sent to Cardinal W. Baum,"[48] and further
equips pastors to address circumstances according to JP2's precedent.

To help get our heads around the sort of situation the Argentine
bishops are thinking of in directive five, consider, for example, the case
of a couple in which at least one of the partners was on the books as
"married" in the Church and that "marriage" has not yet been declared
null, and this new couple is firmly committed to living as brother and
sister until the previous union is declared null. At one time or another,
however, they fail in their honest resolve to live chastely, and they subse-
quently truly repent with the firm resolve to live chastely as brother and
sister from thence onward. In this case and in similar cases, the pastors to
whom such parties come as penitents have an important responsibility to
discern whether to grant absolution. Various factors mitigating culpability and impunity would heighten the possibility of rightly granting absolution—not to a couple that simply rejects the commandment of God, but
to a couple authentically repentant of having, in their actions, rejected
the commandment of God, and are newly resolved to live in accordance
with it. Similar mitigating factors apply to individuals addicted to pornography use, masturbation, or who have attempted suicide for reasons
of psychological duress, as well as to individuals regularly seduced by way
of falling victim to another's manipulative abuse of power. JP2's insistence
that culpability *not be used to justify giving absolution and communion*
to those who have not resolved to live as brother and sister is still on
the books. For JP2's insistence on this matter to remain on the books,
as Francis insists that all previous teaching on the matter does, what
the Argentine bishops identify as the possible place for absolution to be
granted to those who have failed in their resolution to live as brother and
sister—what Francis identifies as the "generous response" which God is
asking of the pair *cannot* refer to committing adultery or fornication. The
generous response called for in such an instance is that of *resolving to live*

47. De Souza, "What Argentina's Guidelines Mean," paras. 15–16.
48. Bishops of Buenos Aires, "Directive," no. 5.

as brother and sister while living together as a family for the good of the children.

The pair in this situation is in a place of heightened vulnerability to fall back into the sin that they have resolved to not fall back into, given the fact that they live under the same roof. This vulnerability, depending on the situation, may be a reason to discern not to live under the same roof; or, the good of the children may require placing oneself in this vulnerable context, though only justifiably so if the pair enters into this vulnerable situation with the firm resolve not to fall into the sin of adultery (or fornication, depending on the particularities of the situation). While this situation does not correspond to the ideal of marriage and family, there may be no other avenue open to the pair for the time being. This indeed may be the most generous response which the Lord is asking of the pair for the time being. This may be precisely what is demanded— according to the positive and negative precepts of the moral law—by justice and charity in such a case.

De Souza proposes that *AL*'s reference to the conscience's capacity to recognize "what for now is the most generous response which can be given to God" "appears to conflict with the teaching of . . . *VS*, which says that an intrinsically sinful act, if understood to be so, can never be done, much less be what God himself is asking."[49] But the generous response called for by Francis is not the mortal sin of adultery or fornication, as though we could ever identify an intrinsically evil act as a generous response. No unjust act, Francis has made clear, can ever be regarded as a generous response that God is asking of someone. No, if Francis is taken for his word that he advocates no change in previous teaching, then the generous response to which he refers coincides with JP2's recognition that even if a marriage bond is on the books as existing with a previous partner, given the circumstances, the most generous response to God's grace "for now" could perhaps be found in raising children with a partner other than one's spouse, and to do so with the firm resolve of living as brother and sister.

What Francis entertains seriously by way of *AL* that previous magisterial documents did not as directly entertain is the quite likely possibility of falling short of what one has resolved to do—to live chastely as brother and sister. Previous magisterial documents did not identify, then, the possible avenues to be discerned in such a case (though JP2 entertained

49. De Souza, "Pope's Amoris Laetitia," para. 22.

this in the above cited letter to Baum) when the fallen though penitent pair seriously returns to their shared resolve to live chastely. The question seriously entertained in *AL* is this: is it ever appropriate for a shepherd of souls to grant absolution and readmission to the eucharistic table in such a case? The answer that *AL* gives is that it may be appropriate, depending on the circumstances, leaving it to the pastor to discern the peculiarities of the circumstances, in close conversation with the penitent pair. Communion may perhaps be granted in a discrete context, so as not to cause scandal to those who may be aware of the previous union, as JP2 had previously directed. However, as the Argentine bishops make clear, access to the sacraments is not simply a guarantee or a right to be demanded. Access to absolution and to receiving the Eucharist is to be *discerned* in a manner that honors the peculiarities of the context, and honors the demands of moral truth as they apply in the particular circumstance.

Let's turn now to *AL*'s famously debated citation of Thomas Aquinas's teaching that general norms are not applicable in all situations. It is well known that these "general norms" refer to positive moral precepts, not negative moral precepts.[50] On a widespread level, it has been insisted that Francis is applying this quote to the negative precept against adultery. It has been supposed, then, that Francis has thus completely misused a Thomist principle, taking it out of context and misapplying it. However, this Thomist principle that the application of positive moral precepts depend upon the particularities of a given circumstance is indeed applicable to the situations to which Francis suggests it be applied, i.e., the situation of a parent whose previous relationship is as of yet still on the books as a marriage, and who has children to raise, and is discerning whether to raise them with a subsequent parenting collaborator of the opposite sex. The question in such a situation, as in all situations of social justice, is *what good is due to whom, and in what manner can the good be rendered to those to whom it is due by those who owe the good in the given circumstances?* General positive moral precepts must be unstintingly honored, and the manner of their application is going to vary from situation to situation, as the Thomist text cited by Francis in *AL* suggests. In the situation of irregular relationships, a key question is *what good is due to the children,* and the positive action to be taken concerns *how to live out the positive moral precepts of the moral law.* The positive precepts of the moral law in such a case may best be pursued by way of living

---

50. *AL*, sec. 304, citing Aquinas, *Summa Theologiae*, I-II.9.4.

under the same roof with a new parenting collaborator, though only with a commitment to living as brother and sister. Or it may be best *not* to live under the same roof. The parties involved stand in need of discerning how to respond to the positive precepts of justice for the children for whom they are responsible. The parties involved must discern how to respond to the positive precept to render the good due to those to whom it is due, particularly to the children and to the previous partner(s). What is due to the previous partner? What is due to the new potential parenting collaborator? What is due to the children involved? Are there children from this more recent union (prior to having resolved to live as brother or sister, or who were conceived in a context in which the couple failed in its resolve to live as brother and sister)? Are there children of a previous union? What is due to all the children involved? What is due to the wider community in which the family is situated? The pastor guiding the couple has to discern with those coming to him for pastoral care the appropriate manner in which to respond to a number of positive moral precepts, taking many questions of justice and charity into consideration, with which the couple must wrestle as well. It's a question of *how to respond to the positive moral precepts of justice*; it's not a question of whether to reject the law of God. Francis's appeal to the Thomist principle is not a proposal that a prohibition against adultery and fornication be loosened, or that such a prohibition is applicable only in some circumstances.

A Critical Conscience for Family Culture and Family Humanism: Francis and JP2 *for* the Moral Truth of Marriage and *against* the Dictatorship of Consumerism

In chapter 8 of *AL*, Francis describes Christian marriage as "a reflection of the union between Christ and his Church."[51] Precisely as such, Christian marriage is the "union between a man and a woman who give themselves to each other in a free, faithful and exclusive love, who belong to each other until death, are open to the transmission of life, and are consecrated by the sacrament, which grants them the grace to become a domestic church and a leaven of new life for society." Here, Francis reiterates perennial themes concerning a Christian view of marriage, and reiterates central themes of the legacy of Paul VI (in *HV*) and JP2.

51. *AL*, sec. 292.

Consistent with his own opposition to relativism, technocracy, and a throwaway culture, Francis, early in chapter 8 of *AL*, laments that "many young people today distrust marriage and live together, putting off indefinitely the commitment of marriage, while yet others break a commitment already made and immediately assume a new one."[52] And this is where Francis really begins to face the question of *How are pastors to care for lost sheep in such circumstances?* Francis identifies as his priority the fostering of "evangelization and human and spiritual growth"[53] for those who live in a manner that contradicts the moral truth concerning marriage. Francis's recognizes that many Catholics who opt for a mere "civil marriage" or a "simple cohabitation" often do so "not motivated by . . . resistance to a sacramental union" but rather do so under the influence of the culture which has formed them—a culture of relativism, technocracy, and disposability. The anxiety of Francis's heart throughout chapter 8 of *AL* is *how to lead today's lost sheep to the pastures of the truth of the meaning of marriage.* It was likewise a fundamental concern that animated JP2 as he penned the Apostolic Exhortation *FC* in 1981. In that text, JP2, in a spirit akin to that of Francis, recognizes that "the family in the modern world . . . has been beset by the many profound and rapid changes that have affected society and culture."[54] As JP2 puts it, while "many families are living this situation in fidelity to those values that constitute the foundation of the institution of the family," there are many others that "have become uncertain and bewildered over their role or even doubtful and almost unaware of the ultimate meaning and truth of conjugal and family life."[55] As Francis would do later in *AL*, so JP2, in *FC*, advocates "the discernment effected by the Church" which results, on the Church's part, in "the offering of an orientation in order that the entire truth and the full dignity of marriage and the family may be preserved and realized."[56]

Like Francis after him, JP2 celebrates positive developments and areas of heightened awareness on a popular level concerning family life:

> On the one hand, in fact, there is a more lively awareness of personal freedom and greater attention to the quality of interpersonal relationships in marriage, to promoting the dignity of

52. *AL*, sec. 293.
53. *AL*, sec. 293.
54. *FC*, sec. 1.
55. *FC*, sec. 1.
56. *FC*, sec. 5.

women, to responsible procreation, to the education of children. There is also an awareness of the need for the development of interfamily relationships, for reciprocal spiritual and material assistance, the rediscovery of the ecclesial mission proper to the family and its responsibility for the building of a more just society.[57]

Also like Francis, JP2 identifies the distortions of family to which we are vulnerable in society today:

Signs are not lacking of a disturbing degradation of some fundamental values: a mistaken theoretical and practical concept of the independence of the spouses in relation to each other; serious misconceptions regarding the relationship of authority between parents and children; the concrete difficulties that the family itself experiences in the transmission of values; the growing number of divorces; the scourge of abortion; the ever more frequent recourse to sterilization; the appearance of a contraceptive mentality.[58]

As Francis has done, so JP2 identifies in his discussion of threats to marriage and family today *a false notion of freedom* as the root of these distortions of family life today. According to these false notions, freedom is "conceived not as a capacity for realizing the truth of God's plan for marriage and the family, but as an autonomous power of self-affirmation, often against others, for one's own selfish well-being."[59] Authentic freedom, for JP2, is found in "realizing the truth of God's plan," and not in "an autonomous power of self-affirmation . . . for one's own selfish well-being."[60]

What JP2 and Francis each have in common, here, is a supreme allegiance to the moral truth concerning marriage and the pastoral challenge of a global flock largely alienated from this truth and radically unequipped to perceive this truth as the good news that it is. Like Francis after him, JP2 identifies the "consumer mentality" as a fundamental source of destruction for the family in wealthy countries.[61] As JP2 observes, "In the countries of the so-called Third World, families often lack both the

57. *FC*, sec. 6.
58. *FC*, sec. 6.
59. *FC*, sec. 6.
60. *FC*, sec. 6.
61. *FC*, sec. 6.

means necessary for survival, such as food, work, housing and medicine, and the most elementary freedoms," whereas "in the richer countries . . . excessive prosperity and the consumer mentality, paradoxically joined to a certain anguish and uncertainty about the future, deprive married couples of the generosity and courage needed for raising up new human life: thus life is often perceived not as a blessing."[62] New life is, sadly, perceived in this context "as a danger from which to defend oneself."[63]

In a turn of phrase, then, appropriate to Catholic social teaching's perennial capacity to both offer prophetically harsh criticism concerning the inhumane aspects of anti-development in society and signs of alliance with authentic human development, JP2 says that "the historical situation in which the family lives therefore appears as an interplay of light and darkness."[64] Indeed, the Church is aware that "history is not simply a fixed progression towards what is better, but rather an event of freedom, and even a struggle between freedoms that are in mutual conflict, that is, according to the well-known expression of St. Augustine, a conflict between two loves."[65] These two loves, as summarized by Augustine and appropriated by JP2, include "the love of God to the point of disregarding self, and the love of self to the point of disregarding God."[66] What is in order in this context, then, is the Church's catechesis offered as an alternative to the powerful educational program forming the hearts of today's youth according to the regime of relativism. For as JP2 puts it, "only an education for love rooted in faith can lead to the capacity of interpreting 'the signs of the times,'" that "are the historical expression of this twofold love."[67]

JP2, like Francis after him, points out the reality that those within the Church are as prone to be affected by the shadows of relativism as are those who explicitly define themselves as independent of the Church. And as Francis does—particularly in *Evangelii gaudium*—JP2 identifies the corporate media as a particularly powerful force in "catechizing" the hearts of society's members according to relativism's regime. As JP2 recounts, "Living in such a world, under the pressures coming above all

62. *FC*, sec. 6.
63. *FC*, sec. 6.
64. *FC*, sec. 6.
65. *FC*, sec. 6.
66. *FC*, sec. 6.
67. *FC*, sec. 6.

from the mass media, the faithful do not always remain immune from the obscuring of certain fundamental values."[68] While what the Church's teaching has on offer, according to JP2, is a "critical conscience of family culture" and a vision for "an authentic family humanism," the faithful do not always "set themselves up as the critical conscience of family culture and as active agents in the building of an authentic family humanism" according to an integral Catholic social vision.[69]

JP2 goes on to recount at this point the "troubling signs" of the existence of the faithful under the shadow of relativism, which through the power of the media especially, disempowers the faithful in their role as spokespersons for an integral humanism and a social conscience.[70] These troubling signs, JP2 says, following the 1980 Synod on the Family, primarily include "the spread of divorce and of recourse to a new union even on the part of the faithful," as a part of what JP2 calls a "consumer mentality."[71] Indeed, the problem that JP2 was up against, and which Francis is now up against, is that this consumer culture has more effectively catechized the hearts of the faithful than has the Church's parishes, schools, communities, ministries, etc. Alongside the spread of divorce followed by the assumption of a new union, among the "troubling signs" of the shadow of relativism's dictatorship over the faithful is the widespread acceptance on the part of Catholics "of purely civil marriage in contradiction to the vocation of the baptized to 'be married in the Lord.'"[72] Another troubling sign identified by JP2 is the widespread "celebration of the marriage sacrament without living faith, but for other motives," and "the rejection of the moral norms that guide and promote the human and Christian exercise of sexuality in marriage."[73]

As JP2 describes sexual chastity in *FC* as "by no means" signifying a "rejection of human sexuality or lack of esteem for it," but rather signifying the "spiritual energy capable of defending love from the perils of selfishness and aggressiveness, and able to advance it towards its full realization,"[74] so the entirety of the theologically rooted social teaching of JP2 and Francis, undergirded by a notion of moral truth upon which they

68. *FC*, sec. 6.
69. *FC*, sec. 6.
70. *FC*, sec. 6.
71. *FC*, sec. 6, 30.
72. *FC*, sec. 6.
73. *FC*, sec. 6.
74. *FC*, sec. 6.

insist, is a teaching that calls for a "spiritual energy capable of defending love from the perils of selfishness and aggressiveness, and able to advance it towards its full realization."[75]

The insistence upon moral truth, proper to the teaching of JP2 and Francis, is aimed precisely at fostering this "spiritual energy capable of defending love from the perils of selfishness and aggressiveness, and able to advance it towards its full realization."[76] Defending love from the perils of selfishness and aggressiveness entails upholding a whole constellation of moral truths, which propose to us generosity over and against selfishness, and authentic gentleness and tenderness over and against aggression and exploitation.[77]

JP2 and Francis against Avoidance, Fashionability, and Resignation: The Weakening of the Family and Threats to Moral Progress

Francis, in his insistence upon moral truth, insists, as we've seen in chapter 2, that "as Christians, we can hardly stop advocating marriage simply to avoid countering contemporary sensibilities, or out of a desire to be fashionable or a sense of helplessness in the face of human and moral failings."[78] Francis suggests that "What we need"—and he's speaking particularly to the concern that it is becoming less common to opt for a definitive marital commitment—"is a more responsible and generous effort to present the reasons and motivations for choosing marriage and the family, and in this way to help men and women better to respond to the grace that God offers them."[79] This is the driving concern of *AL*.

What's up for discussion, for Pope Francis, is not whether to insist upon moral truth—he repeatedly makes it explicitly clear that moral truth is what he's after—but *how* to transmit that truth in a manner in which its full splendor can shine forth before the eyes of the men and women who are today most alienated from that truth due to a false catechesis under the singular regime of relativism and technocracy. The question, for Francis, is never *whether* to pass on the Church's moral teaching or

75. *FC*, sec. 33.

76. *FC*, sec. 33.

77. See Doherty, *Poustinia*, 67.

78. *AL*, sec. 34.

79. *AL*, sec. 34.

whether to insist upon the import of moral truth, but *how* to do this. Transmitting moral truth is key to the task Francis has embraced in his pontificate. That is why he warns against the delusional nature of the secularist line of thought which suggests that "the weakening of the family as that natural society founded on marriage will prove beneficial to society as a whole."[80] It is in view of his commitment to transmitting moral truth that we can make sense of Francis's insistence that the weakening of the family "poses a threat to the mature growth of individuals, the cultivation of community values and the moral progress of cities and countries."[81]

The fundamental problem that Francis perceives in society today, in our loss of moral truth, is the widespread "failure to realize that only the exclusive and indissoluble union between a man and a woman has a plenary role to play in society as a stable commitment that bears fruit in new life."[82] While there is indeed a "great variety of family situations that can offer a certain stability . . . de facto or same-sex unions, for example, may not simply be equated with marriage."[83] For Francis, these alternative fabricated simulations of family simply don't cut it as constituting society's foundation. Francis likewise insists—on behalf of the good of children and on behalf of the good of society which depends upon the family unit as its fundamental building block—that "no union that is temporary or closed to the transmission of life can ensure the future of society."[84]

Francis, feeling the bite of the coldness of a secularized, technocratized, and relativized culture, thus cries out in the streets of a global Athens, prepared to drink the hemlock for having steered the youth of Athens to break the "pieties" of the city gods of autonomy and so-called freedom. And this global Socrates, turning to the core faithful, asks, "Nowadays, who is making an effort to strengthen marriages, to help married couples overcome their problems, to assist them in the work of raising children and, in general, to encourage the stability of the marriage bond?"[85] Not enough of us, this new Socratic pontiff suggests.

80. *AL*, sec. 34.
81. *AL*, sec. 34.
82. *AL*, sec. 34.
83. *AL*, sec. 34.
84. *AL*, sec. 34.
85. *AL*, sec. 34.

9

. . . . .

A Rehabilitation of Marriage and Family

The Papal Trio on the Summit of Creation

IN HIS 2016 ADDRESS to the John Paul II Institute in Rome, commemorating the institute's thirty-fifth anniversary, Pope Francis drew attention to JP2's "wise discernment of the signs of the times," which "has vigorously restored to the attention of the Church, and of human society itself, the depth and delicacy of the bonds that are generated from the conjugal covenant[1] of man and woman."[2] Francis perceives the ways peculiar to "today's context"—economic circumstances included—in which "marital and family ties are in many ways being put to the test."[3] In addition to economic conditions, "the emergence of a culture that exalts narcissistic individualism, a conception of freedom detached from responsibility for the other, the growth of indifference towards the common good, the imposition of ideologies that directly attack the family project, as well as the growth of poverty"[4]—which "threatens the future of so many

---

1. The Italian word "*alleanza*" is translated as both "covenant" and "alliance." Cary has pointed out that the word translated as "helper" or "helpmate" (*ezer*) in Genesis 2:18 (as the NRSV renders it, "Then the LORD God said, 'It is not good that the man should be alone; I will make a helper as his partner'"), in addition to its usage here, is used in the Hebrew Scriptures only in reference to a military ally or to God himself. This gives a sense of what kind of a mighty helper woman is to man, and what kind of alliance or covenant God has placed at the summit of creation. (Cary, "It Was Very Good," paras. 8–9.)

2. Francis, "JP2 Institute," sec. 1.

3. Francis, "JP2 Institute," sec. 2.

4. Francis, "JP2 Institute," sec. 2.

216

families"[5]—are among the primary factors to which Francis attributes the crisis of the family in society today, as a part of the larger crisis in solidarity. For Francis "the uncertainty and disorientation"[6] characteristic of our age is an uncertainty and disorientation pertaining not exclusively to sexuality, but to technology, economics, and ecology, each in integral relation to the other in a singular human-cosmic ecology. It's a disorientation and uncertainty concerning the meaning woven into the deepest ontological framework of our singular cosmic home. As we have been seeing throughout the previous chapters of this book, a key feature of the tapestry of creation in the theologically rooted social teaching of the papal trio is the alliance between man and woman in the sacrament of holy matrimony. In this chapter, we'll see how the theologically rooted social teaching of the papal trio offers an alternative to the all-encompassing disorientation and confusion prevalent in global society today.

Development, for Good and Ill

On the occasion of his 2016 address to the John Paul II Institute, Francis directed the attention of his audience to "the questions opened up by the development of new technologies, which make possible practices that sometimes conflict with the true dignity of human life."[7] The disorientation and uncertainty characteristic of our time of rapid development "touch the fundamental affections of the person and of life," and as such "destabilize all ties, family and social, making the 'I' increasingly prevail over the 'we,' the individual over society."[8] This disorientation "contradicts the plan of God, who entrusted the world and history to the covenant of man and woman."[9]

Francis attributes the disorientation in society today to the very problem that was already identified by Pope Benedict, whom Francis cites on precisely this matter. For Francis as for Benedict, "the deterioration of nature is closely connected to the culture which shapes human coexistence."[10] For this reason, Francis recounts, "Pope Benedict asked

5. Francis, "JP2 Institute," sec. 2.
6. Francis, "JP2 Institute," sec. 2.
7. Francis, "JP2 Institute," sec. 2.
8. Francis, "JP2 Institute," sec. 2.
9. Francis, "JP2 Institute," sec. 2.
10. *LS*, sec. 6, citing *CV*, sec. 51.

us to recognize that the natural environment has been gravely damaged by our irresponsible behaviour,"[11] by our misuse of technological and economic power. For indeed, in Benedict's and Francis's shared analysis, in addition to the natural environment and closely linked with its damage, "the social environment has also suffered damage,"[12] for "both are ultimately due to the same evil: the notion that there are no indisputable truths to guide our lives, and hence human freedom is limitless,"[13] as we already saw in this book's introduction. Francis underscores that "we have forgotten" the very thing that Benedict had alerted us to in his own critique of technocracy: "that 'man is not only a freedom which he creates for himself. Man does not create himself. He is spirit and will, but also nature.'"[14]

Francis continues to recount that "humanity has entered a new era in which our technical prowess has brought us to a crossroads."[15] As is characteristic of the previous popes in their social commentaries on development, Francis too recognizes that "we are the beneficiaries of two centuries of enormous waves of change: steam engines, railways, the telegraph, electricity, automobiles, aeroplanes, chemical industries, modern medicine, information technology and, more recently, the digital revolution, robotics, biotechnologies and nanotechnologies."[16] Quoting JP2's 1981 address to the United Nations University in Hiroshima, Francis voices an enthusiastic support of technological development, suggesting that it is indeed "right to rejoice in these advances and to be excited by the immense possibilities which they continue to open up before us, for 'science and technology are wonderful products of a God-given human creativity.'"[17] For Francis, "the modification of nature for useful purposes has distinguished the human family from the beginning."[18] This distinction of humanity is something which, in and of itself, calls for celebration. "Technology itself," Francis suggests by way of making Benedict's words his own, "expresses the inner tension that impels man gradually

11. *LS*, sec. 6.
12. *LS*, sec. 6.
13. *LS*, sec. 6.
14. *LS*, sec. 6, citing Benedict, "Bundestag."
15. *LS*, sec. 102.
16. *LS*, sec. 102.
17. *LS*, sec. 102, citing JP2, "Hiroshima," sec. 3.
18. *LS*, sec. 102.

to overcome material limitations.'"[19] In Francis's own words, "Technology has remedied countless evils which used to harm and limit human beings."[20] Francis thus asks, "How can we not feel gratitude and appreciation for this progress, especially in the fields of medicine, engineering and communications? How could we not acknowledge the work of many scientists and engineers who have provided alternatives to make development sustainable?"[21]

Francis's Call for Sobriety

While maintaining a capacity to celebrate technological development, Francis goes on to voice in *LS* a call for sobriety and caution, for a temperance proper to the reverence demanded by the dignity of the human being and by the meaning of creation as gift. That is to say, Francis proceeds to recount the danger of what we're calling technocratic lust. Francis recounts that it must "be recognized that nuclear energy, biotechnology, information technology, knowledge of our DNA, and many other abilities which we have acquired, have given us tremendous power. More precisely, they have given those with the knowledge, and especially the economic resources to use them, an impressive dominance over the whole of humanity and the entire world."[22]

Mastery in itself is not the problem. Indeed, it is a part of humanity's ingenuity and task as collaborator with the Creator. The problem is that in today's cultural milieu, "nothing ensures that" our technological power "will be used wisely, particularly when we consider how it is currently being used" today.[23] "Never has humanity had such power over itself."[24] Yet, we have little to no cultural safeguards in place to guide the use of this power. "We need but think of the nuclear bombs dropped in the middle of the twentieth century, or the array of technology which Nazism, Communism and other totalitarian regimes" employed "to kill

---

19. *LS*, sec. 102, citing *CV*, sec. 69.

20. *LS*, sec. 102.

21. *LS*, sec. 102.

22. *LS*, sec. 104.

23. *LS*, sec. 104.

24. *LS*, sec. 104.

millions of people, to say nothing of the increasingly deadly arsenal of weapons available for modern warfare."[25]

When power's "only norms are taken from alleged necessity, from either utility or security,"[26] there is no safeguard against the dehumanizing empowerment of technology put at the "service" of feeding our powerfully felt and experienced disordered desires. The lack of cultural safeguards against the tyranny of our disordered desires, for Francis, is what has facilitated the growth of the technocratic paradigm, while the technocratic paradigm likewise facilitates the unleashing of these disordered desires. Under the reign of the technocratic paradigm, creaturely dignity at large and human dignity in particular becomes subjected to the momentum of technological power and "progress."

For Francis, the "basic problem" is "the way that humanity has taken up technology and its development *according to an undifferentiated and one-dimensional paradigm.*"[27] It's a paradigm of technologically empowered lust with a disinterest in any given object's own meaning and dignity and its relation to the cosmic order. The controlling subject, empowered by technology ordered to the satisfaction of humanity's disordered, vicious hungers, employs "a technique of possession, mastery and transformation."[28] In this situation, "it is as if the subject were to find itself in the presence of something formless, completely open to manipulation,"[29] utterly void of an integral meaning, without regard to any meaning assigned to it by the Creator proper to its own divinely bestowed nature. While "men and women have constantly intervened in nature,"[30] and rightly so, "for a long time this meant being in tune with and respecting the possibilities offered by the things themselves."[31] Many traditions of the world's diverse cultures have cultivated a reverence for what people and things *do* and *do not* offer us. In such an atmosphere of chastity and reverence, "it was a matter of receiving what nature itself allowed, as if from its own hand," as a generous gift from *another*.[32] "Now,

25. *LS*, sec. 104.
26. As we saw in chapter 4.
27. *LS*, sec. 106.
28. *LS*, sec. 106.
29. *LS*, sec. 106.
30. *LS*, sec. 106.
31. *LS*, sec. 106.
32. *LS*, sec. 106.

by contrast, we are the ones to lay our hands on things, attempting to extract everything possible from them while frequently ignoring or forgetting the reality in front of us," Francis laments.[33] According to this technocratic lust, we strive to *remake* reality rather than *receive it for what it truly is.*

Disharmony, Human Dignity, and Chastity

As is proper to the perennial condition of humanity fallen and broken apart and at enmity with itself, technology empowers our violent assaults upon human dignity, particularly by way of modern warfare, abortion, and environmental degradation. As opposed to extending "a friendly hand to one another,"[34] the relationship between human beings "has become confrontational"[35] in an intensified manner by way of technology's appropriation in relations between people and in people's relations with their material surroundings. This is part of a society-wide misapprehension of the fruit of the earth, such that it is perceived as something in relation to which I stand in a posture of violent confrontation as opposed to reverential collaboration. This is exacerbated by the widespread acceptance of "the idea of infinite or unlimited growth, which proves so attractive to economists, financiers and experts in technology"—but a kind of "growth" that comes at the expense of human dignity. We rule powerfully with technology.[36] Thus, the human being, in selling his dignity, is ruled by technology. The dignity of the human subject wielding technological power—from the contraceptive pill to the atom bomb—has been thoroughly compromised, as has the dignity of those blasted away, as it were, by these methods of dealing with (or rather, *not* dealing with) the realities in front of us, in direct contradiction to their meaning.

In Francis's ecological vision, our *households* and *our own selves* are undergoing the same damage that *our common home as a whole* is undergoing. It is human beings who are ultimately reshaped by technocracy. Human dignity is the primary casualty of technocracy. "The effects of imposing" technocracy upon "reality as a whole . . . are seen in the deterioration of the environment, but this is just one sign of a

33. *LS*, sec. 106.
34. *LS*, sec. 106.
35. *LS*, sec. 106.
36. *LS*, sec. 106.

reductionism which affects every aspect of human and social life."[37] If we are to gaze chastely upon humanity within the household of creation, "we have to accept that technological products are not neutral, for they create a framework which ends up conditioning lifestyles and shaping social possibilities along the lines dictated by the interests of certain powerful groups. Decisions which may seem purely instrumental are in reality decisions about the kind of society we want to build."[38] The question Francis wants to get us asking is this: what kind of a society *do* we want to build? One driven by lust? Or one guided by the truth of creation?

Lust empowered by technological power reshapes society and reshapes human hearts according to a manner expedient to the goals of the powerful—including our powerful selves—as those with power (including ourselves) seek to satisfy the threefold lusts of their own hearts (our own hearts) and the hearts of the consumers upon whom we the powerful feed, our own hearts upon which other consumers feed, the threefold lust against which St. John warns—the lust of the eyes, the lust of the flesh, and the pride of life.

Francis's ecological vision seeks to honor the created order and honor human dignity as a key part of it. This seems far-fetched, as Francis is well aware. "The idea of promoting a different cultural paradigm" from that of technocracy, "and employing technology as a mere instrument" at the genuine service of humanity according to humanity's inherent dignity "is nowadays inconceivable."[39] "The technological paradigm has become so dominant that it would be difficult to do without its resources and even more difficult to utilize them without being dominated by their internal logic."[40]

In other words, it's pretty darn difficult today to avoid the domination of the technocratic outlook. It's pretty darn difficult to uphold human dignity in the context of a society ruled by technocratic lust. As Francis puts it, "It has become countercultural to choose a lifestyle whose goals are even partly independent of technology, of its costs and its power to globalize and make us all the same."[41] Technocracy's goals are not goals that take human dignity into account. Technocracy's "power to . . . make

37. *LS*, sec. 107.
38. *LS*, sec. 107.
39. *LS*, sec. 108.
40. *LS*, sec. 108.
41. *LS*, sec. 108.

us all the same"[42]—its drive to homogenization—is a drive that plows over our dignity, utterly indifferent to it. In this context, "technology tends to absorb everything into its ironclad logic,"[43] which tramples upon the meaning of the human person, the meaning of human community and society, the meaning of sexuality, the meaning of family, the meaning of labor, the meaning of the worker, the meaning of authority, the meaning of power, the meaning of responsibility, the meaning of human life, the meaning of production and its means.

Francis, quoting Guardini, laments that man, in pursuit of power, "seizes hold of the naked elements of both nature and human nature."[44] Human responsibility for discernment, according to an integral vision of human freedom, is trampled upon by this technocratic seizure. "Our capacity to make decisions, a more genuine freedom and the space for each one's alternative creativity are diminished."[45]

Technocracy's threat to human dignity makes itself known in the tendency of the technocratic paradigm "to dominate economic and political life," Francis recounts.[46] According to the rationale of the technocratic market, "the economy accepts every advance in technology with a view to profit" that in turn is pursued in view of obtaining more power still, "without concern for its potentially negative impact on human beings," thereby spitting in the face of the human family.[47] "The lessons of the global financial crisis have not been assimilated, and we are learning all too slowly the lessons of environmental deterioration,"[48] inclusive of all that makes up the human-societal environment. "Some circles maintain that current economics and technology will solve all environmental problems, and argue . . . that the problems of global hunger and poverty

---

42. *LS*, sec. 108.

43. *LS*, sec. 108.

44. *LS*, sec. 108. Here, Francis, following Guardini, seems to regard Nietzsche's "will to power" as the fundamental deception of human consciousness—more fundamental than the other two forms of lust identified by Marx (avarice) and Freud (sexual lust) respectively. At base, it seems, in Francis's Guardinian anthropology, Adam Smith's profit motive is fundamentally a power motive. For the rationale of Adam Smith and the liberal market's "profit motive" and an integral Catholic alternative, see Schindler, *Ordering Love*, 2–4, 156.

45. *LS*, sec. 108.

46. *LS*, sec. 109.

47. *LS*, sec. 109.

48. *LS*, sec. 109.

will be resolved simply by market growth."[49] According to this rationale, if we play the game of self-interest in the profit-driven market, that'll solve the problems of hunger, poverty, and environmental degradation, as much as is possible for humanity to solve such problems—if we indeed believe that these are even problems. Such defenders of the market as we know it "are less concerned with certain economic theories which today scarcely anybody dares defend, than with their actual operation in the functioning of the economy," Francis points out.[50] Such supporters of the status quo in finance show "no interest in more balanced levels of production, a better distribution of wealth, concern for the environment and the rights of future generations."[51] If we are indifferent to the ways in which the market today tramples upon human dignity, "maximizing profits is enough."[52]

It is at this point that Francis, true to the ardent defense of human dignity proper to the tradition of Catholic social teaching, insists that "by itself the market cannot guarantee integral human development and social inclusion,"[53] citing Benedict's indictment upon the logic of the market as we know it and Benedict's accompanying prophetic insistence that "if the market is governed solely by the principle of the equivalence in value of exchanged goods, it cannot produce the social cohesion that it requires in order to function well."[54] Francis knows as well as Benedict that *"without internal forms of solidarity and mutual trust, the market cannot completely fulfil its proper economic function."*[55] For, according to Benedict's diagnosis, "today it is this trust which has ceased to exist, and the loss of trust is a grave loss."[56] What we need is a sense of the brotherhood of all, a rehabilitation of trust.

Instead of upholding human dignity in the manner proper to solidarity and fraternity, we trample upon human dignity by way of what Francis, quoting Benedict, calls "a sort of 'super development' of a wasteful and consumerist kind which forms an unacceptable contrast with the

---

49. *LS*, sec. 109.

50. *LS*, sec. 109.

51. *LS*, sec. 109.

52. *LS*, sec. 109.

53. *LS*, sec. 109, citing *CV*, sec. 35.

54. *LS*, sec. 109, citing *CV*, sec. 35.

55. *CV*, sec. 35.

56. *CV*, sec. 35.

ongoing situations of dehumanizing deprivation," which, Benedict says, "some groups enjoy," even in contexts in which they are surrounded by impoverished neighbors.[57] Quick as we are to extol such super development for the sake of market growth, as Francis diagnoses, "we are all-too slow in developing economic institutions and social initiatives which can give the poor regular access to basic resources."[58] We habitually jeopardize and sacrifice human dignity for the sake of the market; all the while we tell ourselves that market growth is what will lift the very poor upon whom we trample by way of our economic practices.

For Francis, the problem is that "we fail to see the deepest roots of our present failures, which have to do with the direction, goals, meaning and social implications of technological and economic growth."[59] For Francis, his economic critique—which is built upon that of Benedict and Guardini—is not merely a matter of advocating democratic socialism over and against liberal capitalism as we know it. It's a matter of diagnosing society's deepest sicknesses, of inquiring into an all-encompassing societal hermeneutic according to the truth of the human person, the truth of society, and the truth of humanity within creation.

Such an economic and ecological vision that upholds the human dignity for which Francis advocates in *LS* and elsewhere, and for which Benedict advocates in *CV* and elsewhere, is the very vision which Paul VI called in *HV* "an integral vision of man."[60] Unfortunately, in our own day, this vision is lost sight of, precisely because of the way in which the technocratic paradigm limits our vision. What this means is that the technocratic paradigm thoroughly limits our capacity to perceive the dignity of the human being, and has a crippling effect upon our capacity to uphold that dignity in the political, economic, and ecological spheres, each of which are a facet of a singular reality of human life within the created order. As Francis recounts, "the specialization which belongs to technology makes it difficult to see the larger picture. The fragmentation of knowledge proves helpful for concrete applications, and yet it often leads to a loss of appreciation for the whole, for the relationships between things, and for the broader horizon, which then becomes irrelevant."[61]

57. *CV*, sec. 22.

58. *LS*, sec. 109.

59. *LS*, sec. 109.

60. *HV*, sec. 7. *TOB*, 4.2.80.

61. *LS*, sec. 110.

226 Part III | The Harmony of Moral Truth against the Cacophony of Relativism

What Francis calls "the fragmentation of knowledge" within the technocratic paradigm, and this fragmentation's consequence of limiting society's hermeneutical vision—particularly as that vision pertains to human dignity—"makes it hard to find adequate ways of solving the more complex problems of today's world, particularly those regarding the environment and the poor,"[62] Francis says, suggesting that "these problems cannot be dealt with from a single perspective or from a single set of interests,"[63] but must be addressed according to an integral vision of humanity, according to an authentic understanding of creation as a singular whole. "A science which would offer solutions to the great issues would necessarily have to take into account the data generated by other fields of knowledge, including philosophy and social ethics."[64] But authentic interdisciplinarity between the hard sciences on the one hand and philosophy and ethics on the other is hard to come by in popular culture.

The Ecological Conversion

Technocracy does not provide an ethos, and the ethos of chastity is not readily perceptible for the technocratically deformed moral imagination. The dictatorship of technocracy is itself the dictatorship of relativism as relativism carries itself out practically. In technocracy's regime, Francis says, there are no "genuine ethical horizons to which one can appeal" such that "life gradually becomes a surrender to situations conditioned by technology."[65] It is in this way that human beings are ruled by technology—contraception and porn taking the lead in making our hearts captive to lust's designs. According to a vision of human dignity, human communities safeguard human agency by way of a temperate determination and intentionality with respect to our use of the tools of society's making. Moral truth is the standard according to which we safeguard the responsible discernment of the manner in which we employ tools, the standard by which we safeguard the intentionality of our course of action in relation to people and things. It is by way of moral truth that we safeguard our own agency, as is proper to chastity, over and against the

62. *LS*, sec. 110.
63. *LS*, sec. 110.
64. *LS*, sec. 110.
65. *LS*, sec. 110.

loss of integrity and responsibility and authentically free agency proper to lust. For our use of technology to be free and chaste rather than an enslavement, we must have truth as our reference point.

As Paul VI perceived in 1970, and as Francis reiterates after him in *LS*, it is "due to an ill-considered exploitation of nature" that "humanity runs the risk of destroying it and becoming in turn a victim of this degradation."[66] Pope Paul's identification of the ecological catastrophe was part and parcel with his overall identification of a catastrophe in morality, which is why, in diagnosing the ecological catastrophe, he, like Francis after him, "stressed 'the urgent need for a radical change in the conduct of humanity.'"[67]

As Francis recounts, for Paul VI, "the most extraordinary scientific advances, the most amazing technical abilities, the most astonishing economic growth, unless they are accompanied by authentic social and moral progress, will definitively turn against man."[68] Francis likewise laments, quoting from JP2's *Centesimus annus*, "that little effort had been made to 'safeguard the moral conditions for an authentic human ecology.'"[69] For Francis, as for JP2, "the destruction of the human environment" according to the dictates of technocratic lust "is extremely serious, not only because God has entrusted the world to us men and women, but because human life is itself a gift which must be defended from various forms of debasement."[70] For Francis, "Every effort to protect and improve our world entails profound changes in 'lifestyles, models of production and consumption, and the established structures of power which today govern societies,'" as JP2 says in *Centesimus annus* (and as Francis quotes in *LS*).[71]

Francis is insistent that "authentic human development has a moral character" and that "it presumes full respect for the human person" and as such "must also be concerned for the world around us and 'take into account the nature of each being and of its mutual connection in an ordered system,'" as JP2 himself said in *SRS*.[72] According to JP2's vision

66. *LS*, sec. 4, citing *OA*, sec. 21.
67. *LS*, sec. 4, citing Paul VI, "F.A.O. 25th Anniversary," sec. 4.
68. *LS*, sec. 4, citing Paul VI, "F.A.O. 25th Anniversary," sec. 4.
69. *LS*, sec. 4, citing *CA*, sec. 38.
70. *LS*, sec. 5.
71. *LS*, sec. 4, citing *CA*, sec. 38.
72. *LS*, sec. 5, citing *SRS*, sec. 34.

appropriated by Francis, "Our human ability to transform reality must proceed in line with God's original gift of all that is."[73]

For Francis, "in the concrete situation confronting us, there are a number of symptoms which point to what is wrong, such as environmental degradation, anxiety, a loss of the purpose of life and of community living."[74] An ecological counterculture of chastity is what is in order, in Francis's clarion call for ecological conversion. He calls, then, for an authentic "ecological culture" that "cannot be reduced to a series of urgent and partial responses to the immediate problems of pollution, environmental decay and the depletion of natural resources."[75] What is needed, rather, is "a distinctive way of looking at things, a way of thinking, policies, an educational programme, a lifestyle and a spirituality which together generate resistance to the assault of the technocratic paradigm."[76] Apart from the development of an ecological culture informed by a robust moral imagination, "even the best ecological initiatives can find themselves caught up in the same globalized logic."[77] Many a new deal, green or otherwise, many a global environmental summit, at which the neoliberal vanguard pat themselves on the back for not being Trump, "seek only a technical remedy to each environmental problem which comes up."[78] This "is to separate what is in reality interconnected and to mask the true and deepest problems of the global system."[79] While new policies must be implemented and new programs indeed need to be backed by government, simply implementing programs by way of a *technocratic mindset*, far from offsetting the ecological catastrophe, perpetuates the very logic responsible for it.

With his eyes wide open to the demanding nature of JP2's call for an ecological conversion, Francis holds out hope that we can indeed "once more broaden our vision" as JP2 had hoped, convinced as Francis is that human beings are equipped, by design, with "the freedom needed to limit and direct technology."[80] In Francis's high anthropology, "We can put it

73. *LS*, sec. 5.

74. *LS*, sec. 110.

75. *LS*, sec. 111.

76. *LS*, sec. 111.

77. *LS*, sec. 111.

78. *LS*, sec. 111.

79. *LS*, sec. 111.

80. *LS*, sec. 111.

at the service of another type of progress, one which is healthier, more human, more social, more integral."[81] This is Francis's proposal for an integral *post*modernity, his progressive vision for an ecological reform proper to the very doctrine of creation that modernity rejected. Francis's plan of recovery from modernity's missteps is one of "liberation from the dominant technocratic paradigm."[82]

In modern anthropocentrism, the cosmos is, in Guardini's words, mere space "into which objects can be thrown with complete indifference"—indifferent, that is, to any inherent meaning and destiny as awe-inspiring gift.[83] With this reduction of created being, "the intrinsic dignity of the world is . . . compromised," for "when human beings fail to find their true place in this world"—when they fail to find the humility of life (as the form of chastity correlating to the pride of life)—"they misunderstand themselves and end up acting against themselves."[84] For Francis and JP2, "Not only has God given the earth to man, who must use it with respect for the original good purpose for which it was given, but, man too is God's gift to man. He must therefore respect the natural and moral structure with which he has been endowed."[85] This cosmo-anthropology of givenness, which is what lays at the heart of the social teaching of JP2 and Francis, contains within itself a call to a human ecology that implies "the relationship between human life and the moral law, which is inscribed in our nature and is necessary for the creation of a more dignified environment."[86]

The Rehabilitation of Marriage, the Summit of Creation

Francis appeals to Benedict's "ecology of man," which is "based on the fact that 'man too has a nature that he must respect and that he cannot manipulate at will.'"[87] For Francis, expounding upon this vision, "Our body itself establishes us in a direct relationship with the environment

81. *LS*, sec. 112.
82. *LS*, sec. 112.
83. *LS*, sec. 115.
84. *LS*, sec. 115.
85. *LS*, sec. 115, citing *CA*, sec. 38.
86. *LS*, sec. 155.
87. *LS*, sec. 155; Benedict, "Bundestag."

and with other living beings."[88] Indeed, "The acceptance of our bodies as God's gift is vital for welcoming and accepting the entire world as a gift from the Father and our common home, whereas thinking that we enjoy absolute power over our own bodies turns, often subtly, into thinking that we enjoy absolute power over creation."[89] The logic of refusing the body-as-gift is the logic that refuses the rest of the cosmic body as gift. "Learning to accept our body, to care for it and to respect its fullest meaning, is an essential element of any genuine human ecology."[90] Reverence for creation begins with reverence for our own skin.

An "ecology of man" entails a receptivity to the meaning of my own body, according to JP2's theology of the human body, and has implications concerning my interactions with my neighbors. "Valuing one's own body in its femininity or masculinity is necessary," Francis insists, "if I am going to be able to recognize myself in an encounter with someone who is different . . . In this way we can joyfully accept the specific gifts of another man or woman, the work of God the Creator, and find mutual enrichment."[91] "It is not a healthy attitude which would seek 'to cancel out sexual difference because it no longer knows how to confront it.'"[92]

In Francis's theology of the family, the family is "the great gift that God gave to humanity with the creation of man and woman and with the sacrament of marriage."[93] Man and woman, Francis says, "stand at the summit of divine creation."[94] Francis's alternative to modern anthropocentrism, which displaces God as creation's center—as the divine gift giver of all—is a theology of man and woman as placed by God at creation's summit. Francis subscribes to an integral theocentrism and *gamokoryphism* (*gamos* being the Greek word for marriage, and *koryph* being the Greek word for summit, suggesting that marriage is at the summit of creation). Francis's cosmology is one with marriage at the summit of creation. His is a *gamokoryphic* cosmology. The Creator, not man, is creation's beating heart and pulsing center, and humanity, as man and woman in the alliance of marriage, is placed by God at its summit. In

88. *LS*, sec. 155.
89. *LS*, sec. 155.
90. *LS*, sec. 155.
91. *LS*, sec. 155.
92. *LS*, sec. 155.
93. "M&F1," para. 1.
94. "M&F1," para. 1.

"the first narrative of creation, in the Book of Genesis," Francis recounts, "we read that God, after having created the universe and all living beings, created his masterpiece, the human being, whom He made in his own image: 'in the image of God he created them; male and female he created them' (Gn 1:27)."[95]

The mystery of sexual differentiation, before which Francis stands with Adam in wonder, is a mystery which humanity holds in common with "many forms of life, on the great scale of living beings."[96] This mystery, proper to a myriad of earth's creatures, manifests itself in a peculiarly wondrous way in humanity, for Francis. "Man and woman alone are made in the image of God."[97] That "man and woman are the image and likeness of God . . . tells us that it is not man alone or woman alone who is the image of God, but man and woman as a couple"—precisely as a couple— "who are the image of God."[98] Thus, "the difference between man and woman is not meant to stand in opposition, or to subordinate," one sex over and against the other, one sex dominating the other, characterized by enmity and strife. Rather, the difference between man and woman is meant "for the sake of communion and generation, always in the image and likeness of God."[99]

In Francis's account, "in order to know oneself well and develop harmoniously, a human being needs the reciprocity of man and woman."[100] While "modern contemporary culture has opened . . . new depths in order to enrich the understanding" of sexual difference, it has also "introduced many doubts and much skepticism."[101] The global Socrates, on the streets of a global Athens, in that global square called St. Peter's, asks "if the so-called gender theory is not . . . an expression of frustration and resignation, which seeks to cancel out sexual difference because it no longer knows how to confront it"[102]—the very question this new Socrates later poses before the entire world in *LS*. "Yes, we risk taking a step

95. "M&F1," para. 2.
96. "M&F1," para. 3.
97. "M&F1," para. 3.
98. "M&F1," para. 3.
99. "M&F1," para. 3.
100. "M&F1," para. 4.
101. "M&F1," para. 5.
102. "M&F1," para. 5. *LS*, sec. 155.

backwards," this Socratic philosopher-become-prophet warns.[103] "The removal of sexual difference in fact creates a problem, not a solution."[104]

Ever sounding a harsh warning proper to the prophetic social critic and ever holding out the hope of recovery, redemption, and growth, proper to a herald of glad tidings, Francis declares that on the basis of respect and cooperation in friendship, "it is possible"—"sustained by the grace of God"—"to plan a lifelong marital and familial union."[105] Such is the possibility offered by Francis in the face of a throwaway culture. "The marital and familial bond is a serious matter, and it is so for everyone."[106] No one who enters into that covenant is spared the hardship of its demands. Francis thus urges "intellectuals not to leave this theme aside"[107]—the theme of the import of the marriage bond as the summit of creation—"as if it had to become secondary in order to foster a more free and just society."[108] Far from it, a free and just society depends upon a robust recognition of the profound seriousness of the marital bond according to an anthropology and cosmology of gratuity.

In a manner similar to his presentation of marriage as the nexus of church and creation in Philadelphia, here in April of the same year in Rome, and in a manner similar to his address to the John Paul II Institute, Francis proposes: "God entrusted the earth to the alliance between man and woman."[109] The failure of this alliance "deprives the earth of warmth and darkens the sky of hope," Francis suggests with apocalyptic urgency.[110] It is to the covenant between man and woman that God the Creator has entrusted the welfare of the cosmos. It is in matrimony that the hope of the cosmos resides. It is in a rehabilitation of marriage that the cosmos finds its rehabilitation. It is in a theology of marriage that an integral ecology reaches its height.

The prophet Francis again cries out in warning, "the signs are already worrisome, and we see them."[111] The global Socrates raises an

---

103. "M&F1," para. 5.

104. "M&F1," para. 5.

105. "M&F1," para. 5.

106. "M&F1," para. 5.

107. "M&F1," para. 5.

108. "M&F1," para. 5.

109. "M&F1," para. 6.

110. "M&F1," para. 6.

111. "M&F1," para. 6.

additional question for the inquisitive youth of Athens: "I wonder if the crisis of collective trust in God," a distrust "which does us so much harm, and makes us pale with resignation, incredulity and cynicism, is not also connected to the crisis of the alliance between man and woman."[112] What Francis calls "the crisis of collective trust in God"[113] is responsible for the crisis of our misperception of the meaning of sexual difference and our misperception of the meaning of marriage, our failure to perceive the meaning of the covenant between man and woman as the cosmos at its highest height.

Francis proceeds to portray the crisis in marriage in view of "the biblical account, with the great symbolic fresco depicting the earthly paradise and original sin,"[114] which "tells us in fact that communion with God is reflected in the communion of the human couple" and speaks of "the loss of trust in the heavenly Father" that "generates division and conflict between man and woman."[115] At the breaking point of harmony found at humanity's primal origins in the Genesis account, we see that the point at which humanity begins to distrust its Creator is the point at which conflict arises between man and woman.

"God's faith in man and in woman, those to whom he entrusted the earth . . . is generous, direct and full."[116] Recounting the creation story, and humanity's place within it, Francis stresses that God "trusts them. But then the devil introduces suspicion in their minds, disbelief, distrust, and finally, disobedience to the commandment that protected them. They fall into that delirium of omnipotence that pollutes everything and destroys harmony," the delirium that is exacerbated by technocracy and which leads to the destruction of harmony that we feel "inside of us."[117] Indeed, "sin generates distrust and division between man and woman."[118] The relationship between woman and man is thus "undermined by a thousand forms of abuse and subjugation, misleading seduction and humiliating ignorance, even the most dramatic and violent kind . . . History bears the scar."[119]

112. "M&F1," para. 8.
113. "M&F1," para. 8.
114. "M&F1," para. 8.
115. "M&F1," para. 8.
116. "M&F2," para. 4.
117. "M&F2," para. 4.
118. "M&F2," para. 5.
119. "M&F2," para. 5.

In this context, Francis identifies "those negative excesses of patriarchal cultures": "think of the many forms of male dominance whereby the woman was considered second class. Think of the exploitation and the commercialization of the female body in the current media culture . . . Let us also think of the recent epidemic of distrust, skepticism, and even hostility that is spreading in our culture—in particular an understandable distrust from women" toward "a covenant between man and woman that" in truth "is capable of refining the intimacy of community and of guarding the dignity of difference."[120]

Francis's fight for orthodoxy consists of his prophetic clarion call, as though pleading with the world to catch a glimpse with him of the mystery of creation, awestruck with Adam in Eden. "If we do not find a surge of respect for this covenant" between man and woman, if we do not find a surge of respect "capable of protecting new generations from distrust and indifference, children will come into the world ever more uprooted from the mother's womb."[121] If we do not find a surge of vigilance for truth fueled by a love that safeguards the meaning of the family, the meaning of the covenant to which man and woman are called, the uprootedness of coming generations will only increase.

A Rehabilitation of Marriage and Family

"The social devaluation for the stable and generative alliance between man and woman is certainly a loss for everyone," Francis declared. The moral truth pertaining to marriage and the family for Francis, then, is foundational for social justice and social charity. "We must return marriage and the family to the place of honour!"[122] According to the call of marriage, "man must leave something in order to" fully find his spouse, which "is why man will leave father and mother to go to her."[123] The meaning of marriage, then, contains within itself a responsibility of magnitude for society: "The responsibility of guarding this covenant between man and woman is ours, although we are sinners and are wounded, confused and humiliated, discouraged and uncertain."[124] Marriage is today a crucible

120. "M&F2," para. 5.
121. "M&F2," para. 6.
122. "M&F2," para. 6.
123. "M&F2," para. 6.
124. "M&F2," para. 7.

as much as ever, if not *more* than ever. It is "for us believers a demanding and gripping vocation in today's situation."[125]

As an icon of the gospel of marriage today, Francis provides *the gospel of God's response*, the gospel of the Creator's care, for man and woman after their fall into sin. Francis recounts: "The same narrative of creation and of sin ends by showing us an extremely beautiful icon: 'The Lord God made for Adam and for his wife garments of skin, and clothed them.'"[126] "It is an image of tenderness towards the sinful couple that leaves our mouths agape: the tenderness God has for man and woman! It's an image of fatherly care for the human couple. God himself cares for and protects his masterpiece."[127] Man and woman, in turn, are called to participate in safeguarding this masterpiece of God's creation.

Francis recounts how "at the beginning of his Gospel, John the Evangelist narrates the episode of the wedding at Cana."[128] In that episode, "Jesus not only participated at that wedding, but 'saved the feast' with the miracle of wine! Thus, the first of His prodigious signs, with which He reveals his glory, He performed in the context of a wedding, and it was an act of great sympathy for that nascent family, entreated by Mary's motherly care."[129] Jesus' sign "reminds us of the Book of Genesis, when God completes his work of creation and makes his masterpiece; the masterpiece is man and woman . . . here at a marriage, at a wedding feast, Jesus begins his own miracles with this masterpiece: a man and a woman. Thus Jesus teaches us that the masterpiece of society is the family."[130] The union of man and woman in the formation of a family is *the* masterpiece of creation and of society, of the cosmos and the polis.

Francis's Alternative to the Culture of the Provisional: An Ecclesio-Sacramental Theology

Reflecting upon God's masterpiece of man and woman in the alliance of marriage as perceived in the narrative of the wedding of Cana, Francis remarks that "since the time of the wedding at Cana, many things have

125. "M&F2," para. 7.

126. "M&F2," para. 7; Gen 3:21.

127. "M&F2," para. 7.

128. Francis, "Family: Marriage (I)," para. 2.

129. Francis, "Family: Marriage (I)," para. 2.

130. Francis, "Family: Marriage (I)," para. 2.

changed, but that 'sign' of Christ contains an ever valid message . . . Today it seems difficult to speak of marriage as a feast which is renewed in time, in the various seasons of the couple's lifetime. It is a fact that progressively fewer people are getting married."[131] Many "young people don't want to get married."[132] "In many countries the number of separations is instead increasing while the number of children decreases. The difficulty of staying together . . . as a couple and as a family—leads to bonds being broken with ever increasing frequency and swiftness, and the children themselves are the first to suffer the consequences."[133] This is the injustice, a grievous and fundamental social injustice, that strikes society a fatal wound at its most foundational level, leading to an array of other social injustices, as the loss of family coherence is a loss of societal coherence. "Let us consider that the first victims . . . the most important victims, the victims who suffer the most in a separation are the children."[134] What family instability communicates to children is the false message "that marriage is a 'temporary' bond," and in receiving this message, "unconsciously it will be so" in the hearts of today's children.[135] As Francis observes, "Many young people are led to reject the very plan of an irrevocable bond and of a lasting family."[136] Francis proposed that in light of this, "we must reflect very seriously on why so many young people 'don't feel like' getting married. There is a culture of the provisional . . . everything is provisional, it seems there is nothing definitive."[137]

As family is foundational for society, as the alliance between man and woman and the children of their union is foundational for society, "this matter of young people not wanting to marry is one of the emerging concerns of today."[138] This new Socrates on the streets of the global Athens proceeds to ask, "Why aren't young people getting married? Why is it that they frequently prefer cohabitation and 'limited responsibility'? Why is [it] that many—even among the baptized—have little trust in marriage and in the family? If we want young people to be able to find the

131. Francis, "Family: Marriage (I)," para. 3.

132. Francis, "Family: Marriage (I)," para. 3.

133. Francis, "Family: Marriage (I)," para. 3.

134. Francis, "Family: Marriage (I)," para. 3.

135. Francis, "Family: Marriage (I)," para. 4.

136. Francis, "Family: Marriage (I)," para. 4.

137. Francis, "Family: Marriage (I)," para. 4.

138. Francis, "Family: Marriage (I)," para. 5.

right road to follow, it is important to try to understand this."[139] He asks, "Why do they have no trust in the family?"[140] Francis suggests that "the difficulties are not only economic, although these are truly serious."[141] Indeed, "the family tops all the indices of wellbeing among young people; but, fearing mistakes, many do not want to even consider it; even being Christians, they do not consider the sacrament of matrimony, the single and unrepeatable sign of the covenant, which becomes a testimony of faith."[142]

Francis inquired into the widespread fear characterizing youth today, in this "culture of the provisional."[143] Francis suggests that perhaps the "fear of failure is the greatest obstacle to receiving the Word of Christ, which promises his grace to the conjugal union and to the family."[144] Francis is insistent that "a marriage consecrated by God safeguards that bond between man and woman that God has blessed from the very creation of the world . . . It is the source of peace and goodness for the entire lifetime of the marriage and family."[145]

The following week, Francis insisted that marriage "is not merely a ceremony in a church, with flowers, a dress, photographs";[146] rather, "Christian marriage is a sacrament that takes place *in* the Church"[147]— which is to say, not just in a church building, but in the mystical body of Christ. It's a sacrament that "*makes* the Church, by giving rise to a new family community."[148] Marriage isn't merely something that takes place within a church building. It is something that both takes place within the mystical body—the Church—and *makes* the mystical body. This is a point Francis would reiterate at the World Meeting of Families later the same year, in a manner reminiscent of Lubac's dictum that the Church makes the Eucharist and that the Eucharist makes the Church. The sacraments arise from the Church, and the Church is what she is by dint of

---

139. Francis, "Family: Marriage (I)," para. 5.
140. Francis, "Family: Marriage (I)," para. 5.
141. Francis, "Family: Marriage (I)," para. 6.
142. Francis, "Family: Marriage (I)," para. 6.
143. Francis, "Family: Marriage (I)," para. 4.
144. Francis, "Family: Marriage (I)," para. 6.
145. Francis, "Family: Marriage (I)," para. 6.
146. Francis, "Family: Marriage (II)," para. 1.
147. Francis, "Family: Marriage (II)," para. 1.
148. Francis, "Family: Marriage (II)," para. 1.

them, arising as she does from the sacramental grace flowing forth from the side of the crucified Christ in his paschal slumber. Indeed, according to Lubac's own rationale, the saying is true of every sacrament, in that, for Lubac, every sacrament makes real, renews, or strengthens the communion of the mystical body,[149] such that it both is affected by the Church and affects the reality of that communion.

For Francis, the sacrificial love inherent to marriage renders this sacrament "a great act of faith and love."[150] It is "a witness to the courage to believe in the beauty of the creative act of God and to live that love that is always urging us to go on, beyond ourselves and even beyond our own family."[151] To enter into and live out this sacrament, in this rationale, is to enter into the mystery of God's creative act. Marriage contains the paradigmatic structure of the Christian vocation at large, in that "the Christian vocation to love unconditionally and without limit is what, by the grace of Christ, is also at the foundation of the free consent that constitutes marriage."[152] Indeed, "the Church herself is fully involved in the story of every Christian marriage: she is built on their successes and she suffers in their failures."[153] Built-up marriages build up the Church; wounded marriages wound the Church. The Socratic Francis, on the streets of the global Athens, asks his fellow Catholics, "do we ourselves as believers and as pastors accept" this identification "of the history of Christ and his Church with the history of marriage and the human family?"[154] That is, do we accept that the story of every marriage is the story of the Church, and the story of the Church is the story of every marriage? For Francis, the history of Christ and his Church and the history of every marriage is a singular history. The mystery of marriage is at the heart of ecclesial existence. This Socratic theologian and social critic continues, asking his fellow Catholics, challenging them with the truth of the Church's doctrine of marriage and family: "Are we seriously ready to take up this responsibility" to go "on the path of the love that Christ has for the Church?"[155] So asks this papal Socrates, rooting a theology

149. Lubac, *Catholicism*, 82.
150. Francis, "Family: Marriage (II)," para. 5.
151. Francis, "Family: Marriage (II)," para. 5.
152. Francis, "Family: Marriage (II)," para. 5.
153. Francis, "Family: Marriage (II)," para. 6.
154. Francis, "Family: Marriage (II)," para. 6.
155. Francis, "Family: Marriage (II)," para. 6.

of marriage within the mystery of creation and within the context of the mystery of the spousal union between Christ and the Church, for which union creation was made "in the depths of this mystery of creation"[156]— this mystery of marriage as creation's summit and as the manifestation and revelation of the love Christ has for the Church. Such is the presupposition of the much needed "decision to 'wed in the Lord.'"[157]

This mystery of Christian marriage entails, Francis says, "a missionary dimension, which means having at heart the willingness to be a medium for God's blessing and for the Lord's grace *to all*."[158] Indeed, "Christian spouses participate"—precisely "*as spouses*"—"in the mission of the Church."[159] Francis insists that "the celebration of the sacrament"[160] calls for the assumption of a "co-responsibility of family life in the Church's great mission of love."[161] As ecclesial collaborators, a great deal is demanded of spouses. As Francis puts it, "it takes courage to love one another as Christ loves the Church."[162] This is why Francis says, when he meets newlyweds, "Here are the brave ones!"[163] The sacrament of marriage demands that the faithful at large courageously support and defend marriage against all that threatens its flourishing.

For Francis, "the life of the Church is enriched every time by the beauty of this spousal covenant" and the life of the Church likewise "deteriorates every time" the spousal covenant "is disfigured."[164] Likewise, to enter into and live the sacrament of holy matrimony is to live as Church, as communion, it is to realize ecclesial communion, it is to enrich the

156. Francis, "Family: Marriage (II)," para. 7.

157. Francis, "Family: Marriage (II)," para. 7.

158. Francis, "Family: Marriage (II)," para. 7.

159. Francis, "Family: Marriage (II)," para. 7.

160. Francis, "Family: Marriage (II)," para. 8.

161. Francis, "Family: Marriage (II)," para. 9.

162. Francis, "Family: Marriage (II)," para. 8.

163. Francis, "Family: Marriage (II)," para. 8.

164. Francis, "Family: Marriage (II)," para. 9. As Lubac says: "Just as redemption and revelation, even though they reach every individual soul, are none the less fundamentally not individual but social, so grace which is produced and maintained by the sacraments does not set up a purely individual relationship between the soul and God." For Lubac, each individual receives the grace of the sacraments by way of being "joined, socially, to the one body whence flows this saving life-stream," which is precisely the joining, the communion, that takes place by way of the sacraments, including marriage. Lubac recounts that "the first effect of baptism, for example, is none other than . . . incorporation in the visible Church." Lubac, *Catholicism*, 82.

Church, to realize and strengthen the Church's communion. Fidelity in married life is the Church's self-realization and enrichment; marital disfigurement is the Church's disfigurement, a detriment to the whole body, a wounding of the whole, a contradiction of her constitutive communion, a sign of humanity's remaining brokenness, humanity's status as yet to arrive at her eschatological ecclesial destiny. "The Church, in order to offer to all the gifts of faith, hope, and love, needs the courageous fidelity of spouses to the grace of their sacrament."[165] To be true to her meaning, the Church depends upon the sacrament of matrimony and the receptivity of spouses to the sacrament's grace.

As the journey of spouses is the journey of the Church, "the People of God need" the "daily journey in faith, in love and in hope"[166] carried out by spouses bound by the sacramental alliance between man and woman. The Church needs this journey to be made, "with all the joys and the toils that this journey entails in a marriage and a family."[167] At the same time, couples can rely on Christ to carry them through, for "Christ does not cease to care for the Church: he loves her always, he guards her always, as himself." Indeed, "the route" of married ecclesial life "is well marked forever, it is the route of love: to love as God loves, forever"—that's what the call to marriage *is*. "Men and women, brave enough to carry this treasure in the 'earthen vessel' of our humanity . . . are . . . an essential resource for the Church, as well as for the world!"[168]

Mercy East of Eden

The treasure carried in the earthen vessel of our humanity is the "radiation of God's power and tenderness" in the testimony of those bound by matrimony. It is the treasure of Christ's fidelity to his Church, his persistent love for her, his refusal to cease removing "stains and lines of every kind from the human face."[169] That icon in Genesis 3, to which Francis appeals, that icon of reconciliation, of the Lord God's loving concern for Adam and Eve, having sinned, consists of the narrative moment when "the Lord God

---

165. Francis, "Family: Marriage (II)," para. 9.
166. Francis, "Family: Marriage (II)," para. 9.
167. Francis, "Family: Marriage (II)," para. 9.
168. Francis, "Family: Marriage (II)," para. 9.
169. Francis, "Family: Marriage (II)," para. 9.

made for Adam and for his wife garments of skin."[170] Mercy doesn't always mean allowing for access to the Eucharist for those living in explicit contradiction to the meaning of marriage, as mercy in the story of Adam and Eve includes a banishment from the garden—*but toward an evangelical end.* The gaze of mercy which Francis commends to the Church's pastors in *AL* chapter 8 is the very gaze of God upon Adam and Eve as he expelled them from Eden.

Francis never fails in his emphatic lamentation of "any breach of the marriage bond" as "against the will of God," and precisely in perceiving this do we perceive "the frailty of many of" the Church's children.[171] It is through "the gaze of Jesus Christ" that the Church is illumined and so "turns with love to those who participate in an incomplete manner" in the Church's life.[172] The maternal Church thus recognizes that "the grace of God works also in their lives by giving them courage to do good"—to carry out justice and charity for their children and for those with whom they have separated and those with whom they now may be raising children—"to care for one another in love and to be of service to the community in which they live and work."[173] And in this context, the Church "constantly holds up the call to perfection, and asks for a fuller response to God."[174] Francis calls upon the Church's shepherds to enter "into pastoral dialogue with these persons" who fall short of living the reality of Christian marriage. The goal of such pastoral dialogue is to begin "to distinguish elements in their lives that can lead to a greater openness to the Gospel of marriage in its fullness."[175] Countering the sexual catechesis on offer in our technocratic, consumeristic, and relativistic culture requires the Church's pastors and the core faithful to be in for the long haul with those whose sexual lives and family lives have come under the rule of technocratic lust, but who nonetheless seek to abide in the fold of the Church, and who know nothing other than a consumeristic, throwaway vision of sexuality. The core faithful and their shepherds must find ways to proclaim the good news that "the earth is filled with harmony

---

170. "M&F2," para. 7, Gen 3:21.

171. *AL*, sec. 291.

172. *AL*, sec. 291.

173. *AL*, sec. 291.

174. *AL*, sec. 291.

175. *AL*, sec. 293.

and trust when the alliance between man and woman is lived properly."[176] The core faithful and their shepherds must find ways of testifying to the truth that "if man and woman seek" this harmony "together, between themselves, and with God, without a doubt they will find" that harmony.[177] "Jesus encourages us explicitly to bear witness to this beauty" of harmony between man and woman, who together constitute "the image of God."[178]

For Francis, children are "the most beautiful gift and blessing that the Creator has given to man and woman."[179] This "great gift" for human-ity[180]—children—unfortunately, is victim to the great scourge of abortion by which thousands are "not even allowed to be born."[181] In the face of the falsehoods of the throwaway culture, which disposes of children, "what is necessary is a more enthusiastic commitment to ransoming" or "rehabili-tating" "this great 'invention' of God's creation"—the family.[182]

It's the sort of commitment needed to combat relativism's dictator-ship of technocratic lust.

176. "M&F1," para. 9.

177. "M&F1," para. 9.

178. Francis, "Family: Marriage (II)," para. 9.

179. Francis, "Family: The Children (II)," para. 1.

180. Francis, "Family: The Children (I)," para. 1.

181. Francis, "Family: The Children (I)," para. 1.

182. Francis, "Address to JP2 Institute," sec. 3.

CONCLUSION

· · · · ·

Prophetic Outcry and Liturgical Praise in the Fiery Furnace of Technocratic Lust

IN DECEMBER 2017, PROFESSOR RENO declared to his "students" in the "classroom" of *First Things* that

> Pope Francis and his associates want to sign a peace treaty with the sexual revolution. They will use whatever arguments and rhetoric are necessary to achieve this goal. One can see the urgency of the task. Reconciling the Catholic Church with the sexual revolution is necessary in order to preserve Catholicism as a bourgeois religion.[1]

Reno's comment led Rod Dreher to dub Pope Francis the "Chaplain of Liquid Modernity,"[2] and to assert that "This papacy is not hard to figure out. Pope Francis and his associates echo the pieties and self-compliment-ing utopianism of progressives."[3] The student in the back row of Reno's classroom, however, has been encountering an entirely different Pope Francis than the one that Reno presents to his students and that Dreher here picks up from Reno's presentation. This student holds Reno respon-sible for broadcasting a misleading presentation of the Francis message. If the above claims of Reno and Dreher were accompanied by a serious exegesis of the pope's own words, then the claims could be taken more seriously. If the above claims were accompanied by a presentation of how

1. Reno, "Liberal Tradition," sec. "Bourgeois Religion," paras. 6–7.
2. Dreher, "Chaplain of Liquid Modernity."
3. Dreher, "Chaplain of Liquid Modernity," para. 8.

Francis lacks any continuity with the JP2-B16 vision of truth, justice, and charity, if they could show that he subscribed to an ethos, spirituality, and theology of a liberal Christianity wholly other than the robust tradition of JP2 and Benedict, then perhaps the student in the back row of Reno's classroom would join the professor in decrying the ways in which the Holy Father is moving in the public square. But the Pope Francis that this student in the back row of Reno's classroom has come to be formed by and whose lead he follows is a Pope Francis who, alongside JP2 and Benedict, offers a robust alternative to the regime of relativism as well as a compelling alternative to the culture warrior Catholic conservatism that Reno's student has come to reject.

Don't get me wrong. The papal trio's song is as much a battle cry as any outcry heard from the ranks of culture warriors duking it out on various media platforms. But more fundamentally, the papal trio's song *is a song of praise*. As a battle cry, it is such at the service of the more fundamental task of cosmic praise that we are called to be leaders in, as cosmic priests, cosmic "shepherds of being," liturgists and cantors in the cosmic church, in awe before the cosmic tabernacle containing God in the flesh, the Word sustaining all things, definitively and irrevocably in our very midst, dwelling among us, flesh of our flesh and bone of our bone.

The three popes are indeed soldiers embroiled in fighting a war. The song they sing and the war they fight is accompanied by their singular battle cry for moral truth, a singular canticle of social justice and chaste love, a hymn of orthodoxy, a prophetic ballad that stands in opposition to the falsehood of the lust of the eyes, the lust of the flesh, and the pride of life. They're singing a song of cosmic chastity within the fiery furnace of technocratic lust.

In the midst of the technocratic paradigm's throwaway culture, we have an alternative *integral,* theologically rooted economic and ecological social vision within our reach in the teaching of JP2, Benedict, and Francis—a vision that is foundational for an integral vision of sexuality, a vision that perceives the sanctity of marriage and of life in the womb. But communities of committed Catholics in North America today tend to form hearts to be highly *suspicious* of environmental concern and of any rhetoric that challenges the logic of capitalism. To express a need for economic and ecological reform today is to play by the playbook of the left—at least, that's what many committed Catholics suppose. For many of the core faithful, to be discontented with the current state of affairs economically and ecologically speaking is to fall for a lie propagated by

our alleged *enemy* in the culture wars. To oppose these movements of
social justice is a temptation to simplistically misidentify the cultural battle between right and left with the spiritual battle between good and evil.
To be discontented with business as usual (with respect to the market) is
thought to be ungrateful for the incredible prosperity of our day brought
to us by capitalism; it's thought to be resentful in the midst of abundant
blessings, resentful like the allegedly resentful socialists, environmentalists, and Black Lives Matter activists who are so easily dismissed in conservative Christian circles as part of what's wrong with the world, part of
an ideological force against which Christianity stands as a polar opposite.
But when we take it for granted that discontentment with business as
usual in the economy is a sure sign of an enemy of Christianity, we miss
the reality that the papal fight against the commercial logic is a fight for
justice, for charity, for truth. Only if we subscribe to a relativistic outlook can we dismiss any protest against that logic as mere ingratitude for
relative prosperity. In the dictatorship of relativism, wealth creation—not
truth, not justice, not charity—is the standard by which we measure the
economic health of a society. But in a communal ethos of chaste love
that prioritizes the common good, there's an actual standard of right and
wrong—not simply degrees of prosperity and relative success or failure
in creating wealth. The neoliberalism that has a choke hold on Demo-
crats and Republicans alike disdains such protest, because neoliberalism
insists upon the measuring stick of relative prosperity, not the measuring
stick of truth, justice, and charity. For the papal trio, the social question
is not how much wealth is being created now relative to other times in
world history, but what good is due to whom, and how we can better
render the good that is due to whom it is due. And for the papal trio, the
pitfall of the liberal market as we know it is that its goals do not include
the works of justice and charity according to the standard of truth, but
wheeling and dealing according to the standards of mere wealth creation
and capital amassment.

Though we have in the Chair of Peter a stalwart warrior fighting
on behalf of the integral human ecology that he inherited from the two
previous popes, many of the core faithful instinctively dismiss him—on
what I regard as superficial grounds—as a figure whose vision is one that
undermines the strength of orthodox commitment. At the same time,
JP2's and Benedict's respective calls for ecological and economic conversion have been disproportionately ignored in conservative Catholic
circles, such that on a popular level, when we hear Francis sound the

same call, our ears aren't trained to recognize its resonance with JP2 and B16, but only its apparent resonance with the demands of bandwagon progressive political correctness.

Reno knows JP2 and Benedict call for ecological and economic conversion, and he's identified points of continuity between Francis and the two previous popes on this score. What I think Reno has missed, however, is the ethical, spiritual, and theological heart of what JP2, Benedict, and Francis each have to say about economics, ecology, and sexuality, and which, when perceived, brings to light the place of Francis as securely within the JP2-B16 tradition of Catholic social teaching.

True to the legacy of JP2 and Benedict, for Francis, business cannot go on as usual. Like the two popes before him, Francis calls for a dramatic transformation of the economic order. This is a key and fundamental aspect of the JP2 and Benedict legacy, an aspect that gets a disproportionately small amount of airtime by some of JP2's and Benedict's most enthusiastic supporters. Francis, in contrast, has faithfully continued this papal cry for economic reform, in integral relation to the entirety of the theologically rooted social vision proper to the two previous popes. What each of these pontiffs have offered is a theological and anthropological ecology with economic implications, in integral relation to the crisis of sexuality, marriage, family, and Christian vocational commitment at large. But how characteristic is it in Catholic circles to discuss the teaching of JP2 in these terms—in terms of ecology and economics?—which is what I take to be the integral context in which JP2 presented his teaching on sexuality. Protest driven by chaste love is protest against injustice and falsehood. That's Pope Francis's alternative to the Religious Right's relativistic alliance with the technocratic paradigm of the liberal market.

As much as Francis's message of cosmic chastity contains within itself a maternal and evangelistic alliance with the best of the impulses of our age and of our society, his message, like that of his predecessors, contains an unsettling call to conversion that is meant to be unsettling for everyone—left, right, center, politically disinterested, or anywhere in between. In sounding this call to conversion to moral truth in an age of technocratic lust, Francis sings the very song that our technocratically deformed and lustful hearts need to hear.

Francis's unsettling call to moral conversion, his call to adhere to moral truth, is fundamentally a call to *responsibility*. The world today— and this is certainly inclusive of the millennial generation and the up- and-coming Generation Z—very much needs to learn the meaning of human responsibility, and in what ways we are called to love. Francis assumes as his own the rationale of JP2's catechesis on humanity as a cosmic *shepherd of being*. We all have a liturgical responsibility, according to our baptismal identity as priests offering the world—which God has given to us—back to God. Collectively and each of us individually, according to our state in life, have a responsibility as shepherds and stewards of what has been entrusted to us, to see to it that the things of the world are cared for according to their meaning and destiny. Francis the teacher, evangelist, prophet, and philosopher-gadfly calls us from irresponsibility to responsibility, inviting us to see with him the splendor of creation in all its truth, to honor that splendor, to honor our own place within it.

The papal trio's call to responsibility as cosmic liturgists *presupposes the liturgical meaning of the universe*. Since the dawn of modernity, Western society, and now globalized society, has stood in need of perceiving the meaning of creaturely existence in reference to God, not merely in reference to pleasure, utility, profit, and the will to power, as though a thing's meaning were determined merely by what I take to be its usefulness to me as a pleasure-seeking consumer or power-seeking, profit-seeking possessor of the means of production.

The world today, as in every age, stands in need of God as revealed in Jesus Christ, and the world can find its ultimate fulfillment only by way of adoring Jesus Christ as God, with all things being subjected to his loving dominion. The song of cosmic chastity that Francis sings with the two previous popes in the fiery furnace of a technocratic age has at its center and object of adoration the "fourth man" in the fire, namely, the Son of Man. In the song of cosmic chastity, *he and his chaste love* is the hermeneutical key to understanding all that exists, revealing the givenness of all being. Jesus Christ is the fourth man in the fire who accompanies the three popes, resembling three young men, with a message characterized by the freshness of youth, singing their praises to the Creator in defiance of lust's tyranny, in defiance of technocracy's false gods, in defiance of lust and its widespread alliance with relativism. Protest and praise: that's what's on offer in Francis's proposal for a renewed sense of meaning.

If St. Francis is the subjective human icon of cosmic chastity, that is, if he is the icon of the human subject who perceives the cosmos chastely, the corollary "objective" icon of cosmic chastity, which is to say, the icon of *the cosmos upon which the chaste eyes of a subject like St. Francis gazes*, is the maternal "pachamama" figure featured prominently at the Synod on the Amazon. What St. Francis beholds with reverence and love is the earth as a fruitful, life-giving mother, pregnant with ever-new life, ever poised to give of herself in the sustenance of new life, ever available as self-giving gift, in maternal communion with the child of her womb, in prepared readiness to deliver her child. We see in this image of purity a personification of life, of maternity, capable of cauterizing the porn-infected eyes and hearts of this technologically fettered generation.[4] To opt for the way of purgation for which St. Benedict opted, the way of asceticism and delight for which St. Francis opted, is to choose the pachamama option—to behold creation for what she is, in all her fecundity, bounty, goodness, and beauty, with the chaste gaze of Sts. Benedict and Francis.

Pope Francis calls us to continue in the prophetic tradition of cosmic reverence, following in the footsteps of Guardini and Lubac, JP2, and Benedict. This prophetic witness to cosmic reverence proper to Christian faith perceives Jesus Christ, the Logos, as the center and source of all creation's grandeur. The project of catechesis and formation in cosmic chastity is a project of reorienting our hearts in relation to "the fourth man in the fire"—Jesus Christ—who is the object of praise in the cosmic liturgy, in the song that the three popes sing, even as the fires of empire, the fires of relativism's dictatorship and technocracy, of lust in its three forms, burn around us. As the "Nebuchadnezzars" of our age (and of our hearts) rage with fury when we refuse to bow to the false gods of the age, we can hold on with a steadfast hope to our song of praise, hold on with steadfast hope to the fourth man present with us in the fire. This fourth man in the fire can awaken in every Nebuchadnezzar an allegiance to the God of Shadrach, Meshach, and Abednego. The papal trio—with their youthful song of cosmic chastity—directs our gaze to the beginning and the end, to the Alpha and the Omega, to the Logos, to the great high priest of the cosmic liturgy, Jesus Christ.

4. It is characteristic of iconoclasm, in its misdirected war on idolatry, to stand in ideological opposition to the very figures that make false deities quake. For a pro-life icon of maternal love is indeed a force against which the myriad idols of lust cannot stand. Such iconoclastic opposition to this pro-life icon was widespread among those who misperceived the image's meaning.

Bibliography

Aquinas, Thomas. *Summa theologiae*. Translated by Fathers of the English Dominican Province, 1955. http://www.newadvent.org/summa/.

Balthasar, Hans Urs von. *The Glory of the Lord: A Theological Aesthetics*. Vol. 3, *Studies in Theological Style: Lay Styles*. Translated by Andrew Louth et al. San Francisco: Ignatius, 1986.

Barker, Jeremiah. "The Poustinik Option: Catherine Doherty's Answer to Violence." *Plough*, August 12, 2021. https://www.plough.com/en/topics/justice/politics/conscientious-objection/the-poustinik-option.

Benedict XVI, Pope. "Address of His Holiness Benedict XVI to Mr. Gilbert Ramez Chagoury, Ambassador of Saint Lucia, Accredited to the Holy See." The Vatican, December 1, 2005. https://www.vatican.va/content/benedict-xvi/en/speeches/2005/december/documents/hf_ben_xvi_spe_20051201_ambassador-santa-lucia.html.

———. "Address of His Holiness Pope Benedict XVI to the Diplomatic Corps Accredited to the Holy See for the Traditional Exchange of New Year Greetings." The Vatican, January 8, 2007. https://www.vatican.va/content/benedict-xvi/en/speeches/2008/january/documents/hf_ben-xvi_spe_20080107_diplomatic-corps.html.

———. *Africa munus*. Apostolic exhortation. The Vatican, November 19, 2011. http://www.vatican.va/content/benedict-xvi/en/apost_exhortations/document/hf_ben-xvi_exh_20111119_afraicae-munus.html.

———. *Deus caritas est*. Encyclical letter. The Vatican, December 25, 2005. https://www.vatican.va/content/benedict-xvi/en/encyclicals/documents/hf_ben-xvi_enc_20051225_deus-caritas-est.html.

———. *Jesus of Nazareth: From the Baptism in the Jordan to the Transfiguration*. Translated by Adrian J. Walker. New York: Doubleday, 2007.

———. "Letter of His Holiness Benedict XVI to Professor Mary Ann Glendon, President of the Pontifical Academy of Social Sciences on the Occasion of the 13th Plenary Session." The Vatican, April 28, 2007. https://www.vatican.va/content/benedict-xvi/en/letters/2007/documents/hf_ben-xvi_let_20070428_scienze-sociali.html.

———. "Meeting of the Holy Father Benedict XVI with the Clergy of the Diocese of Bolzano-Bressanone." The Vatican, August 6, 2008. https://www.vatican.va/content/benedict-xvi/en/speeches/2008/august/documents/hf_ben-xvi_spe_20080806_clero-bressanone.html.

————. "Message of His Holiness Pope Benedict XVI for the Celebration of the World Day of Peace." The Vatican, January 1, 2007. https://www.vatican.va/content/benedict-xvi/en/messages/peace/documents/hf_ben-xvi_mes_20061208_xl-world-day-peace.html.

————. "Visit to the Bundestag: Address of His Holiness Benedict XVI." September 22, 2011. https://www.vatican.va/content/benedict-xvi/en/speeches/2011/september/documents/hf_ben-xvi_spe_20110922_reichstag-berlin.html.

Bishops of the Pastoral Region of Buenos Aires. "Directive of the Bishops of the Buenos Aires Pastoral Region to the Regional Clergy." Translated by Matthew Cullinan Hoffman. September 5, 2016. https://www.lifesitenews.com/wp-content/uploads/2021/03/Basic_Criteria_for_the_Application_of_Chapter_VIII_of_Amoris_Laetitia__September_5__2016.pdf.

Boland, Donald. "Chesterton and John Paul II on Capitalism." *Houston Catholic Worker*, February 1, 2009. https://cjd.org/2009/02/01/chesterton-and-john-paul-ii-on-capitalism/.

Bonhoeffer, Dietrich. *The Cost of Discipleship*. New York: Macmillan, 1963.

Cary, Phillip. "And It Was Very Good." *First Thoughts* (blog), December 11, 2013. https://www.firstthings.com/blogs/firstthoughts/2013/12/and-it-was-very-good.

————. "Gender as Consumer Choice." *First Thoughts* (blog), October 21, 2014. https://www.firstthings.com/blogs/firstthoughts/2014/10/gender-as-consumer-choice-1.

Catechism of the Catholic Church. 2nd ed. Vatican City: Vatican Press, 1997. https://www.vatican.va/archive/ENG0015/_INDEX.HTM.

Compendium of the Social Doctrine of the Church. Vatican City: Vatican Press, 2005. https://www.vatican.va/roman_curia/pontifical_councils/justpeace/documents/rc_pc_justpeace_doc_20060526_compendio-dott-soc_en.html.

De Souza, Raymond. "Pope's Amoris Laetitia Guidelines Get an Upgrade." *National Catholic Register*, December 12, 2017. https://www.ncregister.com/news/pope-s-amoris-laetitia-guidelines-get-an-upgrade.

————. "What Argentina's 'Amoris Laetitia' Guidelines Really Mean." *National Catholic Register*, September 23, 2016. https://www.ncregister.com/news/what-argentina-s-amoris-laetitia-guidelines-really-mean.

Doherty, Catherine. *Poustinia: Encountering God in Silence, Solitude and Prayer*. Combermere, ON: Madonna House, 2012.

Dreher, Rod. "Pope Francis: Chaplain of Liquid Modernity." *American Conservative*, November 9, 2017. https://www.theamericanconservative.com/pope-francis-chaplain-of-liquid-modernity/.

Faggioli, Massimo. "Whose Rome? Burke, Bannon, and the Eternal City." *Commonweal*, October 18, 2018. https://www.commonwealmagazine.org/whose-rome.

Francis, Pope. "Address of His Holiness Pope Francis to the Participants in the General Chapter of the Oblates of Saint Joseph." The Vatican, August 31, 2018. https://www.vatican.va/content/francesco/en/speeches/2018/august/documents/papa-francesco_20180831_oblati-sangiuseppe.html.

————. "Address of the Holy Father Francis to the Academic Community of the Pontifical John Paul II Institute for Studies in Marriage and Family." The Vatican, October 27, 2016. Author's English translation based on Google translate. https://www.vatican.va/content/francesco/it/speeches/2016/october/documents/papa-francesco_20161027_pontificio-istituto-gpii.html.

———. "Address of Pope Francis to Representatives of the Jewish Community of Rome." The Vatican, October 11, 2013. https://www.vatican.va/content/francesco/en/speeches/2013/october/documents/papa-francesco_20131011_comunita-ebraica-roma.html.

———. "Audience with the Diplomatic Corps Accredited to the Holy See: Address Pope Francis." The Vatican, March 22, 2013. https://www.vatican.va/content/francesco/en/speeches/2013/march/documents/papa-francesco_20130322_corpo-diplomatico.html.

———. "Beware of Sliding into Worldliness." Homily. The Vatican, February 13, 2020. https://www.vatican.va/content/francesco/en/cotidie/2020/documents/papa-francesco-cotidie_20200213_bewareof-sliding-into-worldliness.html.

———. "A Big Heart Open to God." Interview by Antonio Spadaro. *America Magazine*, September 30, 2013. https://www.americamagazine.org/faith/2013/09/30/big-heart-open-god-interview-pope-francis.

———. "Closing of the Jubilee for the 800th Anniversary of the Confirmation of the Order of Preachers." The Vatican, January 21, 2017. https://www.vatican.va/content/francesco/en/homilies/2017/documents/papa-francesco_20170121_omelia-domenicani.html.

———. "The Courage of Definitive of Choices." Morning meditation. The Vatican, November 25, 2013. https://www.vatican.va/content/francesco/en/cotidie/2013/documents/papa-francesco-cotidie_20131125_courage-choice.html.

———. "Day of Fraternity, Day of Penance and Prayer." Morning mediation. The Vatican, May 14, 2020. https://www.vatican.va/content/francesco/en/cotidie/2020/documents/papa-francesco-cotidie_20200514_giornodi-fratellanza-penitenza-preghiera.html.

———. "The Family: Marriage (I)." General audience. The Vatican, April 29, 2015. https://www.vatican.va/content/francesco/en/audiences/2015/documents/papa-francesco_20150429_udienza-generale.html.

———. "The Family: Marriage (II)." General audience. The Vatican, May 6, 2015. https://www.vatican.va/content/francesco/en/audiences/2015/documents/papa-francesco_20150506_udienza-generale.html.

———. "The Family: The Children (I)." General audience. The Vatican, February 11, 2015. https://www.vatican.va/content/francesco/en/audiences/2015/documents/papa-francesco_20150408_udienza-generale.html.

———. "The Family: The Children (II)." General audience. The Vatican, April 8, 2015. https://www.vatican.va/content/francesco/en/audiences/2015/documents/papa-francesco_20150408_udienza-generale.html.

———. "General Audience." The Vatican, September 24, 2014. https://www.vatican.va/content/francesco/en/audiences/2014/documents/papa-francesco_20140924_udienza-generale.html.

———. "Healing the World: Solidarity and the Virtue of Faith." General audience. The Vatican, September 2, 2020. https://www.vatican.va/content/francesco/en/audiences/2020/documents/papa-francesco_20200902_udienza-generale.html.

———. "Letter of His Holiness Pope Francis for the Bicentennial of Independence of the Argentine Republic." https://www.vatican.va/content/francesco/en/letters/2016/documents/papa-francesco_20160708_indipendenza-argentina.html.

———. "Mass, Imposition of the Pallium and Bestowal of the Fisherman's Ring for the Beginning of the Petrine Ministry of the Bishop of Rome: Homily of Pope Francis."

The Vatican, March 19, 2013. https://www.vatican.va/content/francesco/en/homilies/2013/documents/papa-francesco_20130319_omelia-inzio-potificato.html.

———. "Meeting with Bishops of Asia." The Vatican, August 17, 2014. https://www.vatican.va/content/francesco/en/speeches/2014/august/documents/papa-francesco_20140817_corea-vescovi-asia.html.

———. "Meeting with Indigenous People of Amazonia." February 2, 2021. https://www.vatican.va/content/francesco/en/messages/pont-messages/2021/documents/papa-francesco_20210202_messaggio-forum-popoli-indigeni.html.

———. "Meeting with the Leaders of Other Religions and Other Christian Denominations at the Catholic University 'Our Lady of Good Counsel.'" The Vatican, September 21, 2014. https://www.vatican.va/content/francesco/en/speeches/2014/september/documents/papa-francesco_20140921_albania-leaders-altre-religioni.html.

———. "Message of His Holiness Pope Francis to the Young People Gathered in Medjugorje for the Annual Meeting." The Vatican, June 29, 2020. https://www.vatican.va/content/francesco/en/messages/pont-messages/2020/documents/papa-francesco_20200629_messaggio-giovani-medjugorje.html.

———. "Message of the Holy Father Francis to the Organisers and Participants at the Fifth Global Meeting of the Indigenous Peoples' Forum." The Vatican, February 2, 2021. https://www.vatican.va/content/francesco/en/messages/pont-messages/2021/documents/papa-francesco_20210202_messaggio-forum-popoli-indigeni.html.

———. "Message of the Holy Father Francis to the XXV General Assembly of the Spanish Conference of Religious Men and Women (CONFER)." The Vatican, November 5, 2018. https://www.vatican.va/content/francesco/en/messages/pont-messages/2018/documents/papa-francesco_20181105_messaggio-confer.html.

———. "Meeting for Religious Liberty with the Hispanic Community and Other Immigrants." Speech. Independence Hall, Philadelphia, September 26, 2015. https://www.vatican.va/content/francesco/en/speeches/2015/september/documents/papa-francesco_20150926_usa-liberta-religiosa.html.

———. "Meeting with the Volunteers of the XVIII WYD: Address of Pope Francis." The Vatican, July 28, 2013. https://www.vatican.va/content/francesco/en/speeches/2013/july/documents/papa-francesco_20130728_gmg-rio-volontari.html.

———. "Message of Pope Francis on the Occasion of the 50th Anniversary of the Foundation of the Pontifical Council for Interreligious Dialogue." The Vatican, May 19, 2014. https://www.vatican.va/content/francesco/en/messages/pont-messages/2014/documents/papa-francesco_20140519_messaggio-50-dialogo-interreligioso.html.

———. "Midday Prayer in the Monastery of the Discalced Carmelites." The Vatican, September 7, 2019. https://www.vatican.va/content/francesco/en/homilies/2019/documents/papa-francesco_20190907_omelia-madagascar-oramedia.html.

———. "Participation at the Second World Meeting of Popular Movements." July 9, 2015. https://www.vatican.va/content/francesco/en/speeches/2015/july/documents/papa-francesco_20150709_bolivia-movimenti-popolari.html.

———. "The Prayer of the Psalms." General audience. October 14, 2020. https://www.vatican.va/content/francesco/en/audiences/2020/documents/papa-francesco_20201014_udienza-generale.html.

———. "Prayer Vigil for the Festival of Families: Address of the Holy Father." The Vatican, September 26, 2015. https://www.vatican.va/content/francesco/en/speeches/2015/september/documents/papa-francesco_20150926_usa-festa-famiglie.html.

———. "Press Conference of His Holiness Pope Francis Onboard the Flight from Colombo to Manila." Interviewed by Jerry O'Connell. Papal Flight. The Vatican, January 15, 2015. https://www.vatican.va/content/francesco/en/speeches/2015/january/documents/papa-francesco_20150115_srilanka-filippine-incontro-giornalisti.html.

———. "Solemnity of All Saints: Homily of Pope Francis." The Vatican, November 1, 2014. https://www.vatican.va/content/francesco/en/homilies/2014/documents/papa-francesco_20141101_omelia-ognissanti.html.

———. "Thanksgiving Mass for the Canonization of Saint Jose de Anchieta, Professed Priest of the Society of Jesus." Homily. The Vatican, April 24, 2014. https://www.vatican.va/content/francesco/en/homilies/2014/documents/papa-francesco_20140424_omelia-san-jose-de-anchieta.html.

———. *To All Consecrated People on the Occasion of the Year of Consecrated Life.* Apostolic letter. The Vatican, November 21, 2014. https://www.vatican.va/content/francesco/en/apost_letters/documents/papa-francesco_lettera-ap_20141121_lettera-consacrati.html.

———. "The Well-Mannered Evil One." Homily. The Vatican, October 9, 2015. https://www.vatican.va/content/francesco/en/cotidie/2015/documents/papa-francesco-cotidie_20151009_the-well-mannered-evil-one.html.

Francis, Pope and Ahmed Al-Tayyeb, Grand Imam. *Document on Human Fraternity for World Peace and Living Together.* The Vatican, February 4, 2019. *L'Osservatore Romano,* February 4-5, 2019, 6.

George, Robert P. "Unity, Truth, and Catholic Social Thought." *First Things,* July 13, 2018. https://www.firstthings.com/web-exclusives/2018/07/unity-truth-and-catholic-social-thought.

Gorman, Michael J. *Elements of Biblical Exegesis.* Peabody, MA: Hendrickson, 1998.

Guardini, Romano. *The End of the Modern World.* New York: Sheed and Ward, 1956.

Guggenheim, Davis, dir. *An Inconvenient Truth.* Beverly Hills, CA: Lawrence Bender Productions, 2006.

Hanby, Michael. "The Gospel of Creation and the Technocratic Paradigm: Reflections on a Central Teaching of Laudatio Sí." *Communio* 42.4 (Winter 2015) 724–47. https://www.communio-icr.com/files/42.4_Hanby_website.pdf.

———. "Technocracy and the Body." *Humanum Review* 4 (2018). https://humanreview.com/articles/technocracy-and-the-body.

John Paul II, Pope. *Address to Scientists and Representatives of the United Nations University.* Hiroshima, February 25, 1981. https://www.vatican.va/content/john-paul-ii/en/speeches/1981/february/documents/hf_jp-ii_spe_19810225_giappone-hiroshima-scienziati-univ.html.

———. *Ecclesia in Africa.* Apostolic exhortation. The Vatican, September 14, 1995. https://www.vatican.va/content/john-paul-ii/en/apost_exhortations/documents/hf_jp-ii_exh_14091995_ecclesia-in-africa.html.

———. "God Made Man the Steward of Creation." General audience. The Vatican, January 17, 2001. https://www.vatican.va/content/john-paul-ii/en/audiences/2001/documents/hf_jp-ii_aud_20010117.html.

———. "Homily of His Holiness John Paul II: Boston Common." The Vatican, October 1, 1979. https://www.vatican.va/content/john-paul-ii/en/homilies/1979/documents/hf_jp-ii_hom_19791001_usa-boston.html.

———. "A Meditation on Givenness." *Communio* 41 (Winter 2014) 872–83. https://www.communio-icr.com/articles/view/a-meditation-on-givenness.

———. "No Peace Without Justice, No Justice Without Forgiveness: World Day of Peace Message." January 1, 2002. https://www.vatican.va/content/john-paul-ii/en/messages/peace/documents/hf_jp-ii_mes_20011211_xxxv-world-day-for-peace.html.

———. *Redemptoris custos.* Apostolic exhortation. The Vatican, August 15, 1989. https://www.vatican.va/content/john-paul-ii/en/apost_exhortations/documents/hf_jp-ii_exh_15081989_redemptoris-custos.html.

———. *Redemptoris missio.* Encyclical letter. The Vatican, December 7, 1990. https://www.vatican.va/content/john-paul-ii/en/encyclicals/documents/hf_jp-ii_enc_07211990_redemptoris-mission.html.

———. *Spiritus Domini.* Apostolic letter. The Vatican, August 1, 1987. https://www.vatican.va/content/john-paul-ii/fr/apost_letters/1987/documents/hf_jp-ii_apl_19870801_spiritus-domini.html.

Lubac, Henri de. *Catholicism: Christ and the Common Destiny of Man.* Translated by Lancelot C. Shepherd and Elizabeth Englund. San Francisco: Ignatius, 1988.

Martino, Renato Raffaele, and Giampaolo Crepaldi. "Presentation." In *Compendium of the Social Teaching of the Church*, Pontifical Council for Justice and Peace. https://www.vatican.va/roman_curia/pontifical_councils/justpeace/documents/rc_pc_justpeace_doc_20060526_compendio-dott-soc_en.html#PRESENTATION.

Maurin, Peter. "The Personalist Communitarian." *Catholic Worker* 83.3 (May 2016) 1.

Mayor, Tom, dir. *Seven Deadly Sins, Seven Lively Virtues.* Los Angeles: Word on Fire Institute, 2007.

Neusner, Jacob. *A Rabbi Talks with Jesus.* Montreal: McGill-Queen's, 2000.

Pentin, Edward. "Full Text and Explanatory Notes of Cardinals' Questions on '*Amoris Laetitia*.'" *National Catholic Register* (blog), November 14, 2016. https://www.ncregister.com/blog/full-text-and-explanatory-notes-of-cardinals-questions-on-amoris-laetitia.

Paul VI, Pope. "Advertising in the Mass Media: Benefits, Dangers, Responsibilities." Message for World Social Communications Day. May 12, 1977. https://www.vatican.va/content/paul-vi/en/messages/communications/documents/hf_p-vi_mes_19770512_xi-com-day.html.

———. *Ecclesium suam.* Encyclical letter. The Vatican, August 6, 1964. https://www.vatican.va/content/paul-vi/en/encyclicals/documents/hf_p-vi_enc_06081964_ecclesiam.html.

———. "Visit of Pope Paul VI to the F.A.O. on the 25th Anniversary of Its Institution." Speech. November 16, 1970. https://www.vatican.va/content/paul-vi/en/speeches/1970/documents/hf_p-vi_spe_19701116_xxv-istituzione-fao.html.

Ratzinger, Joseph. "Europe's Crisis of Culture." In *The Essential Benedict XVI: His Central Writings and Speeches*, edited by John F. Thornton and Susan B. Varenne, 325–35. New York: HarperOne, 2007.

———. "Homily at the Mass for the Election of the Roman Pontiff". In *The Essential Benedict XVI: His Central Writings and Speeches*, edited by John F. Thornton and Susan B. Varenne, 21–24. New York: HarperOne, 2007.

Reno, R. R. "Building Bridges, Not Walls." *First Things*, November 2017. https://www.
firstthings.com/article/2017/11/building-bridges-not-walls.

———. "The Civility Trap." *First Things*, March 2019. https://www.firstthings.com/
article/2019/03/the-civility-trap.

———. "Crisis of Solidarity." *First Things*, November 2015. https://www.firstthings.
com/article/2015/11/crisis-of-solidarity.

———. "Empire of Desire: Outlining the Postmodern Metaphysical Dream." *First
Things*, June 2014. https://www.firstthings.com/article/2014/06/empire-of-desire.

———. "A Failing Papacy." *First Things*, February 2019. https://www.firstthings.com/
article/2019/02/a-failing-papacy.

———. "Francis's Improv Theology." *First Things*, June 2016. https://www.firstthings.
com/blogs/firstthoughts/2016/06/franciss-improv-theology.

———. "Francis Stands Firm." *First Things*, February 2020. https://www.firstthings.
com/web-exclusives/2020/02/francis-stands-firm.

———. "How to Limit Government." *First Things*, December 2013. https://www.
firstthings.com/article/2013/12/how-to-limit-government.

———. "Liberal Tradition, Yes; Ideology, No." *First Things*, December 2017. https://
www.firstthings.com/article/2017/12/liberal-tradition-yes-ideology-no.

———. "A Militant Church: Ecumenism of Hate and a Case against *Cardinal*." *First
Things* (podcast), July 2017. Hosted by Julia Yost. With Matthew Schmitz. https://
www.firstthings.com/blogs/firstthoughts/2017/07/a-militant-church.

———. "Schools of Thought." *First Things*, November 2010. https://www.firstthings.
com/article/2010/11/schools-of-thought.

———. Series preface to the *Brazos Theological Commentary on the Bible*. In *Genesis*,
edited by R. R. Reno, 9–14. Grand Rapids: Brazos, 2010.

———. "The Weakness of *Laudato Si*." *First Things*, July 2015. https://firstthings.com/
web-exclusives/2015/07/the-weakness-of-laudato-si.

Second Vatican Council. "Dogmatic Constitution on the Church, *Lumen gentium*,
21 November, 1964." The Vatican, November 21, 1964. https://www.vatican.va/
archive/hist_councils/ii_vatican_council/documents/vat-ii_const_19641121_
lumen-gentium_en.html.

———. "Pastoral Constitution on the Church in the Modern World, *Gaudium et
spes*, 7 December, 1965." The Vatican, December 7, 1965. https://www.vatican.
va/archive/hist_councils/ii_vatican_council/documents/vat-ii_const_19651207_
gaudium-et-spes_en.html.

Schindler, D. C. "*Quaerere Deum*: Work as Love of God and World." *Humanum Review*
Issue 1 (2017). https://humanumreview.com/uploads/pdfs/quaerere-deum-work-
as-love-of-god-and-world.pdf.

Schindler, David L. "Conscience and the Relation Between Truth and Pastoral Practice:
Moral Theology and the Problem of Modernity." *Communio* 46 (Summer 2019)
333–85. https://www.communio-icr.com/articles/view/Moral-Theology-and-the-
Problem-of-Modernity.

———. "Habits of Presence and the Generosity of Creation: Ecology in Light of
Integral Human Development." *Communio* 42 (Winter 2015) 574–93. https://
www.communio-icr.com/articles/view/habits-of-presence-and-the-generosity-
of-creation-ecology-in-light-of-integ.

———. *Ordering Love: Liberal Societies and the Memory of Love*. Grand Rapids:
Eerdmans, 2011.

Schmitz, Matthew. "How I Changed My Mind about Pope Francis." *First Things*, December 8, 2016. https://www.firstthings.com/web-exclusives/2016/12/how-i-changed-my-mind-about-pope-francis.

Seewald, Peter. *Benedict XVI: A Life*. Vol. 1, *Youth in Nazi Germany to the Second Vatican*. Translated by Dinah Livingston. New York: Bloomsbury, 2020.

———. *Benedict XVI: A Life*. Vol. 2, *Professor and Prefect to Pope and Pope Emeritus: 1966–the Present*. Translated by Dinah Livingston. New York: Bloomsbury, 2021.

———. *Light of the World: The Pope, the Church, and the Signs of the Times*. Translated by Michael J. Miller and Adrian J. Walker. San Francisco: Ignatius, 2010.

Snell, R. J. *Acedia and Its Discontents: Metaphysical Boredom in an Empire of Desire*. Kettering: Angelico, 2015.

———. "Laudato Si' and the Feverish Summer." *Front Porch Republic*, August 20, 2015. https://www.frontporchrepublic.com/2015/08/laudato-si-and-the-feverish-summer/.

Waldstein, Michael. Introduction to *Man and Woman He Created Them: A Theology of the Body*, by Pope John Paul II, 1–128. Translated by Michael Waldstein. Boston: Pauline, 2006.

Walker, Adrian J. Foreword to *Not as the World Gives: The Way of Creative Justice*, by Stratford Caldecott, xv–xviii. Kettering, OH: Angelico, 2014.

———. "'What God Has Conjoined, Let No Man Put Asunder': A Meditation on Fruitfulness, Fidelity, and the Conjugal Embrace." *Communio* 41 (Summer 2014) 372–79.

Weigel, George. "*Caritas in Veritate* in Gold and Red." *National Review*, July 7, 2009. https://www.nationalreview.com/2009/07/caritas-veritate-gold-and-red-george-weigel/.

———. "Charity in Truth." *National Review*, July 13, 2009. https://www.nationalreview.com/2009/07/charity-truth-george-weigel/.

Wenders, Wim, dir. *Pope Francis: A Man of His Word*. Lugano, Switzerland: Palindrome, 2018.

West, Cornel, and Keeanga-Yamahtta Taylor. "America's Moment of Reckoning." Interview with Amy Goodman and Nermeen Shaikh. *Democracy Now!*, July 3, 2020. https://www.democracynow.org/2020/7/3/americas_moment_of_reckoning_keeanga_yamahtta.

West, Cornel, and Robert P. George. "The Politics of the Gospel." Interview with Peter Mommsen. *Plough Quarterly* 24 (Spring 2020) 17–23.

Wilhelmsen, Frederick D. Editor's introduction to *The End of the Modern World*, by Romano Guardini, 3–13. New York: Sheed and Ward, 1956.

Wikipedia, The Free Encyclopedia, s.v. "No justice, no peace," (accessed February 8, 2023), https://en.wikipedia.org/wiki/No_justice,_no_peace.

Index

Abel, 74
abortion,
  as assault on human dignity, 221
  children victimized by, 242
  Francis on, 71, 211
  as household mismanagement, 114
  as objectification of another, 114
  as technocratically-empowered
    irreverence, 116
Abraham, xi
absolution, 205, 206, 208
Al-Tayyeb, Ahmed, Grand Imam, 84
anthropology, 78, 21
  agency and, 76
  Augustinian, 121
  biblical (scriptural), 150, 183–84
  capitalism's false anthropology, 129
  concupiscence and, 149
  cosmo–, 76, n33, 229
  cosmology and, 83, 138, 232
  de Lubac's, 75
  ecology and, 9
  false development and, 138
  Francis and, 76, 223, 228–29
  freedom and, 76
  Freudian, 183
  of givenness, 63, 229
  gratuity and, 232
  of Guardini, 113n44
  of hope, 183
  of humanity–as–gift, 39
  of JP2, 7, 9, 80, 83, 91, 121, 128–
    29n38, 135, 149–50, 183–84
  of responsibility, 76
  of the Sermon on the Mount, 150

  of sexual chastity, 8
  technocratic lust and, 138
  theology of the body and, 7, 9
  theology of creation and, 7
  truth and, 8
  work and the worker and, 135

Benedict XVI, Pope (B16/Joseph
    Ratzinger),
  on abortion, 135
  on Africa, 133
  in *Africae munus*, 133
  on agriculture, 97
  on arms trafficking, 135
  on availability of consumer goods,
    72
  on Babel, 95, 97
  on Bacon, Francis, 98–101, 105
  on Baconian modernity, 103, 105
  on Benedict, St., 9, 157
  Benedictine social vision of, 96–97
  on Bernard of Clairvaux, St., 96–98
    104
  on "book of nature," 86
  budgetary policies and, 73
  call for re-examination of develop-
    ment, 138
  capitalism and, 120
  caricature of, 4
  Caritas in veritate and, xvii, 28, 32,
    78, 224–25
  on Catholic social teaching, 39
  charity (love) and, 30–33, 78, 126,
    134, 158

(Pope Benedict XVI continued)

chaste love and, rationale of, 35, 157, 191,

on children, exploitation of, 135

Christian identity and, 158

on commercial logic, 3n3

on the common good, 34, 133

on communion, 32

on communism's collapse, 138

on community, 157

competition between States and, 72

on conflict, 133

conservative Catholics and, 5, 245

consumeristic development and, 224–25

consumption of creation and, 10n22

on contemplatives, 96

contraception and, 70

cosmic chastity and, message of, xiii, xvii, 5, 7, 10, 31–32, 34, 158

on creation, 78, 134

on the Creator, 135

culture and, 157

de Lubac and, 13, 94, 98

on the Decalogue, 189

dehumanization and, 224–25

deprivation and, 224–25

on deregulation of the labour market, 72–73

on destructive capacities of man, 134

in *Deus caritas est*, 158

on development, 134, 138

dialogue and, xi, 133

dictatorship of relativism and, 38

on dignity, 73–74, 120, 133

on dignity of workers, 73–74

on discovery of the New World, 99

on displaced people, 135

on the distribution of goods/resources, 133, 135

on the domestic market, 72

on dominion over creation/matter, 101, 103, 157

on drug trafficking, 135

on duties, 32,

on the earthly city, 31–35, 105

ecological message of, 7

ecclesiology and, 98

ecological conversion and, 245

economic conversion and, 245

on economic development, 133

economic function of the market and, 224

on economic "freedom," 73

on economic injustice/justice, 86, 133, 135, 138

economic life and, 126,

on economic utility, 73

emerging countries and, 73

environment and, 10, 134,

on environmental change, 134

eschatology and, 96, 102

on eternal life, 158

evangelization and, 157

on exploitation, 138

on exploitation of children, 135

on exploitation of creation, 103

on faith, privatization of, 102

family of Abraham and, xi

on fiscal regimes, 72,

on foreign businesses, 72,

on forestry, 97

Francis, Pope, and, xiii-xvi, 2, 4–5, 11, 13, 39, 52, 65, 67, 69–70, 73–74, 86, 91, 103, 107, 138, 158–59, 168–70, 189, 193, 217–18, 224–25, 229, 244–46, 248

on freedom, 52, 76, 100, 218

on freedom of labor unions, 73

on freedom of workers, 73

Gaudium et spes and, 35

on the global market, 72

on the global village, 133

on the good, 34

governments and, 73

on gratuity/gratuitousness, 32–33

Guardini and, 13, 98

harmony and, 102

on Hebrews (Epistle), 95

Hesse, Herman and, 167, 191

hoarding of resources and, 134

on hostilities, 135

on human ecology, 134

Humanae vitae and, 225

on human trafficking, 135
humanism of, 133
on hunger, 135
on individualism, 98, 158
on integral human development,
    31–33, 96–97, 136
integral vision of man and, 229
interdisciplinary approach of, 134
international financial institutions
    and, 73
on injustices, 135
on international community,
    133–134
in *Jesus of Nazareth* ix, 148
John Paul II, Pope (JP2), and, xiv,
    1–5, 7, 11, 17, 32, 39, 52, 65–67,
    69–70, 74, 91, 120, 126, 133, 138,
    244–46
on justice, 30–34, 78, 126, 133–34,
    159, 245–46
on kingdom of God, 105
on labor, 96–97, 104
labour unions and, 73
law of Moses and, xi
in *Laudato si'*, 86
legacy of, 246
on the limitation of resources, 134
logic of capitalism and, 120, 133
on the logic of giving and forgiving,
    32
on low-cost production/labor costs,
    72, 74
on the market, 72, 126, 224
market logic and, 70–71, 224
on mercy, 32
on modern civilization, 133
on modernistic eschatology, 102
on modernistic "theology," 101–2
on modernity, 98–104
on monasticism/monks, 95, 98,
    104, 158
on Monte-Casino, 157
moral truth/moral norms/morality
    and, 25, 52, 120, 133–34
mutual trust and, 224
on nationalism, 133
on natural capital, 134
natural resources and, use of, 133

on nature, 100–101, 218, 229
on negotiating capacity of labour
    unions, 73
Neusner and, Jacob xi, 148
on outsourcing production, 72
on paradise, 96, 102
Paul and, St., 29,
Paul VI and, Pope, 4, 33, 70, 107,
    225
on peace, 133
on politics, 159
political piety of, 35
on poor countries, 73, 135,
    137–138,
Popularum progressio (Paul VI)
    and, 72
on poverty, 135
powerlessness of citizens and, 73
on price reduction, 72
on progress, 101, 104–5, 133,
    135–36
prophetic cry of, 30
protection for workers and, 73
on purchasing power, 72
on purification, 157
on racist attitudes, 133
on rate of development, 72
on reconciliation, 133
on redemption, 102
on re-examination of development,
    138
on refugees, 135
on relationships, 32
relativism and, 10, 25, 169, 193, 244
religious right and, 4
Reno and, R.R., 246,
resignation of, x
on resources, 133–34
on responsibility, 95, 133, 15
restoration and, 157,
on rich countries, 72, 135
rights and, 32, 72, 135
on right of workers to organize, 73
on salvation, 95, 98
on scientific progress, 99
Seewald on, Peter, 167–68
social cohesion and, 224

(Pope Benedict XVI continued)
social justice and, 65, 72–73, 95, 126
on social security, 72–73
social spending and, 73
social State, and the, 72
social teaching of, 74
social vision of, 97
socialism and, 135
on solidarity, 72, 95, 98, 133, 224
on solitude, 157
on soteriology, 95, 98
in *Spe salvi*, 94, 103, 103, 158n103
on standard of living, 133
Steppenwolf (literary figure), 167
Der Steppenwolf (Herman Hesse), 168
at Subiaco, 157
super development and, 224
supporters of, 245
on sustainability, 134
on technocracy, 9, 70, 157, 191, 218
technocratic lust and, 5–6
on technological control, 101, 103, 157
on technology, 218–19
on trafficking, 135
on "triumph of art over nature," 99
trust and, 224
on truth, 100, 120, 136, 218
on truth about work, 120
on the unborn, legal protection of, 135
wasteful development and, 224–25
on wealth, 133
on wealth production, 135
on welfare, 72
Weigel and, 86n84
on "winds of doctrine", 26
on work, 133
on workers, 72–74
workers associations and, 73
on xenophobic attitudes, 133
on zeal, 157–58
Benedict of Norcia, St. 9–10, 14, 157–58, 248
Bergoglio, Jorge (see Francis, Pope)
Black Lives Matter 2, 245

Brazos Theological Commentary on the Bible, xii
business as usual, xvi–xvii, 113, 245

Caldecott, Stratford, 6n9, 83–84n69
capital,
labor and, 24, 67, 125, 127, 130–32
capitalism,
industrial, 22, 128, 132
John Paul on, 22, 100, 120, 124–37, 244
Leo XIII and, 22, 67, 125, 129
capitalist market, 24
caritas in veritate/charity in truth (notion of),
Cary, Phillip, xi, 49n58, 56n102, 60n124, 188n187, 216n1
Catholic social teaching/Catholic social doctrine/Church's social doctrine/teaching
aim of articulating, 7
as amphitheatre, xiii, 6, 13, 17, 91, 162
ecology and, 9n15
moral doctrine and, 22
in opposition to technocratic lust, xii
and Paschal mystery, 23
as a whole, xii
Centesimus annus (John Paul), 124–26, 134n84, 135n85, 138, 227n69 and n71, 229n85
John Paul's fidelity to Leo XIII in, 22
on Leo XIII's rationale, 22
on *Rerum novarum*, 24
charity, 12, 14n30, 38, 53–55, 59–60, 62, 64, 68, 91, 93, 99, 123, 126, 129, 144, 169–70, 177, 179, 188, 193, 203–4, 207, 209, 234
Benedict on, 28–34, 134
evangelization and, 29
at heart of Church's social doctrine, 28
truth and, 28
chastity
agency and, 226
all-encompassing, 200

antidote to household mismanagement, xvii
Benedict on, Pope, 9–10, 34, 138
Benedict and, St., 9
broadest sense of, xvii
Caldecott, Stratford on, 6n9
contesting with lust, 12
cosmic, xii–xiii, xv–xvii, 5–10,
   12–14, 17, 21, 31, 33–35, 38, 65,
   79, 81, 99, 109, 123, 138, 142,
   145n24
the cry of the poor and, 179
counter culture of, 228
demands of xv, 7
Doherty and, Catherine, 14
disharmony and, 221–226
earthly city and, 33
ecological, 228
of the eyes, 6, 185
ethos of, 8, 13–14, 226
in every sphere of life, 153, 158
of the flesh, 6
Francis and, Pope, 10–11, 138,
   142–43, 145–47, 153, 158–63,
   220
Francis and, St., 10–11, 14, 67, 74,
   84, 138, 156–158, 161
human dignity and, 221–26
humility of life and, 229
Joseph and, St., 138, 142, 144–47,
   160–61, 163, 169, 247–48.
justice and, 33, 151
opposite of possessiveness, 160
paradigm of, 138
polity and, 6n9
pride of life and, 229
reverence and, 220
rehabilitation of, 151–52, 154
resentment and, 151
right of citizenship in our hearts,
   151
safeguarding the gift, 5, 11, 87
sexual, xiv, 3, 8, 146, 213
spirituality of, 13–14
and technocracy, 226
theology of, 13–14,
three forms of/three–fold 6, 151
as a virtue, 151

Walker on, Adrian, 6n9
Zacchaeus and, 163
Christ (*see also* Francis, *subsection*
   Christ's call and *humanism*,
   Christ as measure of),
   friendship with, 28, 156
   fullness of Christ/maturity of/in,
      25–27
   redeeming work of, 24
commerical logic, 13, 245
   Benedict XVI on, 3n3, 134
   of neoliberalism, 13
commodities/commodity/commodifi-
   cation/commoditized, 11, 54, 59,
      61, 71, 73
common home, xvi, 23n23
Commonweal (magazine), xi
communal/cultural formation, 24, 47,
      50, 65
concupiscence (*concupiscenza*), 6n8,
   21
conflict between capital and labor, 24,
   125, 132
consumer(s), xv, 11, 59–61, 64, 72,
   109, 125, 222, 247
consumerism/consumeristic, xvi, 33,
   37, 47, 49–51, 53, 56, 60–65, 93,
   147, 155–56, 198–99, 209–14,
   224–25, 241
consumption, 8, 10n22, 116, 125–26,
   155, 160, 174, 227
control, 11
cosmic chastity,
   against relativism, 21
   and the good, 21
   John Paul's song of, 21
cosmic gentleness, 14, 214
cosmic tenderness, xx, 22, 214
cosmology,
   rooted in truth, 8
cosmos (*kosmos*),
   meaning of, 10n20
   as mother, 11
   reverence for, 11
   as sister, 11
creation,
   Benedict on, 10n22
   beauty of, 20

(creation continued)
creation–as–gift, 7
dignity of, 11
doctrine of, 7
as mother, 11
as sister, 11
Creator,
splendor of the, 20
Creighton University, Jesuits at, 4
culture wars, xiii, xvii, 1–5, 13, 67, 72, 74, 82–83, 86, 88, 91, 109, 170n19
culture warrior(s) 17, 244–45
as genre of Catholicism, 244

Daniel, prophet, 84n69, 91–93, 106–107
de Lubac, Henri,
de Souza, Raymond xiii, 205, 206n47, 207
democratic socialists, 2
dignity,
moral truth and, 27
relativism and, 27
rights and, 21
Doherty, Catherine, 14
Douthat, Ross, xiii

ecological crisis/environmental crisis/ deterioration, xvi, 10, 87, 93, 120, 223
ecology, xv–xvi, 8–9, 11, 13, 24, 66, 97, 114, 118, 134, 155, 167, 194, 217, 227, 229, 230, 232, 245–46
theological, 8
economic/financial crisis, xvi, 120, 223
economic injustice, 13, 120, 126, 131, 138
economic justice, 23–24, 125, 132–33
economic libertarianism, 24
The End of the Modern World (Guardini), 92, 107–108, 112–113
environment,
social, 10
truth of its being, 10
Ephesians, St. Paul's Letter to the, 25–28

Faggioli, Massimo xi
family, xv
Farrow, Douglas, xiii
First Things ix, xi–xiii, 202, 243
Francis, Pope (Jorge Bergoglio),
Abel and, 76, 79
abortion and, 71, 114, 116, 221, 242
abuse and, xvi, 85, 87, 110, 114, 160, 233
Adam and Eve and, 81, 160, 240–41
adult children and, 40
Africa and, 49–50, 65, 74
African bishops, 49–50, 65
agency and, 51, 76, 108, 226–27
All Saints Day and, 115–117
Al-Tayyeb, Grand Imam Ahmed and, 84
air and, 85, 154
airplane interview(s) and, xv, 109–11
Amazonia/Amazon and, 38n97, 82,110, 247
Amazon Synod and, 81–82, 247
America magazine and, 109
American Catholicism and, xi, 2–3
Amoris laetitia (AL) and, xv, xx, 56–57, 60–64, 201–215, 241
ammunition (literal), 84
ammunition (political ammo) and, 2,109
anthropological changes and, 48, 56–57, 93, 99, 181, 218, 227, 235–36
anthropology and, 39, 63–64, 75–76, 79–80, 83, 223n44, 232
Aparecida and, 82, 85
apocalypse and, 112–19
Argentina and, 40, 110, 171, 205, 206
Argentinian Supreme Court and, 110
arms build-up and, 84
Asia and, Asian bishops, 50, 65, 181–82, 187–88
assisted suicide (see euthanasia)
atom/atomic, and and,112–13, 221
autonomy and, 70–71, 108, 215
Babel and, 66–69, 73

Baconian modernity and, 101, 103

Beatitudes and, 118

beauty and, 81–82, 111, 146, 157, 180–83, 194, 238–39, 242, 248

belonging, 53, 77–79, 209

Benedict XVI, Pope and, x, xii–xvii, 1–7, 10–13, 38–39, 52, 65–67, 69–70, 73–74, 78, 84, 86, 91, 94, 101, 103, 107, 120, 137–38, 157–59, 168–70, 189, 191, 193, 217–18, 224–25, 229–30, 243–48

on Ben Franklin Parkway (Philadelphia), 58–59, 79, 141–42

Bible/Scripture/biblical stories and, 55, 74–77, 79–81, 84, 86, 92, 103, 107, 117, 139–47, 149, 154–57, 159–63, 179, 216, 233

blaming young people and, 41

blood of the Lamb and, 117

book of nature and, 86

boldness of speech and, 43

boomers and, 2

borders and, 71

bounty and, 80–81, 248

bourgeois religion and, 1n1, 243

bread and, 117

bridge-building and, 1n1, 3–4n4, 55, 170–71, 181–82

brotherhood/fraternity and, 74–77, 79, 118n123, 158–59, 170–71, 190–91, 224–25

Buenos Aires and, 40

Buenos Aires and, Bishops of Pastoral Region of, 202, 204–06

Cain and Able (story of) and, 76, 79

Caldecott, Stratford and, 83–84n69

canticle of St. Francis and, 83–84

capital and, 69–70, 128, 130

capitalism and, 66–67, 128, 225, 244–246

care/giving a damn and, 10, 69, 77, 109–10, 116, 169, 174, 210, 230, 235, 240–41

caricature of, xiii, 1–5, 243–46

Caritas in veritate (Benedict XVI) and, xvi–xvii, 77–78, 86, 137, 138n105–6, 217n10, 219n19, 224n53–54, 225

cataclysmic occurrences and, 117

Catholic social teaching/Church's social teaching/social doctrine and, xiii, 1, 7, 12–14, 17, 38–40, 65, 67, 74–77, 84, 86, 91–92, 97, 142, 199, 212–13, 217, 224, 229, 246

challenges and, 42–44, 48, 52, 56, 71, 107–108, 192, 211

chaos and, 112–13

Charles Borromeo Seminary (Philadelphia) and, 141

chaste love and, xvii, 6, 10, 12–14, 81, 86–87, 91–93, 142–49, 157–61, 163, 244, 246–48

chastity and, xvii, 5–6, 11, 13, 87, 139, 142–47, 153, 159–61, 163, 200, 213–14, 220–21, 226–29

chastity and, paradigm of, 138

child-rearing and, 12, 40–43, 53–55, 93, 142–44, 169, 198, 202–11, 215, 234, 236, 241–42

children and, 12, 40, 53–54, 69, 71, 116–17, 143, 169, 198, 202–11, 215, 234, 236, 241–42

children of God and, 118

choice(s)/choose/choosing and, 59, 62, 69, 92–93, 108, 139, 158, 173, 178, 189, 192, 214, 222

christ's call/God's call/divine call/Gospel's call and, 13, 55, 57, 61–62, 75–77, 110, 139–43, 159–63, 174–75, 177, 179, 185–186, 201, 234, 240–41

church's credibility and, 52

civility and, 77

clichés of, 1n1, 3–4

climate change and, 109–113

conservative North American Catholics and, xiv–xv, 245–46

commitment and, 12–13, 40–43, 48–49, 50–53, 57, 60–64, 66, 93–94, 120, 138–63, 168, 177, 182, 187–88, 192–93, 195–96, 204n43, 210, 214–15, 242, 246

common good and, 39, 52, 60, 70, 85, 158, 216, 245–46

(Pope Francis continued)

common home and, xvi, 23n23, 83–85, 93, 158–59, 221, 230

Commonweal and, xi

communion (of persons, with God, etc.) and, 45, 54–55, 231–33, 237–40, 248

communion/reception of the Eucharist, 199, 205–206, 208, 241

condemning young people and, 41

conscience and, 107, 155, 178, 202–214

consumerism and, xv–xvi, 4–7, 10, 49, 60–61, 63–65, 93, 155–56, 198, 209

control and, 11, 84, 101, 109, 115–16

cosmic chastity and, xii–xiii, xv, xvii, 5, 7, 10–14, 38, 65, 79–81, 109, 142, 158–59, 161–62, 182–83, 193–94, 244, 246–48

cosmic harmony and, 87, 107

cosmic praise and, 84

cosmo-anthropology of, 76n33

cosmology and, 44–45, 80, 83, 85, 230, 232

cosmos and, 11–12, 44–45, 66, 76, 81–84, 86, 87, 113, 118–19, 153, 161, 232–33, 235, 247

courage and, 41–42, 92, 193, 238–41

creation and, xv–xvii, 5–7, 10–11, 36, 39–40, 44–47, 61, 67, 76–85, 87, 94, 101, 103, 109–16, 118–19, 138, 147, 155, 157, 216n1, 217, 219, 222, 225–26, 229–35, 239, 242, 247–48

creation-as-gift and, xv, xvii, 5–7, 19, 39–40, 46–47, 67, 77–79, 138

creator and, 5–6, 77–83, 85–87, 155, 161, 219–20, 230, 232–33, 242, 247

creatures and, 46, 77, 79, 85, 87, 110, 112–13, 153, 161, 231

Creighton University and, 4

crisis of communal commitment and, 48, 51–52, 64, 93–94, 120

cultivation of corn and, 111

cultivation (non-cultivation) and, 111–113

cultivation (post-cultivation) and, 111–12.

cultivation (un-cultivation/uncultivation) and, 109–12, 168

cultural changes and, 48, 56, 235–36

culture(s) and, xvi, 39, 41–43, 46, 48–51, 56, 59–61, 63–64, 66, 69, 70, 74–75, 77, 79, 109, 112–15, 171–72, 175, 179, 182, 189, 193, 195, 198, 202, 216–17, 220, 228, 231, 234–37, 241

consumer culture and, 213

culture of the ephemeral and, 64, 182, 187, 191–92

culture and, media, 180

culture and, popular, 226

culture and, relativistic, 241

culture and, throwaway/of waste, 70, 93, 116, 193–94, 205, 210, 215, 241–42, 244

as culture warrior, 13, 193

culture wars and, 66–67, 82, 83, 193, 244

Daniel (prophet) and, 92–93

deforestation and, 110

de Lubac and, Henri, 13, 45, 75, 76n33, 91, 94, 237–39n164, 248

democratic socialists and, 2, 225

destruction and, 38, 86–87, 108, 112–18, 145, 168, 211, 227, 233

determinism and, 76–77

devastation and, 116–118

development and, 52, 54–55, 70, 97, 107–08, 137–38, 168, 195, 217–20, 224, 227–28

dialogue and, 3n4, 168–71, 176–78, 181–82, 187–88, 190, 193, 197, 241

dignity and, 5–6, 11, 47, 49, 51–52, 56, 63, 73, 69–70, 73, 76, 79, 85, 87, 109, 117, 147, 161, 168, 196, 217, 219–26, 229, 234

direction provided by, xiii

disabled children and, 71

discarded populations/people and, 79, 116–18

dismissal of, xiii, xvii, 2–4, 245

dissonance and, x

dispossession/dispossessive and, 13, 139, 142, 159, 163

distress and, 84, 117

distribution and, 84

dominion and, 101, 103

dream (of universal fraternity) and, 74–75

dubia and, xv, 201n31

earth and, 78, 80, 85, 87, 110–15, 118, 144n21, 154, 158, 170, 179, 181, 221, 229, 232–33, 241

ecclesiology of, 39, 44–47, 48, 56, 80, 118, 142, 209, 232, 235–40

ecological awareness and, 81–82, 85

ecological catastrophe/crisis and, 86–87, 118, 120, 227–28

ecology and, 13, 66–67, 81–82, 85, 114, 118, 155, 167, 194, 217, 227, 229–30, 232, 245–46

economic dysfunction and, 86

economic growth and, 86

economic interests and, 84, 155, 168, 224

elderly and, 70, 172

End of the Modern World (Guardini) and, 92, 107–08n71, 112–13n92–93

ends and means and, 47, 67, 69–71, 75, 128

enmity and, 74–77, 79, 94, 110, 170, 197, 221, 231

enslavement/slavery/slaves and, 67, 69, 92, 156, 227

entrustment and, 92–93, 110, 196, 217, 227, 232–33, 247

environment and, 10–11, 66–67, 69, 82–83, 86, 109–13, 217–18, 221, 223–24, 226–30, 244

ethic(s) and, 49, 54, 65, 91, 109–12, 114, 172, 179, 226, 246

euthanasia and, 70, 116

Evangelii gaudium (Francis) and, 48–55, 64–65, 78, 155–159, 168, 179–81, 183, 197n16, 212

evangelization/Gospel/Good News/as evangelist and, 43–48, 52–54, 93, 147, 155, 169, 172–81, 183, 189–90, 195–96, 201–03, 210–11, 241–42, 246–47

expendability and, 67, 193

exploitation of children and, 69

exploitation of the gift and, 87, 103

exploitation of nature and, 86, 99, 101, 103, 109–12, 227

exploitation of women and, 69, 234

Faggioli, Massimo and, xi

faithfulness, 92–93, 188–89

familial love and, 12, 55, 63, 75, 158–59, 202, 209, 234, 238–41

family/families and, 11–13, 38–48, 50, 52–67, 71, 73, 75–77, 86, 117–18, 158–59, 167–68, 172, 192, 195, 197–98, 202–07, 209–18, 223, 230–42, 246

farming/farms and, 85, 110–11

fatalism (*see also* determinism) and, 76–77

Father, God the, and, 55, 118, 159, 173–75, 230, 233, 235

fear of commitment and, 12, 40, 60–61

fear of future and, 84

fear of God and, 111

fear of loneliness and, 63

fear of mistakes and, 237

fear of monstrous technological power and, 112

fear of others and, 182

fear of starting families/matrimony and (*see also* Francis, reluctance to marry and), 40–41, 60, 71, 192, 237

fidelity and, 46, 52, 60, 62–63, 189, 204, 240

First Things and, xi, xiii, 202, 243

food and, 85, 212

Foucault, Charles de, and, 74–75

Francis of Assisi, St. and, 10, 67, 74, 84, 138

"Francis option," 67

fraternal love and, 74–75

(Pope Francis continued)

fratelli devastori (devastating brothers/destroying brothers), 118n123

Fratelli tutti (FT) and, 11, 74–77, 79, 83n69, 84n71, 144, 158–59, 161

fraternity and, 75–76, 79, 118n123, 171, 190–91, 224

freedom and, 37n95, 38–39, 52–53, 65, 76–77, 108, 139, 142

French bishops and, 54

Galatians, Letter of St. Paul to the, 55

generosity (generous) and, 41–42, 62, 78, 155, 172, 203, 205–07, 214, 220, 233

Genesis, Book of, 67, 76, 80, 154, 216n1, 231, 233, 235, 240–41

gift(s) and, 5, 11, 13, 39–40, 44, 46–47, 61–62, 67, 70, 76–78, 80–82, 87, 109, 111, 113, 115–16,138, 141–43, 145–46, 155, 158, 162, 168, 178, 183, 193, 195, 197, 200, 219–20, 227–30, 240, 242, 247

givenness and, 63, 70–71, 77–80, 142–43, 229, 247

globalization and, 38, 49, 54–55, 174, 222, 228, 247

glory of God and (*see also* Francis, Splendor of the Creator and), 81, 235

God the Father and, (*see* Francis, *subsection* Father and, God the)

good/goodness and, 39, 47, 49–50, 52, 60, 64–65, 70, 80, 82, 116

Good Samaritan and, 75, 79

Gore, Al and, 112

gratitude and, 82, 110, 219

greed and, 69

Guardini, Romano and, 13, 36n94, 37n95, 93–94, 107–108, 111–13

guidance of, xv

Hadyn's *The Creation* and, 81

harmony and, 79–80, 83, 107, 118–19

hermeneutic of continuity and, xiii

hermeneutics of, xiii, xvi, 1, 44, 116

hiring an assassin and, 71

hope and, 84, 115, 118, 172, 190, 228, 232, 240

hormones and, 85

Huffington Post and, 1n1

human relationships and, 46–47, 54–55, 59, 63–64, 76, 80, 145, 170, 210–11, 221, 233

Humanae vitae and, 70, 209, 225

humanism of, 128, 182–83, 209–14

humanity as custodian and, 110

human ecology and, 66–67, 114, 194, 227, 230, 245

humanity-as-gift and, 39

human person and, 56, 62, 70, 75, 144, 217, 223, 225, 227

hungry people/hunger and, 67, 116–17, 223–24

idolatry and, 69, 189, 248n4

Ignatian style/manner of, 115, 173

indifference and, 39, 48, 62, 65, 76–77, 79, 144, 216, 234

individualism and, 41, 50–51, 55–58, 62–63, 70, 158, 216

individual gain and, 48–49

industrialism and, 86, 108

injustice and, 10–11, 50–53, 69, 71, 75, 78–79, 84–85, 120, 168–69, 172, 236, 246

integral ecology and, xv, 13, 155, 167, 232

integral human development and, 70, 224

irreverence and, 110, 116, 174

Jesuits and, 4

John XXIII and, Pope, 4–5

John Paul II and, Pope, x–xvi, 1–13, 17, 36–40, 49–50, 52–53, 56n97, 65–67, 69–70, 72, 74, 77, 79–84, 86–87, 91, 94, 120, 128, 130, 137–39, 141–43, 145–47, 151–54, 160, 163, 167, 177–78, 182, 184–85, 187, 190, 194, 198–200, 213–18

John Paul II Institute and, xv, 216–17, 242n182

John and, St. (the revelator), 77, 117, 120, 222

Joseph and, St., 55, 138, 142–47, 155–63, 183

justice and, xvii, 2, 7, 10, 51, 53–55, 59–60, 62, 65, 73, 75, 78–79, 91, 93–95, 110, 114, 128, 144, 154–55, 159, 170, 177, 179, 187, 203–04, 207–09, 234, 241, 244–46

labor and, 57, 97, 117, 128, 223

Latin American bishops and, 82

Laudato si' and (*LS*, Francis), xvi, 5n7, 10–11, 23n23, 67, 79–80, 83–87, 103, 107–109, 141n21, 154–55, 158–59, 168, 217–31

left and, xvi, 2, 4, 67, 84, 86, 113, 244–46

Leo XIII and, xii, 14, 67, 97

Let Us Dream (Francis, *LUD*), 67, 69–71, 77–83, 85, 87, 130n51

liberal capitalism and, 66

liberal elite and, xiii, 1n1,

liberals and, 4

life and, value of, 70

limits and, 87, 107, 109, 112

liturgical crisis and, 118

liturgical hermeneutics of being and, 83

liturgical ontology of praise and, 66, 80–82

love and, 87

Luke (Gospel of) and, 141

Lumen gentium and, 45

lust and, xvii, 87, 118, 139

man-god and, 118

Manila (Philippines) and, 108–111

manipulation and, 103

market and, 38–39, 60, 63–67, 69–71, 108

market liberalism and, 67, 69–71, 75, 108

marriage and, 13, 39–47, 53–54, 57–65, 141–42

mastery and, 70

meaning and, 91

means and ends, 69–71, 75, 128

media and, 50, 64, 65, 179–80, 212, 234, 244

mercy and, 69, 118, 198, 201, 240–41

message of, x, xii–xv, xvii, 1–5, 39–40, 138, 205, 243, 246

migrant/immigrant and, 69, 71, 73

millennial moment and, 1

misapprehension of, 5

modernity and, 93, 101, 107

money and, 43, 69, 188

monocultural farming and, 111

moral norms and, 36, 51–52, 208

moral progress and, 86, 214–15, 227

moral truth and, 13, 40, 54, 65

moral values and, 52, 64

morality and, 51, 75, 118, 201, 227

mother earth/nature and, 110, 113–14, 247–48

multiculturalism and, 61

National Catholic Reporter and, 1n1

natural resources and, 84, 111

nature and, 36n94, 53, 78, 103, 110, 112

neocolonialism and, 38, 49–50n64, 66–67, 109

neo-Darwinist ideology and, 70

neo-Marxism and, 2

nitrogen replenishment in the soil and, 111

Obergefell and, 58

O'Connell and, Jerry, 109–110

ontology of, 39, 63–64, 87, 138

opposition to, xi, 2

orthodoxy and, xv, 5

outdated, 1

pachamama and, 80–81, 247–48

Paglia and, Cardinal Vincenzo, xv

pain and, 71, 115

parents and, 40, 53–54, 71, 204, 208

Patmos, isle of and, 117

Patris corde (Francis) and, 142

Paul VI, Pope, and, 70, 74n29, 86, 107

peace and, 117

people and, 69, 87

permanent decisions and, 57

(Pope Francis continued)
persecution and, 117
personalism of, 61
Philadelphia (Philly) and, 40–48,
    53, 57, 78, 141–43
Philippines and, 109
pleasure and, 69
plundering the earth and, 78
polis and, 76, 83–84n69, 87
political correctness and, 39
political crisis and, 84
Populorum progressio and, 74n29
possessiveness and, 87, 139, 144
poverello and (see St. Francis), 74
poverty and, 78
power and, 69, 87, 107–109, 115
praise and, 80–81, 84
prenatal diagnosis and, 70
pressure not to marry and, 41, 43
profit and, 69–70
progress and, 55, 86, 107, 137
progressivism and, 1, 61
prophetic outcry of, xvii
pro-family environmentalism of, 66
prostitution and, 69
protest and, 84
Psalms and, 84n72, 87
reexamination of development and,
    138
relativism and, 13, 38–39, 46,
    48–49, 51, 53, 60–61, 64–65, 215
reluctance to marry and (*see also*
    fear of starting families and),
    141–42
Reno, R.R. and, xii–xiii, 1, 3n4,
    4–5, 77n38
Rerum novarum (Leo XIII) and, 97
responsibility and, 46, 76, 107–108,
    139, 144
restoration and, 80
Revelation and, book of, 115–16
rich young man/ruler and,
    138–139, 141–42
right (political/religious) and, 1,
    4, 67
rights and, 51–52, 55
"Risk of fruitfulness and life" and,
    39–40, 42

Rohingya and, 78
ruffling feathers, x
sacramental grace and, 45–46
Salta (Argentina) and, 110
alvation and, 117
Sanders, Bernie and, 2
scientific advances and, 86
sea and, 115
secularism and, 52, 65
security and, 107–108
self-centeredness and, 60
self-gift and, 142
self-interest and, 108
selfishness and, 79
self-restraint and, 109
self-sufficiency and, 78
sex/sexuality and, 60, 86
sexual liberalism and, 66–67, 75
shepherds of being and, 110
sick people and, 117
sin and, 65, 75, 85, 87, 95, 118–19
singleness and, 40
sinners and, 117
sister earth and, 110
social ethic of, 91
social justice and, 54
social justice warriors and, 2
social message of, xii, 60, 65, 69–70,
    74, 76, 94
society and, 91
soil and, 85, 111
solidarity and, 39, 41, 52–53, 55,
    75, 78, 118, 138–39
soteriology and, 75
soy and, 111
spirituality and, 109
spite and, 79
Sri Lanka and, 109
supermarket and, 58–61
Tartagal (Argentina) and, 110
technical abilities and, 86
technocracy and, xvii, 11, 69–70,
    75, 93, 101, 103, 107, 118
technocratic lust and, xvii, 5, 38,
    78, 118
technocratic logic/mindset/para-
    digm and, 6, 11, 66, 93, 108, 118
tension and, 84

thanksgiving and, 82
three young men and, 92
throwaway culture and, 66, 69
trees and, 115
tribalism and, 5
tribulation and, 117
Trinity and, 55
triumph of the fittest and, 69
trust and, 46, 59
truth and, 10–11, 13, 40, 51–52, 94,
    107, 128
truth about work and, 128
universal brotherhood and, 74
unknown saints and, 117
unplanned pregnancies and, 71
U.S. and, 139
U.S. Bishops and, 51–52
U.S. Congress, address to, 41
usefulness/utility and, 107–108
values and, 107
Verano Cemetary and, 115
violence and, 85, 108, 117
vocational commitment and,
    12–13, 138
war and, 55
water and, 85
wealth and, 69, 78, 87
weaknesses of, xv, 3n4
welfare (wellbeing), and, 107
West, Cornel and, 71n18
Woodstock and, 2
work and (see labor)
worker and, 67
world and, 77
World Meeting of Families
    (Philadephia, 2015) and, 57–58,
    78, 141–43
worries about, 2
young adult Catholics and, 3
youth and, 139
Zacchaeus and, 138, 141–42
Francis of Assisi, St., 10–11, 14, 67,
    74, 84, 138, 156–158, 160_161,
    169, 247–248.
"free" market, 11
freedom,
    abuse of, 23
    anthropology of, 76

and arbitrariness, 22
Benedict on, 32–33, 73,
Centesimus annus and, 22
economic "freedom," 71
Francis on, 52, 62
god of, 71–72
John Paul on, 19–25, 27, 31, 35–37
justice and, 21
liberation of, 23
modernity's false notion of, 38
passions and, 22
truth and, 22
of workers and labor unions, 73

givenness, 8
God's art, 31
good, the, 21
    due to me, 21
    of our common home, 23
    of the human community, 23
    and human flourishing, 21
    of the individual, 23
    John Paul's advocacy for, 21
    and justice, 21
    the truth of, 21
gratuity, 6
Guardini, Romano, 13, 36n91&94,
    37n95, 53n81, 91–94, 98, 106–8,
    111–13, 153, 168, 223, 225, 229,
    248

Hanby, Michael, 108n70
harmony, x, 13–14, 17, 31, 52–53,
    74–77, 83, 99–101, 107, 118, 167,
    233, 241–42
    triad of, 30–31, 79–80, 87, 102, 104,
    106, 134–35
heart(s),
    appetites of, 147, 154
    distortion/deformation of, 66
    fickleness of, 27, 47–50, 93, 189
    relativism and, xv, 12–13, 20, 25,
    27, 36, 46–47, 51, 61, 64, 93,
    121–22, 161, 170, 175, 177, 180–
    82, 187, 189, 191–93, 199–200,
    213, 226, 246, 248
    unmusical discord in, 25
hermeneutic of continuity, xiii

household management
    macro and micro xvi
Huffington Post, 1n1
human nature,
    common to all, 23
humanism,
    against relativism, 27
    Christ as measure of, 27
humility of life, 6, 33, 185, 229
    John Paul on, 7–9, 151–52

idol(s),
    relativism as, 20, 189
industrial capitalism,
    John Paul on, 22
    Leo XIII and, 22
Irenaeus, St., 30–31, 79–80, 87, 100

Jeremiah, Prophet, 30, 121, 190
Jesus of Nazareth (Benedict XVI), x-xi
John XIII, Pope,
    caricature of, 4
John Paul II, Pope (*see also* anthropol-
        ogy *subentry* JP2; Benedict XVI,
        Pope, *subentry* John Paul; Cent-
        essimus annus; *see* Francis, Pope,
        subentry John Paul; *see* Veritatis
        Splendor; *see* social justice *suben-
        try* John Paul),
    anthropology of, 7–9, 21, 69, 80, 83,
        121, 128–29n38, 135, 147–50,
        183–84, 229, 246
    caricature of, 4
    ecological catastrophe and, 86
    on freedom, 19–20, 22–25, 31,
        35–38, 52, 65, 99–100, 124–25,
        139, 184, 210–12, 228
    on God's art, 31, 79, 100
    the good and, 20–21, 105, 122–23,
        125, 130, 152–53, 178
    industrial capitalism and, 22, 128,
        132
    on injustice, 12, 22, 30, 121–22,
        126–27, 129–31, 135–36, 138
    on moral decay, 30
    on oppression, 30
    on progress, 31, 227

relativism and, xiv, 13, 20–21,
        37–38, 49–50, 121–22, 153, 200,
        212–14
    on triad of harmony (*see also*
        harmony, *subcategory* triad of),
        30–31, 80, 106
    truth and, 8, 19–25, 30–32, 35, 40,
        65–66, 81, 100, 105, 120–23,
        127–31, 140, 143, 148, 185, 190,
        194, 200–201, 210–11, 213–14
    on violence, 30, 120–21, 123, 185
    on war, 30, 68
Joseph of Nazareth, St., xx, 55, 138,
        142–47, 155–63, 183
justice,
    and charity, 29–34, 54n87, 126, 134
    freedom and, 20–25, 27, 31, 35–38,
        53, 60, 62, 64–65, 71–73, 76, 99,
        105, 124–25, 168
    harmony and, 30–31, 135
    human flourishing and, 21, 62,
        68n7, 71
    moral decay and, 30
    Paul VI on, 30, 33, 72
    toward the creator, 6, 9, 123, 155
    truth and, 30

labor (see work)
Laudato si' (Francis) (*see also* Francis,
        subsection Laudato si'), 5n7, 80,
        83, 85
    Companion to *Caritas in veritate*
        (Benedict), xvi
left (Leftists)
    ecology and economics, xvi
    Francis and, 2–3
    papal trio and, xvi
Leo XIII, Pope (*see also* Leo *subsec-
        tions for* capitalism, *Centesimus
        annus*, industrial capitalism,
        Rerum novarum, Francis, *subsec-
        tion* Rerum novarum)
    Centesimus annus and, 22
    John Paul and, 22
Let Us Dream (*LUD*, Francis), 67,
        69–71
liberal Catholics, 1–2
liturgical ontology, 13

love (see also charity)
  disordered, 23
  of self, 23
marriage, xv, xvi, 12, 13, 38, 40, 42–
  48, 50, 53–54, 56–65, 67, 75, 78,
  84n69, 93, 142, 146, 159, 167–68,
  192, 197–99, 201–11, 213–16,
  229–30, 232–42, 244, 246.
Mary of Nazareth, xx, 142, 145–147,
  155, 159, 183, 235.
moral discernments, 23–24
moral doctrine,
  Catholic social teaching and, 22
moral standards, 23, 36, 51
moral theology, 22, 24, 100, 200, 205
morality, 26–27, 75, 118, 122–23, 129,
  201, 227
  public, 22–23
Moses, xi, xiv, 121.

National Catholic Reporter, 1n1
Nebuchadnezzar, 93, 248.
neoliberal, neoliberalism 13, 67, 110,
  228, 245.
Neusner, Jacob x, xi, xi n3, 148.
New Evangelization, xiv

pachamama, *see* Francis, *subsection*
  pachamama
paschal mystery, 23–24
Paul, St. (Apostle), 14, 25–29, 55, 58,
  172–173, 184.
peace/peaceful, xiii, xvii, 30–31,
  32n78, 52, 68, 114, 117, 133,
  169–71, 178, 193, 197, 237, 243
postmodern hospitality, xi
Paul VI, Pope, 4–5, 18, 33, 70, 72,
  74n29, 86, 107, 156, 160, 176–77,
  209, 225, 227
  Caricature of, 4
poustinia/poustinik, xx, 14
Princeton Theological Seminary, ix,
  142n18
Princeton University, ix–x
progressive/progressives, xvi, 61
  Dreher's characterization of Francis
  as, 243
  Francis's ecological vision as, 229

"hymnal," 1n1
imagination, 52
millennial moment, 1, 2
A Rabbi Talks with Jesus (Neusner),
  x–xi
regulation (of market), 24, 33, 72–73
relativism, xi, xiii–xvi, 3, 10, 20–21,
  23, 25–27, 36, 39, 46, 48–61,
  63–65, 93, 121–22, 153, 156, 161,
  163, 168–72, 174–81, 187–200,
  202, 210, 212–14, 226, 241,
  244–48
  Benedict on *see* Benedict XVI,
    subsection, relativism
  desire and, 27,
  dictatorship of/regime of, 12–13,
    38, 242
  ego and, 27
  environmental crisis and, 10
  fickle-heartedness of, 27, 47, 93,
    189
  as idol, 20
  John Paul on (*see* relativism *subsec-
    tion of* John Paul II, Pope)
  moral relativism (in contrast to
    Francis's message), 1–2
  moral standards and, 23
  moral truth and, 27
  teleology and, 27
religious right, 4, 246
Reno, R.R., ix–xiv, 1–5, 59n119,
  77n38, 170n19, 181n90,
  243–244, 246
  on biblical interpretation, xii
  on tradition, ix,
  on Princeton Theological Seminary, ix
responsibility, 3n3, 24, 28, 51, 72,
  76–77, 82, 96, 98, 104–108, 114,
  122, 125–26, 139, 144–45, 150,
  159, 162, 185–87, 206, 211, 216,
  223, 226–27, 234, 236, 238–39,
  246–47
Rerum novarum (Leo XIII), 22, 97,
  132, 135
  Centesimus annus and, 22
  false freedom and, 22

reverence, 36–38, 81, 110–11, 116,
    138, 151–53, 155, 219–20, 230,
    247–48
  for the cosmos, 11
  proper to integral ecology, 8
rich young man/ruler, 138–43, 153,
    156, 159, 163, 185–187, 201
right(s), 21–22, 27, 32, 37, 51–52, 55,
    63, 72–74, 78–79, 123, 126, 129,
    133, 135, 137, 151, 154, 158, 170,
    186, 199, 208, 224
right (political) xvi, 2, 4, 67, 84, 245,
    246
right–wing tribalism, 5

Sanders, Bernie, 2
Schindler, DC, 10n20
Schindler, David L., 9n1
Schmitz, Matthew xiii, 202, 205
self–indulgent, 23, 41, 144, 161
self–interest, 23, 108, 224
sexuality, xv–xvii, 7, 24, 38, 48, 50, 56,
    60–61, 67–68, 75, 86, 146, 148,
    150, 183–84, 200, 213, 217, 223,
    241, 244, 246
  gift-of-self/self-gift and, xv–xvi,
    61, 146
sin, 11, 20, 23, 31, 65, 69, 75, 85, 87,
    94–96, 101, 103, 106, 116, 118,
    123, 149, 154, 184, 188–89, 203,
    205, 207, 233, 235
  mortal, 207
  truth and, 20
Snell, RJ, 58n113, 59n119
social justice, 6n9, 21–23, 27, 35, 54,
    59, 65, 72–73, 75, 78, 93, 95, 99,
    121–23, 126–27, 131, 136, 170,
    208, 234, 244–45,
  demands of, 23, 54, 73, 93, 99, 121,
    123, 208
  John Paul and, 21–23, 35, 65, 121,
    123, 126, 127, 131–32, 136
  Truth and, 21–23, 27, 35, 54, 59, 65,
    73, 78, 93, 99, 121, 123, 126–27,
    131, 170, 208, 234, 244
social justice warrior(s), 2
socialism, 100, 125n21, 138, 225
  atheistic, 22, 100
Son of God, 25, 27, 147

true measure of humanism, 27
soviet communism, 194
  followed by relativism, 20
stewardship, 8, 66, 72, 74, 82–83, 93,
    97, 104, 163, 174
technocracy's regime of lust, xii, 185,
    226
technocratic approach, 110
  Francis on, 11
technocratic lust, xii, xv–xvii, 5–6, 8,
    11–13, 17, 36–38, 78, 81, 87, 91,
    93, 101, 108–109, 116, 118, 138,
    147, 155–56, 160, 163, 185, 193,
    219–22, 227, 241–42, 244, 246
technocratic paradigm, xvii, 6, 9, 11,
    36–37, 66, 108, 112, 138, 154,
    156, 168, 220, 223, 225–26,
    228–29, 244, 246
technocratic unchastity, 6
theology of the body, 3, 7, 9, 77, 150,
    201, 230
theology of the cosmic body, 9, 230
three young men (Shadrach, Me-
    shach, and Abednego), 84n69,
    91–92, 247–48.
triad of harmony, 30–31
truth, 6
  commitment to, xiv, 11–13
  of cosmic chastity, 8
  demands of, 23
  of the environment, 8, 10,
  of the givenness of creation, 8
  and the good, 20, 24
  about humanity, 23
  and the individual, 23
  John Paul on, 19
  justice and, 20
  social justice and, 23
  reverence for, 11
  about social justice, 23
  submission to, 12
  universal, 27
  Veritatis splendor and, 21
  yearning for, 20

Veritatis splendor (*VS, Splendor of
    Truth,* John Paul),
  Amoris laetitia and, 207

Augustine in, St., 121
beauty and, 123
cosmos and, 121
de Souza on, 207
on development, 123
encounter with God and, 19
on enslavement, 123
on freedom, 13, 36–37, 53n81, 99,
    105,
on the good, 123
on human dignity, 123
on evil, 123
on the human person, 123
on idolatry, 13
on intentionality, 122
and justice, 121
knowledge of truth, 13
on life, 123
man (humanity) and, 19
meaning and, 201 (add)
on morality/moral life, 122–123
on moral theology, 200
natural law and, 121
on nature, 36–37, 99–100
on obligations, 122
on profit, 123
prayer of the Psalmist and, 20
relativism and, 13, 27n45

rich young man and, 201
on rights, 123
on sin, 13, 123
social justice and, 21
on temperance, 123
Thomas Aquinas in, 123
on truth, 13, 105, 121, 123, 201
on violence, 123
on vocation, 123
works of the Creator and, 19
violence, 30, 55, 85, 108, 114, 117,
    120–21, 123, 147, 154, 170, 185
vocation/vocational commitment,
    xv–xvi, 12–13, 31, 34, 97, 114,
    122, 123, 138, 144, 146, 158,
    162–63, 186–87, 192, 195, 213,
    235, 238, 246

Waldstein, Michael, 6n8
Walker, Adrian, 6n9, 44n36,
    44–45n36, 83n69
war, 30, 55, 68, 108, 112, 114, 116,
    118, 120, 133, 158, 220–21
Weigel, George xiii, 86n84

Yost, Julia xiii

Zacchaeus, 138, 141–143, 156, 163.